Ida Rubinstein
(1885-1960)
A THEATRICAL LIFE

Michael de Cossart

LIVERPOOL UNIVERSITY PRESS

For
G.T.

Liverpool Historical Studies, no. 2
General Editor: P.E.H. Hair

Published in Great Britain, 1987,
by the Liverpool University Press,
Senate House, P.O. Box 147, Liverpool L69 3BX,
on behalf of the Department of History, University of Liverpool.

British Library Cataloguing in Publication Data are available.

ISBN 0 85323 146 X

CONTENTS

ILLUSTRATIONS

(between pages 113 and 120)

(The cover design incorporates the Portrait of I.R. by Romaine Brooks, 1917.)

ACKNOWLEDGEMENTS

A work as complex as a study of Ida Rubinstein's life and career would be an impossible task for an author working in isolation. I, therefore, must acknowledge with grateful thanks the practical help, advice and encouragement afforded me by a number of kind individuals. While responsibility for any views, ideas and interpretations contained in this volume rests entirely with myself, the following people generously helped me in various different ways during the course of my research:

Dr Edward Acton, Sir Frederick Ashton, Mr Philip Bell, M. Bernard Biancheri, Mr William Chappell, Miss Mary Clarke, M. Jean Claude, M. Doda Conrad, Mr Ronald Crichton, Mr Roy Davison, the Lady Donaldson of Kingsbridge, Mr David Dougill, M. Jean-Claude Eger, Mrs Lynn Garafola, the Lord Hastings, Mr A. Hourvitch, Mr Oleg Kerensky, Mme Madeleine Milhaud, the Duchesse de La Rochefoucauld, née Fels, Mr David Leonard, the Lord Moyne, Mr Rollo Myers, Mme Dominique Nabokov, Dr Roger Nichols, Mr Alexander Poliakoff, Dr Richard Ralph, Dr John Rogister, Mrs Meryle Secrest-Bainbridge, the Marchioness of Normanby and Mr Igor Vinogradoff.

I am particularly grateful to Mme Renée de Monbréson and to Mrs Véra Russell for supplying me with a great deal of information about Ida Rubinstein's family background.

M. Serge Lifar kindly gave me permission to quote at length from his own works on Diaghilev and the Ballets Russes. As I mention later, Mr Keith Lester generously permitted me to read, prior to its publication, his article on the Ida Rubinstein that he knew.

A number of cherished friends and acquaintances, old and new, gave me invaluable encouragement with my work during the various stages of this volume's preparation. In particular I should like to thank Mr Richard Buckle, Mr Clement Crisp and Mr Raleigh Trevelyan. Their advice on what pitfalls (human and otherwise) to avoid proved to be entirely sound. Finally, an especially warm word of thanks must go to Dr Robert Orledge, without whose help and moral support my task would have been infinitely more difficult and less enjoyable than it was in fact.

With a work in which a number of personalities of Russian origin inevitably figure prominently, one has the perennial problem of how to transliterate their names. At the risk of appearing inconsistent or even contradictory, I have tried hard to resolve the dilemma by using the westernized form of their names that they themselves came to employ in their professional capacity in the English- or French-speaking worlds. The result may irritate purist but, none the less, I hope that clarity is achieved and confusion avoided as much as possible.

Illustrated material is almost all no longer in copyright, although every effort has been made to trace copyright owners. Any omission of due acknowledgement is entirely unintentional and will be rectified in any subsequent edition of this volume. Other than photographs in the author's possession, such material appears by courtesy of the Bibliothèque Nationale, Paris (nos 9-14, 16 and 17), and by courtesy of the National Collection of Fine Arts, Smithsonian Institution, Washington (no. 6 and cover).

MICHAEL de COSSART.

CHAPTER 1

The Baptist's Head, 1885-1908

The year was 1908. A young woman of twenty-two, strikingly beautiful, tall, thin with flowing brown hair, made her way at the head of a small party across the Syrian desert towards Palestine. Her only real companion was an elderly kinsman, brought along to act as a guide and, more important, as a chaperon. The rest of the party was made up of a handful of servants, including a hairdresser whose sole function it was to take care of her hair and undo the havoc caused by the fierce desert winds. The local tribesmen were struck with almost superstitious awe by the vision of this ravishing stranger having her tresses tended by the light of the stars. One of their princes was so captivated that he promptly approached her escort with a proposal. Could he have the girl? In exchange he was prepared to offer him a number of women, several caravans and - the **pièce de résistance** - a fine gold watch and chain. These considerable inducements were courteously declined: the lady had a higher goal in life than that of becoming a Syrian prince's concubine. She was on her way to the Holy Land to assimilate the atmosphere of the place. Then she would return to her home-town, St Petersburg, where she intended to star in her own production of Oscar Wilde's exotic verse-drama **Salomé** - an event that caused more scandal than the Syrian potentate's ingenuous importuning.

Ida Rubinstein was born in Kharkov on 5 October 1885 - according to the Gregorian calendar. Her parents, Lvov and Ernestine Rubinstein, gave her the formal Biblical name of Lydia but immediately shortened to the more endearing one of Ida. And so it remained for the rest of her life. Lvov came from a well-established Ashkinazim Jewish family which had made a vast fortune from multi-faceted commercial activities in the Ukraine. His own specialty was the grain trade but he was also closely connected by marriage and business interests with the Raffalovich and Poliakoff families, whose achievements in the field of international finance and railway construction were of vital importance to the economic development of nineteenth-century Russia. Because of this and their willingness to assimilate the mores of Orthodox society these families were cushioned against much of the anti-semitic feeling rife during the reigns of Alexander III and Nicholas II. They adopted a life-style that made them indistinguishable from the rest of top-ranking society.

Ida was scarcely more than an infant when tragedy struck her family. Both her parents died in an epidemic and she and her elder sister were brought to St Petersburg to live with their aunt Madame Horwitz in her grand house on the Angliskaya, the fashionable street overlooking the River Neva. There, surrounded by innumerable cousins, Ida first came in contact with the cultural world. The capital was a haven of sophistication and comparative tolerance where her aunt and one of her uncles, Daniel Rubinstein, grouped round themselves leading members of the Russian intelligentsia, musicians, artists and writers. Contact with them taught Ida some useful early lessons in artistic expression and feeling that were to stand her in good stead in later years when she established herself as an actress and dancer and as one of the twentieth century's most far-sighted patrons of the arts. Madame Horwitz's extensive collection of paintings - none of them too avant-garde - gave Ida's childhood environment the air of an art gallery. She became used to having beautiful and precious objects around her. And at night she went to sleep lullabied by the distant strains of musical masterpieces performed by excellent musicians in her aunt's salon.

There was also a more formal side to her education. At an early point a keen intelligence and rapier-like agility of mind manifested itself. This was subjected to the rigours of academic discipline. Without much difficulty she mastered a list of languages including English, French, German and Italian. Later on, as an adolescent, she became so interested in Greek history and classical antiquity that a Hellenistic scholar was employed to teach her Greek. She also developed a passion for Russian literature, a passion that remained with her all her life. She loved to discuss the merits and demerits of her favourite authors and, in later years, though meticulously 'westernized', she would outrage her friends by arguing that Dostoyevsky was more of a genius than Shakespeare. Serious or not, she could certainly argue the point because she knew her Shakespeare (as well as her Dostoyevsky) backwards. She was equally familiar with the work of other great European writers: she could recite pages of Goethe and Nietzsche by heart.

Lessons in music and dancing occupied an important place in her curriculum. Ironically, dancing was the one subject in which she made little progress as a child, possibly because it was taught in much too rigid and stilted a fashion for somebody with as wide-ranging an imagination as herself. On the other hand she was fascinated by the art of communication through dramatic gestures and poses. Domestic storms blew up whenever she was discovered posing in front of her bedroom-mirror and she was expressly forbidden to linger there longer than necessary. Frustration and disappointment at being misunderstood did nothing to stop the girl being fascinated by her own image and by the plasticity of her body. If anything, it reinforced a narcissistic fixation that motived her throughout her entire life.

Her aunt clearly did not realize that there was a connection between these childish posturings and a serious interest in acting, because within a few years she began to encourage her interest in the stage by taking her regularly to St Petersburg's great theatres. This fired Ida with such a passion for acting that she was allowed to take private drama lessons with artistes from the imperial theatres. Monsieur Ozarovsky, the director of the Alexandrinsky Theatre, became her main tutor, teaching her acting technique by making analytical studies of leading roles in the classical repertoire.

Satisfied with her own progress, Ida presented herself one day, quite unannounced and with only a governess tagging along behind, at the studio of the designer Leon Bakst. They had a mutual acquaintance in the person of Count Benckendorff, the tsar's court chamberlain, and she knew and admired Bakst's work for the theatre. She had a proposition to make: would he design sets and costumes for a production of Sophocles's **Antigone**, which she was planning to mount? Bakst was stunned by the vision before him. He had seen Ida pass in her carriage in the streets of the city. He had admired her from afar as she took the conventional promenade down the Naberezhnaya Admiralteystva. But seeing her at close quarters for the first time, he was overwhelmed. And he remained infatuated with her slender, almost androgynous beauty until his dying day. As he later remarked, 'this is a fabulous being. We are blessed to have her among us...I might love the whole of humanity, every living being like a flower of the Lord, but she I adore like a beautiful tulip, insolent and dazzling, proud of herself and shedding pride around her' (Tosi, 1948b, p. 2). Bakst had a preconceived image of her as a sixteen-year-old girl - the boyish slimness of her body was deceptive - whereas at the time, 1905, she would have been nineteen years old. (In later years Ida did nothing to correct Bakst's impression. With each repetition of the story her real age became less certain.)

Bakst recovered from his surprise. Her proposition? Why **Antigone**? After all, a cycle of plays by Sophocles and Euripides had only just finished at the Alexandrinsky Theatre. But Ida insisted. What she wanted was a new production, spectacularly beautiful and entirely independent of any previous one. She had distinctive ideas on the subject and intended to do them justice. She had just visited Greece. Taking only her maid and her Greek teacher as guide, she had descended upon Athens and spent days on the Acropolis. There her mentor had evoked for her the city's magnificent history. How could one fail to appreciate the sublime shades of the past, Pericles and Phidias before the Parthenon, Socrates in his prison nearby, Aeschylus, Sophocles, Euripides and Aristophanes, whose marble theatre still survived on the flank of the hill, and Saint

Paul? She had returned at night to admire the Parthenon by moonlight, 'the columns of unreal vegetation..., Ida brushing these stone trees with her slender hands, the nocturnal breeze making her scarf shiver on her body. She resembled a Victory taking flight,...carrying off the secrets of divine beauty to the western world' (Nozière, pp. 11-12). Ida had, so to speak, plundered the monuments of Ancient Greece, questioned the Apollonian statues and meditated upon the golden treasures from the Mycenean tombs and now, back in St Petersburg, was ready to give concrete expression to her ideas by mounting a new version of **Antigone.**

At this point Bakst managed to gain some control over the situation. He succeeded in convincing her that, to begin with, she should attempt only one act of the play and that, rather than become involved with the commercial theatre, she would be better advised to give a private performance. Ida agreed and two months later their **Antigone,** with lavish new sets and costumes, was presented to an invited audience. Flocks of society people, all seasoned theatre-goers, turned up to see the young woman's début. As Bakst recalled, 'in the room there was a good number of sceptics who could ask for nothing better than to pass comments on the audacious young thing in the event of her falling flat on her face. But...her success was immediate and decisive' (Thomas, p. 92). Years later the critic and writer André Levinson recorded his impressions of the occasion: 'I clearly remember this unique production. And I see again the proud maiden as she is wrapped in the numerous and complicated folds of her black mourning robe. In working out this conception Bakst had drawn his inspiration from a tombstone or else had deciphered the clever pattern from a Greek vase' (1923, p. 156). More important, the performance made a lasting impression upon another member of the audience, Sergei Diaghilev.

Antigone's success had a fundamental effect upon the careers of both Ida Rubinstein and Bakst. It was the prelude to a collaboration that lasted until his death in 1924. Levinson commented upon their relationship (pp. 156-7):

> This young woman with her disconcerting and mysterious beauty, this mystical virgin, voluptuous yet frigidly cold, with a will of iron underneath a fragile frame, and possessed of a haughty and cold intelligence..., became one of the Muses of our artist. Hers was the gift of driving his imagination to exasperation...she held for him the all-powerful attraction of the strange, of the unreal, of the supernatural. His Muse - perhaps that is not the right term: rather, his Friendly Demon.

If Ida drove Bakst to accomplish feats of creativity on her behalf, she certainly did not spare herself. She was prepared to spend enormous sums and risk her reputation to satisfy her artistic cravings. As Alexandre Benois put it, 'she was unspeakably beautiful and gifted in every way,...a creature of genius; she was also unbelievably wealthy. She was very eccentric; and to achieve her artistic goal was ready to go to the limits of decency, as far as appearing in public without any clothes on' (1964, p. 243). The project that demanded this display of nudity was Wilde's play **Salomé**, whose production she began planning hot on the heels of her triumph in **Antigone**. But it was a production that demanded a lot of work and careful preparation before it reached the stage in December 1908. It also caused a major upheaval in Ida's life.

Taking her script with her, she set off on her first visit to Paris, where her sister Irène now lived with her husband, the celebrated doctor Professeur Lewinsohn. Ida immediately entered a new world focused almost entirely upon the arts. She was fortunate enough to be the niece of the Warshawski sisters, Julia Cahen d'Anvers and Marie Kann, whose passion for painting, music and anything (or anybody) avant-garde had prompted that notorious anti-semite Jean-Louis Forain to label them and their friends Ernesta Stern and the Baronne Gustave de Rothschild 'the Jewesses of Art'. Ida inhaled a whiff of the heady atmosphere in which they lived and this may have distorted her sense of social values because it encouraged her to announce her intention of becoming a professional actress. Her sister and brother-in-law were horrified. Violent arguments took place. No girl fom her background could make a career for herself on the stage: that was almost synonymous with becoming a courtesan. But Ida insisted. Hysteria reigned. Lewinsohn made a clumsy attempt to save the family reputation. Acting in his professional capacity, he pronounced Ida mentally ill and sent her to a special clinic run by a Docteur Sollier at Saint-Cloud. And there she stayed until her family in St Petersburg heard the news and insisted on her being sent back to Russia.

Ida simply exchanged one prison for another since the basic problem remained: she had no intention of abandoning her plans for a stage career and her family had no intention of sanctioning them. There was only one solution for it. She could gain her freedom by marrying a compliant husband - not normally the easiest of prey to trap but one was to hand. Vladimir Horwitz, one of the cousins with whom she had grown up, was completely besotted with her and willing agreed to marry her on her own terms: it must be a marriage in name only and he must allow her to pursue a career in the theatre. The marriage ceremony took place with due pomp. The satisfied couple set up house in a huge apartment on the Angliskaya. And Ida immediately gave her undivided attention to the business of mounting **Salomé**.

First of all the play itself had to be translated from its French original into Russian. None of the richness of the hyperbolic language must be lost, so she employed a seasoned translator to do the job. The play needed incidental music, so she approached Alexander Glazunov, a formidable figure in his official role as director of the St Petersburg Conservatoire and a difficult one: he could be extremely rude, drunk or sober - usually the former. Ida was undaunted: he was one of Russia's leading composers, Rimsky-Korsakov's spiritual heir, and she had faith in his work. Her faith was rewarded by the composition of some impressive music of symphonic proportions. Glazunov even agreed to conduct the music at the first performance. Meanwhile, Bakst was put to work on the sets and costumes.

For her own part Ida redoubled her efforts to perfect her acting and diction and went to great lengths to improved her technique as a dancer. For some time she had been taking private lessons with Michel Fokine and from the beginning of the 1907 season they began to work together on the choreography for **Salomé**. Ida refused to let him rest, even while he was on holiday in Switzerland in the summer of 1908. One can sense a mixture of admiration and irritation in his comments on the subject: 'She was anxious to play the role of Salomé...and to perform the Dance of the Seven Veils. This resulted in her working daily with me and devoting a great deal of effort to her work. When my wife and I went to Coux for our vacation, she followed us there. One has to give the artist credit. I have seldom seen such energy and persistence' (p. 137). This was very necessary because, as Fokine put it (pp. 137-8):

> The work on the Salomé dance was unique in my life. I had to teach
> Rubinstein simultanteously the art of dance and to create for her
> the Dance of Salomé...Before this, she had studied dancing very
> little...Her energy and endurance were of great assistance, as was
> her appearance. I felt it would be possible to do something
> unusual with her in the style of Botticelli. She was tall, thin
> and beautiful, and was interesting material from which I had hopes
> of moulding a unique scenic image.

But the choreography turned out to be the least of Ida's problems. Russia in the 1900s was country in turmoil. Psychologically unsure of itself after its disastrous defeat in the Russo-Japanese War of 1904-1905 and shaken by the 'Bloody Sunday' revolution of 22 January 1905 and by the strikes and street-fighting that continued throughout that year, the tsarist establishment failed to regain its grip on the situation. Even the granting of a constitution and the setting up of a legislative Duma did little to ease the tension. As a result the authorities resorted to repressive measures and clamped down on anything that gave the slighest sign of upsetting the equilibrium of society. The Holy Governing Synod of the Russian Orthodox Church lent its support and acted as an instrument of state. Since it was effectively manipulated by lay officials, the authority of the church could be used to help counteract any moral or ideological force that threatened to prove disruptive. This was the institutional stone-wall that Ida Rubinstein came up against just as she was on the point of unveiling her **Salomé** before the public.

Leading clerics were up in arms: it was sacrilege to show the head of John the Baptist on stage. (To make a three-dimensional representation of the saint's head was tantamount to making a sacred image and that went very much against the Orthodox interpretation of the second commandment.) The Holy Synod acted swiftly and banned the performance. But Ida had her contacts in high places and, while her enemies remained implacable, the Holy Synod modified its outright ban. Instead, it simply prohibited the actors from reciting the text of Wilde's play on stage. Everybody assumed that the effect would be the same. A performance was virtually out of the question and it was a very gloomy group of artists that gathered at Ida's apartment to discuss the crisis. The auditorium of the Conservatoire was booked for 20 December. St Petersburg's leading actors were prepared. Ida had made her trip to Palestine - but all to no avail. To make matters worse, public interest had been so great that all seats had been sold a long time before.

It was Bakst who came up with a solution that met with universal acclaim - and relief. Ida was a first-rate mime, so why should the whole play not be mimed? The entire action could be conveyed by gestures and poses. The plan went ahead and, in the meantime, copies of the play were widely circulated so that few in the audience would be ignorant of what was happening on stage. Public excitement mounted: not only was there the promise of a fantastic ballet, liberally laced with outrageous moments, but also a distinct snook was being cocked at the civil and ecclesiastical authorities.

But a final hurdle still had to be negotiated. Two hours before the performance the Prefect of Police of St Petersburg arrived backstage in search of Bakst (Thomas, p. 94):

'Where is the head of Saint John?'

'How should I know?' shrugged Bakst. 'Probably in the properties room.'

'Bring me the head of Saint John!'

'What do you want with it?'

'I forbid anyone to display it on stage.'

And so the wrangle went on. Bakst's promise that it would not appear on stage was not enough. The Prefect refused to budge until he had the papier-mâché head in his hands. Escorted by a bevy of underlings, he bore it off in truimph, as though he had finally delivered the death-blow to the production. In effect, this simply provided yet another foil for Ida's talent as a mime. The audience had no difficulty in seeing the severed head in the mind's eye as the empty platter was presented to Salomé. Everybody knew that after the Dance of the Seven Veils, her reward had to be something extraordinary. Never before had the St Petersburg public been treated to the spectacle of a young society woman dancing voluptuously to insinuating oriental music, discarding brilliantly coloured veils until only a whisp of green chiffon remained knotted round her loins, even though, as Benois admitted, this 'final reprehensible moment of the dance was dissimulated by means of a lighting trick' (1941, p. 278). The audience applauded wildly.

Even without its audacious moments **Salomé** would have been a genuine artistic triumph. It fully justified its enormous cost in terms of money and effort. And Ida had fulfilled her desire to incarnate the heroine of her dreams. At the same time she made herself into something of a legend as the woman for whom no extravagance was too much in her pursuit of beauty and perfection. She also established herself firmly as a professional performer and was accepted as such even by the most critical and sceptical.

But she achieved all this at considerable personal expense. Her audience may have relished the sight of a society woman depicting a depraved and amoral adolescent on stage. But Ida's family was outraged and cold-shouldered her. She also quickly discovered that marriage provided no immunity from the hypocritical disapproval of certain sections of St Petersburg society. For a time, however, she continued to attract round her a circle of artists, musicians, writers and intellectuals, creating a little cultural enclave with herself at the centre, like a Renaissance princess, beautiful, mysterious and taciturn. Yet this provided only limited scope for somebody like herself who saw her role in life as an apostle of beauty. She began to set her sights beyond the frontiers of Russia towards Western Europe. And before long she found herself being drawn into a career as a dancer and mime and deflected away from her chosen one as an actress.

She would have some cause to regret - as well as relish - the long-term consequences of the controversy over a papier-mâché head of John the Baptist.

CHAPTER 2

Russian Ballets, 1909-1910

Ida Rubinstein's spectacular appearance in **Salomé** came at a key-point in the history of Western theatre. Sergei Diaghilev was then in the middle of preparations to take a company of dancers and singers from the Mariinsky Theatre to Paris for his first full season of Russian ballet and opera and one of the ballets on the projected programme, **Une nuit d'Egypte**, was causing the artistic committee particular problems. For a story about the exotic Cleopatra the title was limp. The music by Arensky was less than satisfactory. And Ludmilla Barach, the dancer who had been the Egyptian queen at its première in St Petersburg on 21 March 1908, had not lived up to expectations. The title was quickly changed to the more eye-catching **Cléopâtre**. Arensky's score was cut and suitably oriental sounding passages of music by Taneyev, Rimsky-Korsakov, Glazunov and Mussorgsky were successfully tacked together. Nicholas Tcherepnine was asked to write completely new music for the ballet's finale, now suitably altered to heighten the dramatic effect. The problem of finding a replacement for the old Cleopatra, in what was rapidly becoming a completely new ballet, was not so easy to solve.

Two of the committee members did have a suggestion, but enthusiasm for it was not universal. Prince Peter Lieven gave a slightly sceptical account of the event (p. 53):

> Bakst and the choreographer (Fokine) whispered to each other a great deal behind the backs of the others. Eventually it appeared that the subject of their whisperings was one of Fokine's private pupils - a handsome, talented and rich young girl, Ida Rubinstein. Bakst, with his peculiar Jewish loyalty, was loud in her praises. 'She is a goddess,' he would shout, and Fokine, too, spoke highly of her. The friends discussed the possibility of giving her the part of Cléopâtre.

Everybody was prepared to go along with the idea except the old General Alexander Bezobrazov, the 'godfather' of the St Petersburg ballet and one of Diaghilev's closest advisers: 'Being a very strict balletomane, he considered that no one except professionals should be admitted into the company, and disapproved of amateurs. The committee tried to point out that there was unfortunately no suitable dancer for the part at the Mariinsky; but he was not convinced and went on grumbling for some time' (Grigoriev, p. 20). However, Diaghilev was convinced and that was all that mattered. He had seen Ida's performances in **Antigone** and **Salomé** and had been impressed by her stage-presence. Her sensational reputation, bordering on notoriety, could only be good for publicity. Besides, with her money, she could be counted on to work for nothing.

Fokine's part in this episode may seem inconsistent because he had already considered and rejected the idea of casting Ida in the original **Nuit d'Egypte**. But he probably changed his mind while working with her on **Salomé**. Certainly there was no denying that she had style - and enthusiasm. As if his working-vacation at Coux were not proof enough of that, the following summer Ida pursued the Fokines even further afield to Sorrento in order to continue work on her dances.

Ida Rubinstein's success in **Cléopâtre** is now legendary. But when she arrived in Paris at the beginning of May 1909, she was an unknown quantity. Even the ballet company scarcely knew her since she had not rehearsed with them in St Petersburg: Fokine had trained her for the part behind locked doors, so the ballet finally took shape only in the few weeks before the **répétition générale** (the full public dress rehearsal traditional in the French theatre) on 2 June and the première on 4 June. In the meantime, rumours about an extraordinary artistic happening began to circulate round Paris - although Benois always insisted that the ballet's success had nothing to do with any suggestive element in it: 'It is true,' he admitted, 'that the Egyptian queen...gradually discarded all her veils and gave herself up to the ecstasy of love before the eyes of the whole audience'. Only at the most critical moment the helpful court ladies...surrounded the couch with curtains, and by doing so they really emphasized the point' (1941, pp. 295-6). But, he insisted, this had none of the smuttiness of dubious moments common in popular operettas and farces (p. 296):

> The disrobing took place to the beautiful but terrifying music of (Rimsky-Korsakov's) **Mlada**. Slowly, in accordance with the complicated court ritual, one by one, the covers were unwound, disclosing the divine body omnipotent in its beauty...when the slight figure émerged covered only by the wonderful transparent garment invented by Bakst, one experienced a feeling of awe. Here was not a pretty artiste appearing in frank **déshabille**, but a real, fatal enchantress, in the tradition of the cruel and grasping Astarte.

Fatal indeed because, after allowing her court to indulge in a full-blown bacchanal, she insisted that her lover Amune (danced by Fokine) should take poison as the penalty for his infatuation. She then callously departed, leaving his real love (Anna Pavlova in the guise of a slave girl) to weep over his corpse.

The audiences that packed themselves into the Théâtre du Châtelet - and even willingly sat on the stairs - were stunned by the ballet. No other work in that season's programme achieved quite as much success and no artist more universal acclaim than Ida Rubinstein. This was all the more remarkable because her role was essentially a static one in which a series of poses was used to convey the irresistible but cold and cruel fascination exercised by Cleopatra. Peter Lieven described the effect: 'Her long, youthfully slender, peculiarly angular body seemed to have just descended from an Egyptian bas-relief, and her marvellous Eastern profile with its narrow eyes was very appropriate to the role' (p. 97). As prima ballerina, Pavlova should have been the centre of attention but was quite overshadowed - to her intense chagrin. (This may account for her reluctance to work for Diaghilev in future seasons.)

Although Cleopatra's decadence and sadism left audiences trembling with excitement, life behind scenes at the Châtelet did have its mundane moments. Michel Calvocoressi recorded one. At the climactic end of the bacchanal when Ida and Fokine (p. 213)

collapsed onto a couch around which the slaves held up a curtain...one could feel a thrill running through the auditorium. A Frenchwoman said to me one day: 'Last night, I had a seat right at the side of the dress circle. I was glad of that because from there I could see Rubinstein and Fokine behind the curtain...I expected to see them continuing their love-making. Not at all: they were drinking beer!'

Ida certainly could not have coped with a glass of beer at the start of the work when she was carried on stage in a sarcophagus-like palanquin, from which she emerged wrapped tightly in veils like a mummy. The effect was deliberate but problematic. One evening, as the curtain was going up (Lieven, p. 80),

Benois approached Ida Rubinstein where she lay wrapped up and asked her: 'Well, Ida Lvovna, how are you feeling?'

'All right, thank you,' she replied from the coffin, 'but I can't move.'

If fire had broken out, the hapless Cléopâtre would certainly have perished.

Even without her wrappings she was not very mobile. A twenty-two-year-old Jean Cocteau was so bowled over by her appearance on stage that he began furiously jotting down notes, recording the impression of the moment in the hope that 'a vividness, of which the memory is incapable, may atone for their incoherence.' The vision of her, as she stood revealed 'with vacant eyes, pallid cheeks, and open mouth, before the spell-bound audience, penetratingly beautiful, like the pungent perfume of some exotic essence', compelled him to leave his seat at the end of the performance and become one of the permanent back-stage hangers-on. From his new vantage point he could watch her performance and assist at 'a wonderful experience...the draping of Madame Rubinstein before the curtain rises. Silent stage-hands and "supers" form a respectful circle round her, and melt gradually away as she disappears beneath the wealth of veils' (1913, pp. 27-8). Cocteau's own moment came one night when, as he put it, 'I had the honour to escort Madame Rubinstein for the process, for she cannot walk alone on her pattens, and, as I felt the light weight of her trembling palm in mine, I thought of Flaubert's Cleopatra with her blue hair, her rapid breathing, her delicate discomfort' (p. 28). In every way a sublime experience! As he concluded, 'disposed as I already was to admire Rimsky-Korsakov's music' - the bacchanal must have said most to him - 'Madame Rubinstein has fixed it in my heart, as a long blue-headed pin might impale a moth with feebly fluttering wings' (p. 28).

Nor was Cocteau the only fluttering moth transfixed by Cleopatra and by her extraordinary powder-blue wig, designed by Bakst to complete the vivid polychromatic fantasy of the décors. The Comte Robert de Montesquiou, amateur poet and professional arbiter of elegance, with one of the most vitriolic tongues in the business, could think only of the most honeyed phrases to describe his impressions as he sat through every performance of **Cléopâtre** that season.

His first 'introduction' to Ida had been startling. As he sat waiting for the curtain to rise on the first night, he overheard an acquaintance of his say to a neighbour: 'She is an immensely rich Russian Jewess, who asks for nothing more than to come to Paris for the pleasure of showing herself completely nude' (1923, pp. 123-4). Montesquiou left the theatre that night determined to forestall Ida's critics, salacious and prudish alike (1912, pp. 215, 226):

> Madame Rubinstein's costume...might be described as 'suggestive' by a provincial newspaper. The lady is nude, under bejewelled veils, just like these scarfs by Fortuny with which our Parisian women have fallen in love...I know no person of taste who has not been deeply impressed by this extraordinary spectacle; and some have come up to me to say: 'This is the most beautiful thing that I have ever seen!'

Montesquiou expressed his feelings about Ida in a poem entitled 'La Dame bleue' and published it in **Le Figaro Littéraire** on 19 June 1909 (1909, p. 2):

> Devant votre beauté, notre vue est fleurie
> Comme d'un clair printemps qui serait éternel.

His arch lines clearly reflected general feeling about Ida's Cleopatra and letters of congratulation from distinguished men such as Albert Robin, Albert Flament and Reynaldo Hahn accumulated in his files (BN,

15163, fols 141, 147-55). But however artificial the paradise inhabited by Montesquiou, his admiration for Ida Rubinstein was real enough. He was infatuated with her. He even loved her - platonically, of course. At last he had found his long-sought ideal beauty. As Philippe Jullian remarked, 'was she not the flat and cruel hermaphrodite of whom he had dreamed when he was twenty? Thus...this fifty-year-old man was suddenly impelled into an international demi-monde, the women of which, with their multi-coloured aigrettes, seemed to have escaped from a harem kept by pashas who speculated on the stock exchange' (1967, p. 223).

When the time came for Montesquiou to meet Ida to express his devotion to this epitome of beauty, his verbal springs, which normally gushed incessantly, suddenly dried up. Afterwards he made no attempt to gloss over the incident. He admitted that 'a very unusual and pretty humiliating thing happened'. While he was waiting in the salon of her hotel suite, he was 'struck by the sensation that the atmosphere was impregnated with beauty, like the East, with scent, the air of a little garden, where at night indiscernible tuberoses bloom. One does not see them, but...can swear that they are there' (1913, p. 220). In a word, by the time Ida appeared, Montesquiou was too keyed-up emotionally to speak. The moment when she turned to him and said, 'Monsieur, sit down!' was one of 'indescribable beauty'. The artist Romaine Brooks, to whom he gave an account of this incident, insisted that 'to him this was no anti-climax. He was experiencing over again in his imagination...that quality which gave distinction to everything she said or did' (quoted Secrest, p. 241). Nobody else would have gone to such lengths to invest a social commonplace with such an exalted significance.

Once Montesquiou had recovered his powers of speech, the conversation quickly elevated itself onto a higher plane where - one suspects - it remained until his death in 1921. And to be fair, the friendship that grew up between them was undoubtedly genuine, resilient and creative. Unlikely though it may seem, their relationship was as significant as almost any other in either of their lives. Why? Both shared the same ideals: they were committed to the pursuit of beauty, or rather to the manifestation of beauty in artistic activities in which Ida's body would be the instrument of its expression. They both sought to escape from the banality of everyday life. A reaction to the times, the diametrical opposite of Alfred Jarry's response, which consisted in investing his King Ubu's surprising dietary predelictions with a social message, it involved the evocation of the past, reliving its glories and recreating them through the best modern media.

But these aims were achieved only gradually over the next three decades. In the meantime, Montesquiou encouraged Ida to concentrate upon her work for Diaghilev and upon cultivating a public image designed to give the impression that nothing vulgar ever intruded upon her consciousness. As a very young girl 'the high-priestess of fashion', Diana Vreeland, found her first glimpse of Ida breathtaking: 'I'd never seen Russian boots before - remember this was 1909. She came in black suède Russian boots, black coat, a big band of fox fur, hair like Medusa, all held in black tulle. She took off the tulle and her eyes were blackened with kohl...fantastic!' (Howell, p. 47). Romaine Brooks painted a verbal picture of an equally stunning Ida (quoted Jullian, 1972, pp. 223-4):

> She seemed to me even more beautiful when off stage; like some heraldic bird delicately knit together by the finest of bone structures giving flexibility to curveless lines. The clothes she wore were beyond fashion, for without effort everything contributed to make her seem like an apparition. The banality of her surroundings, to which she paid no attention, made the effect more striking. I remember one cold snowy morning walking with her around the Longchamps race course. Everything was white and Ida wore an ermine coat. It was open and exposed the frail chest and slender neck which emerged from a white feathery garment. Her face was sharply cut with long golden eyes and a delicate bird-like nose; her partly veiled head with dark hair moving gracefully from the temples as though the wind were smoothing it back...she possessed...mystery. Hers was a mask whose outward glow emanated from a disturbed inner depth.

Rumours about her singular life-style circulated widely. She was said never to wear any of her couture dresses twice. Many believed that she drank champagne out of Madonna lilies. Indeed, some thought that she lived on nothing but champagne and biscuits. Decades later this myth still persisted: André de Fouquières whispered that at her sumptuous dinner parties she would 'try only a biscuit in a glass of champagne' (p. 178) - the lilies, after all, must have proved impracticable!

Ida deliberately fed gossip about herself. Soon after her arrival in Paris she commissioned Valentine Serov, an artist friend from Moscow, to paint a full-length portrait of her, lying on a divan in the nude. A crisp, elegant composition with her head turned to the right looking over her boyishly thin shoulder, it was sensational enough in itself but additionally piquant when people learned that she had posed for it in a former monastery on the Boulevard des Invalides. The artist's studio had once been the chapel and was still pervaded with an ecclesiastical chill, which the naked Ida give no sign of noticing.

Distinctive accessories to her exotic image were her wild animal pets.

A black panther cub was the first among many that she paraded around with an equanimity that nobody else shared. In time it would prove a less than successful idea but, in the short term, it added considerably to her reputation for eccentricity, although some were rather suspicious about her motives - Peter Lieven for one: 'Apparently her main aim was to attract people's notice, and the question of good taste did not trouble her' (p. 119). His comment must have surprised Ida since she saw herself as defining or redefining good taste. And did she not have the backing of Montesquiou, whose taste was impeccable? Did he not idolize her? Images of her were seldom far from his thoughts. He had seen her by the fountains at Versailles 'where the white plumes on her hat and flounces of lace fought victoriously with the spray of the jets and the cascades,' or 'under a spring sunset, she in violet and her silhouette, against the lilies of the Trianon's Perseus, all powdered with mauve, making a cameo of her outline;' or again 'in the street, as she passes, one sees eyes widen, people stop in their tracks, words die away, as if...silence were the only worthy way of...worshipping the unique' (1913, pp. 220-1).

Admittedly the Montsquiou-Rubinstein friendship did have its ups and downs - scarcely surprising considering the count's hypersensitivity. But whereas others who gave offence, real or imagined, were usually irrevocably struck off his visiting-list, Ida managed to weather the storms of his indignation. The first came within weeks of their introduction.

Montesquiou was moving from his house in Neuilly, the Pavillon des Muses (it was permeated with too many memories of his dead boy-friend Gabriel Yturri), and he wanted to have a farewell **matinée**. Nine well-known actresses were engaged to play the Nine Muses in a classical tableau. Eugénie Segond-Weber was to be Thalia, with Ida Rubinstein heading the cast as Terpsichore. He approached Fokine and Bakst for help with the choreography and production. They were amenable. Bakst replied graciously: 'I accept your kind invitation with pleasure and tomorrow we shall decide with you the small details of the production for the dance of Cleopatra, transformed into Terpsichore!' (BN, 15163, fol. 86).

When Fokine, Bakst and Ida learned what minor details Montesquiou had in mind, they were secretly amused. He wanted to represent a classical scene against a simple black backcloth, like a fragment from an Etruscan vase. They brushed the idea aside and began describing the huge, elaborate and enormously costly set that they had in mind. Montesquiou listened in terror until the joke dawned on him. Undaunted, he took up the thread of his own argument again: there were yards and yards of black material stored in the vaults of the Madeleine. It had been used only once - at the funeral of Alfred Chauchard (one of the founders of the Magasins du Louvre, so the cloth was of high quality!) The count now intended to get some more wear out of it by using it as his set. The others could not restrain a smile as their interest visibly waned. Montesquiou muttered angrily that the road to Hell was, indeed, paved with good intentions.

Worse was to come. On 16 June 1909, the very day of his gala, messages arrived to say that both Madame Segond-Weber and Ida Rubinstein were unable to take part in the performance. Montesquiou only saved the day by offering himself as a substitute in the part of Thalia - the Muse of Comedy. His guests applauded the suggestion enthusiastically, probably hoping that he might also tackle Terpsichore's dance. He did not record how he overcame that difficulty. Nor did he record why Ida absented herself (1923, pp. 125-7). La Segond-Weber was stricken with unseasonable influenza. Ida almost certainly had been required for rehearsals. Since Diaghilev's season was still in full swing, why this 'outside' engagement had been given serious consideration in the first place is a mystery. The count complained bitterly: 'Our Terpsichore **manquée**...ended up by pleasing everybody...except me' (p. 124).

But he forgave, if he did not forget. He scribbled an account of the incident in his memoirs - in the heat of the moment, he freely admitted - but, although his fury soon abated, the passage remained unaltered and was thrust before the public eye when published posthumously in 1923. In the months following this initial 'hiccup' in his relationship with Ida, Montesquiou's magnanimous 'forgiveness' seems to have had the effect of cementing their friendship. And eventually he and Ida became very dependent upon each other. Neither would make a major decision on artistic matters without first seeking the other's advice.

Throughout the summer months of 1909 they saw a great deal of each other. He sent her volumes of his verse. **Les Perles rouges** arrived at her hotel in August and she wrote back saying that it would be 'like a talisman' to her (BN, 15214, fol. 188). He gave a dramatic reading from the manuscript of his memoirs - carefully selected passages, of course - and she confessed herself profoundly impressed by the experience (BN, 15228, fol. 255). They spent hours, days together in the Louvre. She accepted with alacrity his invitation to visit the Musée Gustave Moreau (BN, 15284, fols 129-30). They alternated in inviting each other to see plays and occasionally took Bakst - also restored to favour - with them to the Théâtre Français (BN, 15162, fol. 113).

In the meantime, Ida was fulfilling a remarkable number of theatre engagements herself. The Ballets Russes season ended with some of the stars' taking part in a gala performance at the Paris Opéra in aid of the city of Messina, which had been devastated by an earthquake in 1908. Ida with Nijinsky and Karsavina held the stage with Sarah Bernhardt, Sacha Guitry, Réjane, Felia Litvin and George Robey - mixed company, but the result was described as 'one of the most inspiring presentations ever planned' (Bourman, p. 210).

After disrupting Fokine's holiday in Sorrento, Ida made a series of music-hall appearances, performing dances of the **Cléopâtre** genre. She scored a great success at the Olympia in Paris and in September she came to the London Coliseum to take part in an 'all-star' music-hall programme, which included the Russian Balalaika Court Orchestra and Seymour Hicks 'as Scrooge'! But her London début was postponed, as she explained to Montesquiou with some pride: 'Sir Edward Moss (the Chairman of these theatres) who is, besides, a cultivated and very kind man, attended my rehearsal last Monday. He was so impressed by the music and the dance that he begged me to delay my début for a week to allow time to change the whole programme, to obtain a large orchestra for me and to prepare the public through the newspapers, as he said, for the "most beautiful thing that London will ever have seen"' (BN, 15333, fols 21-2). Ida remarked that this was extraordinary for a theatre administrator and added: 'Even more extraordinary...is that they send me my money each day as if I were dancing.' And all that for four days of performances (twice daily) between 27 and 30 September! But meanwhile, as she idled her time away in the Grand Hotel in Trafalgar Square, she confessed to feeling 'very alone and almost lost' (fol. 22).

In time London would become a more familiar place but for the moment, despite her triumph, she was glad to return to Paris to discuss an engagement in New York with the conductor of the Metropolitan Opera House. On 13 November she set sail for the United States to fulfil her contract (fols 35-6, 39-40). Other engagements in France and Italy followed on her return.

Ida derived a degree of satisfaction from her success. Even the fact that she was being paid for her efforts was psychologically uplifting: it was a token of her arrival as a professional artist. But not everybody approved. Montesquiou gave her some half-hearted encouragement, although clearly he did not see variety theatre, however respectable, as her proper milieu. A close friend, the actress Cécile Sorel, wrote to him in very blunt terms: 'Tell me why, in the Devil's name, does our beautiful idol transform herself into a music-hall caryatid like this, instead of waiting for the realization of your beautiful dream?...It is a betrayal over which I grieve with your soul, which communes so divinely with mine' (BN, 15163, fol. 145).

Even if she were conscious of not living up to Montesquiou's expectations, Ida began to feel the strain of her 'private' schedule. Back in St Petersburg she fulfilled her official duties with the troupe and would arrive back at her house at 24 Dvortsovaya Naberezhnaya too worn out to concentrate on dances designed for private audiences: 'I was too tired to compose anything without the aid of my master (Fokine). And how can I show myself before an élite public without knowing what I am doing and without rehearsing?' (BN, 15333, fols 17-18).

Besides, she knew that as a star in major stage productions, such as Diaghilev organized, she attracted much more public attention than in any other way. On 20 May 1910, when the company began a two-week season in Berlin, it gained instant acclaim. Kaiser Wilhelm II attended the first night and was so impressed by 'the fresh aspect Bakst gave Egyptian antiquity in **Cléopâtre**...like a surprising discovery in the field of archaeology...that he...called together the members of the Society of Egyptologists of which he was president to talk to them about the cultural significance of the ballet and to urge them to study Bakst's **mise-en-scène**' (Kochno, p. 37). What they thought about Ida's powder-blue wig is not recorded, but there was no doubt that she - and it - were the centre of attraction.

But before long the success of **Cléopâtre** had been overshadowed by the triumph of a new ballet, **Schéhérazade,** which opened Diaghilev's season at the Paris Opéra on 4 June 1910. The Paris public, its appetite whetted by the previous season, gorged itself on a feast of oriental decadence. Ida and Nijinsky, its stars, became the talk of the town.

The music for the ballet was Rimsky-Korsakov's, an obvious choice, although his widow and son did everything they could to prevent this. The story was simple. The Sultan (Alexis Bulgakov) sets out for war and leaves his harem behind. His favourite wife Zobeïda (Ida Rubinstein) faints on being separated from him. But she and her fellow concubines quickly recover and before long have bribed the chief eunuch with pearls to open the door to the apartments of the negro slaves. The women fall into their arms and even Zobeïda is swept off by the Golden Slave (Nijinsky). 'Then,' said Cocteau, 'begins an orgy of mad caresses' (1913, p. 30). Romola Nijinsky's description was even more colourful (p. 94):

> Zobeïda's...gestures were a combination of dignity and sensuality, and expressed the essential languors of a woman who demands sexual satisfaction. The Slave, a superb, golden animal,...with one movement possesses her. His jump is a tiger's, once caged, now freed for his victim. He bounds with her on to a divan for the maddest, fiercest activity of love...voluptously wild, a cat caressing, a tiger devouring, now at her feet, now at her breasts

and mouth, stroking and exciting her.

Lincoln Kirstein described what happened as virtual rape (p. 42).

Willing or unwilling, Zobeïda reaps the inevitable retribution. The Sultan returns unexpectedly. Mayhem ensues. The harem women, the negro slaves and the eunuchs are all slaughtered. Only Zobeïda remains untouched. Her tears momentarily soften her master's heart but his fury returns. He commands his men to kill her. But she eludes their scimitars and stabs herself with her own dagger. There is a final telling moment. She drags herself to expire at her master's feet as though the slave, who died for her love, had never existed. The Sultan is overwhelmed with grief.

If the plot was rather melodramatic, the sheer brutal impact of the production excused everything. Bakst's sets and costumes assaulted the eyes with unbelievable force. In Richard Buckle's words, 'not form but colour reigned, and its reign was as debauched as that of Heliogabalus...An unheard-of violence of peacock-green and blue was the main theme (which gave the jeweller Cartier the idea of setting sapphires and emeralds together for the first time since the Mogul Emperors), but this was defied by the subsidiary theme of coral-red and rose-pink' (1979, p. 171). The impact was such that Parisian taste and colour-sense changed overnight and the soft hues and respectable forms of the reigning Louis-Seize style received a body-blow.

Fokine was overjoyed by the extent to which his choreography contributed to the ballet's success. He was lavish in his praise for Ida Rubinstein's Zobeïda (p. 155):

My creation...and her performance of the role were remarkable for giving powerful impressions accomplished by the most economical means. Everything was expressed with one single pose, with one movement, one turn of the head. Nevertheless, everything was outlined and drawn clearly. Every line was carefully thought out and felt...She stands in front of a door through which her lover is momentarily to emerge. She waits for him with her entire body...Then (and to me the most dramatic scene) she sits utterly still while slaughter takes place around her. Death approaches her, but not the horror nor fear of it. She majestically waits hers - in a pose without motion. What powerful expression with no movement!

Sergei Grigoriev's comment on the part played by Diaghilev in the creation of the ballet is perceptive: 'In **Schéhérazade** Diaghilev attained an aim once dreamt of by Noverre, when he said, "If only the painter, the composer, and the choreographer could work together in harmony, what one wonders would they not show the public!"...It is impossible to describe the reception of this ballet. It took no little time for the audience...to calm down' (pp. 46-7).

In the end of the day the work was too successful. The very fact that it had such an influence on popular taste was a problem. Arnold Haskell put his finger on it: simply because it 'launched a fashion, brightened the colours of shop windows and women's clothes, and has lightened the tone of every stage décor...and spread to revue and music hall, Diaghilev himself was forced to fly from it.' And Haskell added an interesting anecdote: fifteen years later a ballot for the most popular of Diaghilev's ballets was held in London. **Schéhérazade** came top of the poll - despite the fact that it was not listed on the ballot-paper (1955, p. 222).

Although **Schéhérazade** continued to bring Ida the wildest acclaim throughout the season, for her too it brought to an end a stage in her personal and artistic development. There could be no going back. Even the repetition of her success in another type-cast role as a statuesque **femme fatale** would ultimately prove pointless and frustrating. The question as to what she should do next did not wait long for an answer.

CHAPTER 3

Saint Androgyne, 1910–1911

Gabriele d'Annunzio, poet and professional womanizer, soon to be Italy's patriotic superman, entered Ida Rubinstein's life at this crucial moment.

Nobody ever agreed on how he first heard of her. Robert de Montesquiou befriended him in the spring of 1910 as soon as he arrived in Paris, a refugee from his creditors in Italy, and must have mentioned her to him. The Comtesse de Béarn, music-lover, balletomane and Ida's fervent admirer and friend, cannot have failed to draw his attention to her – unless she feared a rival. Very late in the day Jacques Rouché, the director of the Paris Opéra, brushed aside all other claims. They were pure gossip: 'It was I. I told him about this Cleopatra's appearance in Paris, about her débuts, about her passion for art, about her life' (p. 116).

Whatever the truth, something was said that sent d'Annunzio rushing to the Opéra specifically to see Ida dance in **Schéhérazade.** His secretary Tom Antongini was certain about that fact: the poet had no desire to see the first half of the programme. He arrived five minutes before the curtain rose on the Rubinstein ballet; settled down in the third row of the stalls and waited (pp. 285–6):

> As soon as Ida Rubinstein appeared on the stage, he ceased to have eyes for anyone else, and from the moment the performance was over till we returned to the hotel at four o'clock in the morning...he talked to me only of Ida Rubinstein, of the harmony of all her movements, the grace of her attitudes, and, above all, of the plastic perfection of her legs.
>
> 'Here,' he exclaimed, 'are the legs of Saint Sebastian for which I have been searching for years!'

Antongini did not understand him. What was the connection between the saint's legs and this Russian dancer's beautiful limbs? Something had clearly whetted d'Annunzio's poetic imagination, something more than the stories of Ida's originality. Montesquiou had supplied some information: 'She is...very difficult to approach, and...her life is full of mystery. No one has ever seen her in the company of man or woman...she only leaves her hotel to go to the theatre, or to go for solitary motor drives in the forest of Saint-Cloud or other isolated spots in the vicinity of Paris, where she leaves her car, and walks for an hour or so, before returning to the hotel...When she leaves Paris, she goes lion-hunting in Africa' (Antongini, p. 286). That alone was enough to set d'Annunzio on Ida's trail. He dashed off a note formally introducing himself. She replied in equally formal terms and a few days later the poet and his secretary presented themselves at her suite in the Hôtel Carlton.

Considering the warmth of their subsequent friendship, this first meeting was very cold and unrelaxed. But soon d'Annunzio and Ida were spending a great deal of time in each other's company and much of their talk centred on the connection between Saint Sebastian's and her own remarkable legs. He raved about her to his friends. Beautiful? She was more than beautiful. She was 'lost in the midst of the frivolous actresses in Paris, like a Russian icon among the trinkets of the rue de la Paix' (Tosi, 1948b, p. 2).

Their friendship soon became public knowledge. Marc Chagall, a new arrival in Paris, went backstage at the Opéra to see his old master Bakst and could not help noticing that 'near him d'Annunzio, short, with a thin moustache, was flirting tenderly with Ida Rubinstein' (p. 105). Or he might be seen watching her before a performance, 'sitting in silence, seated like a Sibyl who waits for the god inside her or already hears him in her' (Tosi, 1948b, p. 2). During the performance he would join the audience. The writer Elisabeth de Gramont, the Duchesse de Clermont-Tonnerre, remembered his coming into Romaine Brooks's box to relive the experience of **Schéhérazade**, although the vision of Ida apparently faded quickly on that occasion. After the performance, 'descending the staircase of the Opéra, he whispered to a lady swathed in a fur wrap, her head bristling with diamonds, "Come with me, we shall have a night of profound bliss." But,' the duchess gathered, 'the moment was not propitious' (1932, p. 332).

However surprising it may seem - considering d'Annunzio's voracious sexual appetite - he and Ida were not lovers and almost certainly never became so. It made their friendship all the more intriguing. Not knowing what to think, some joked about it. D'Annunzio tried to solve his financial problems by having his furniture and **objets d'art** auctioned in Florence. When a very large crucifix with an extemely thin figure of Christ came under the hammer, a wit exclaimed: 'There's Ida Rubinstein!' (Jullian, 1972, p. 193).

Indeed, the real Ida Rubinstein had become part of the furniture of d'Annunzio's public life. Within weeks of their meeting she figured prominently in a scheme to realize his dream of creating a festival theatre in Paris. The Comtesse de Béarn, Montesquiou, Sarah Bernhardt, Romaine Brooks - the list went on - were organized into committees and issued with subscription forms. The project was grand, too grand because it did not survive the summer of 1910, although for many years to come d'Annunzio, encouraged by Ida, kept alive the idea of creating a theatre of his own.

At the same time Ida was also involved in a 'plot' to introduce d'Annunzio to Maurice Barrès. Barrès was one of France's most acclaimed writers, the poet who associated his name with patriotism. D'Annunzio led the poetic field in Italy, if not yet the patriotic one: that would come soon. It was only logical that they should meet. But there was a problem: Barrès, the ascetic upholder of authority and conventional religion, distrusted d'Annunzio and disliked him without having met him: 'I see him as part of the faded tradition of the Jean Lorrains and the Wildes of this world...But he is something more. What? A businessman looking for a provider of funds' (p. 335).

Cécile Sorel took matters into her own hands. She enlisted the help of Ida, Montesquiou and Anna de Noailles - the French Sappho - and on 30 June held a grand dinner party for Barrès. D'Annunzio, as arranged, slipped in almost unnoticed with the soup. Barrès was outraged and his hostess only just dissuaded him from leaving. D'Annunzio set to work: without addressing a direct word to Barrès, he treated the whole company to a brilliant display of his rhetoric. Even the waiters were transfixed, forgot their work and stood listening. The service was held up but nobody noticed. Barrès sat still, inexpressive, glacial, determined not to be impressed, but before the end of the evening even he was conquered. As Cécile Sorel noted with some satisfaction, although 'the outer ice held..., within everything was flaming with exaltation and enthusiasm' (p. 94). In time even the outer ice melted and the two men became firm friends. Before a year had passed d'Annunzio did Barrès the honour - a slightly embarrassing one - of dedicating to him that masterpiece of aestheticism, his French verse-play **Le Martyre de Saint Sébastien.**

Ida Rubinstein's dramatic entry into d'Annunzio's life had been the thing that finally triggered off the mechanism set to produce this major work. Its creation became the focal point of their friendship from the moment of its inception. D'Annunzio had long dreamt of writing a work based on the legend of Saint Sebastian, whose martyrdom at the hands of the Emperor Diocletian's archers had inspired countless poets and painters. Over the centuries the saint, pierced with arrows and with a look of languid ecstasy on his face, had become the personification of the syncretic union between the suffering and patient Christian and the handsome, sexless ephebe of classical antiquity. D'Annunzio, whose own sexual instincts were generally very conventional and not in the least transcendental, was fixated by the image of this latter-day Adonis.

As early as 1884, at the age of twenty-one (still not sophisticated enough to know better), he had been fascinated by the love-bites left on his chest by his mistress Olga Ossani. They looked like fresh arrow-wounds and, for the first time, the image of Saint Sebastian pierced with arrows rose up before his eyes. But not until his first sight of Ida Rubinstein - who had not even been conceived in 1884 - did his vision of the saint assume a bodily form. She became not only the inspiration for a work of literature but also the agent of its expression in a dramatic form. She had the ideal body, he decided, the ideal legs, the ideal air of sexual ambiguity for the saint. The transvestite nature of the role would subtly underline the androgynous and passive image of his beautiful masochistic anti-hero.

D'Annunzio was slow to start writing **Le Martyre**. Not until December 1910 did he make a serious attempt to seek the expert advice of Gustave Cohen on the medieval antecedents to the 'mystery' that he intended to construct and it was not until **the** same month that definite arrangements were made to commission music for the production, which had already been fixed for May 1911.

During the summer of 1910 d'Annunzio had retired to his villa at Arcachon to meditate upon reproductions of Old Masters depicting the saint. (They had been borrowed from Montesquiou's extensive collection of prints.) He also developed an interest in archery. Walking in the forests near his villa, he had been fascinated by the sight of pine trees gashed by resin-collectors: they seemed to be suffering their own martyrdom, their wounds bleeding like those of the divine Sebastian. And when Ida descended upon Arcachon to spend a few days at the Grand Hotel, she found herself having to humour him by shooting arrows at pine trees. The local people were amazed at the sight of the willowy figure of a woman stretching a bow as tall as herself. But the poet was inspired. Preliminary jottings began to fill his notebooks. He became totally absorbed in the work and for a time everything that did not relate to it was neglected. A tortoise with a heavily gilded shell, a present from Ida, crept into a patch of funereal tuberoses and died unnoticed. Living it may have lacked style; dead it had no choice: its shell became an attractive centre-piece on the dining-room table at Il Vittoriale, the villa on Lake Garda later acquired by d'Annunzio.

But a major distraction forced itself upon the poet whether he liked it or not. During the summer he had been living with the melancholic American artist Romaine Brooks. As a child alternately neglected and terrorized by her family, as a young woman the heir to a large fortune, she had plunged into a marriage of convenience with an English member of Capri's homosexual community. But she left him to make her name in London and Paris as a painter of remarkable portraits, brooding and dark-toned. She also caused something of a sensation by designing the décor of her houses in stark black and white.

Romaine was an unusual woman by any standard but her liaison with d'Annunzio was even more extraordinary because it represented an unexpected deviation in an otherwise entirely lesbian existence. At the time she was on the rebound from a psychologically problematic involvement with a fellow American, the renowned music-lover, the Princesse Edmond de Polignac. Romaine had not felt comfortable in her social circle. At the same time she had become too dependent upon her as a mother-substitute - which the princess did not find flattering. And when the honey-tongued and passionate d'Annunzio took Paris by storm in 1910, he swept Romaine along with him. She did, however, manage to keep some control over the situation. She was quite capable of maintaining her emotional and financial defences - since the poet had a nose for money as well as beauty. And, as André Germain put it, 'she knew how to bite as well as he knew how to claw' (1951, p. 115).

But it was an external force that disrupted their relationship. Natalie de Goloubeff, a mistress of some years standing, was still besotted with the poet and was insanely jealous of any rival. 'Donatella', as he called her, arrived at the gates of his villa brandishing a couple of pistols and threatening all in sight. D'Annunzio collapsed in a state of panic. Romaine was glacially amused and, although she remained emotionally attached to him for some time, she wrought a strange revenge on him by 'stealing' the one object capable of stimulating his creative imagination - Ida Rubinstein.

The subsequent love-affair between Ida and Romaine caused a considerable stir. Romaine's propensities were well enough known but few had suspected Ida of having lesbian tendencies. True, the story of her unconsummated marriage had leaked out and her husband had conspicuously faded from the scene. True, her own brand of aestheticism came very close to **fin-de-siècle** decadence - now highly suspect. But since her appearance in Paris, only male 'protectors' had been in evidence. An elderly admirer Antoine Mavrocordato, a millionaire Roumanian nobleman, kept a watchful eye on her. Many believed that Diaghilev extracted large sums from him to subsidize his projects but nobody knew for certain and, besides, Diaghilev was always on the look-out for potential backers. There was something rather sinister about the man. The impresario Gabriel Astruc described him as 'the sombre Mavrocordato', one of 'the three archers' (with d'Annunzio and Montesquiou) surrounding Ida (1929, p. 295). He did nothing to dispel his gloomy aura by appearing at a costume ball dressed as Othello. Ida did not play Desdemona to him: on that occasion the role was left to his notoriously flirtatious wife. Montesquiou was less inclined to take Mavrocordato seriously and always insisted on calling him 'Cold jellied crow'.

However, by the end of the 1910 season Mavrocordato had been replaced as Ida's protector by a young, much more dashing and infinitely richer man. This was Walter Guinness, the third son of the Earl of Iveagh, who had made and continued to make a fortune from brewing stout. Walter was always described as one of the richest men in England, although he devoted much more of his time to public service than to the family business. When he first met Ida, he was thirty years old and had already been the Unionist member of parliament for Bury St Edmunds for three years. (He continued to pursue an active parliamentary career, occupying a number of senior ministerial posts in successive governments. He was elevated to the peerage as Baron Moyne of Bury St Edmunds in 1932 and between 1941 and 1942 he held the post of Leader of the House of Lords. He died, dramatically, still in public service as Deputy Minister of State in Egypt in 1944.)

But there was also an active 'unofficial' side to his life. His cousin by marriage, Sir Henry ('Chips') Channon, stressed this balance in a colourful description prompted by the news of his death (pp. 396-7):

> Walter Moyne was an extraordinary man, colossally rich, well meaning, intelligent, scrupulous, yet a viveur, and the only modern Guinness to play a social or political role, being far less detached than most of his family. He collected yachts, fish, monkeys and women. He had a passion for the sea, and for long expeditions to remote places. He had a curious frenzy for the very early Gothic, and all his houses were in that style, and hideous...Walter with his steely-grey hair, turquoise eyes, had a distinguished appearance, and also the curious Guinness money traits. He was careful of his huge fortune, though he probably had about three millions.

Chips Channon was wrong on two counts - apart from the fact that, when Ida first met Walter Guinness, his hair was not yet steely-grey. One of his houses was not a mock-Gothic horror: to be close to Ida he kept the lease on a house in Paris at 12 rue de Poitiers in the classically restrained and aristocratic Faubourg Saint-Germain. And when his will was probated, it transpired that his fortune amount to two (not three) million pounds. Many conjectured (and long before the offical figues were known) that the other million had been spent on Ida Rubinstein. Although she was very rich in her own right, he gave her a fortune in jewels and is said to have borne much of the financial brunt of her extravagant theatrical productions in the three decades and more that their friendship lasted. 'Guinness was good for her' (1972, p. 66). Many agreed with Arnold Haskell's comment but did not express it quite so crudely.

For her part Ida seldom seemed to give much thought for money, her own or anybody else's, just as long as it was in plentiful supply. Her relationship with Walter Guinness was based on more than just a financial foundation. She shared a great many of his interests and found him a lively and exciting companion. And, as Philippe Jullian coyly put it, 'what little desire she had for men she offered to her protector' (1972, p. 228).

Ida's love for Romaine Brooks had only a passing effect upon her relationship with Walter Guinness, although it did smoulder on for several years and the two women's friendship lasted a lifetime. This is all the more surprising because their affair seems to have precipitated Ida into a crisis. She fell deeply in love with Romaine. Romaine saw in Ida her ideal of female beauty but she was not quite so emotionally involved and, having used her as a foil against d'Annunzio, she became alarmed when Ida began to talk about buying a farmhouse deep in the country where they could live alone together. She would give up everything for her, her career, her ambitions, her property, her friends. Romaine back-pedalled and made strenuous efforts to control Ida. She diverted her by painting several studies of her in the nude, such as **Azalées blanches** (1910) and **Le Trajet** (1911), which said a lot more about Romaine's psychological state (particularly her mother-fixation) than about her sitter's. Ida's slender form fed Romaine's addiction to elongated lines and curves to a point of exaggeration worthy of El Greco. But these nude studies did represent a completely unique phase in Romaine's development as an artist. Generally her subjects hid themselves behind a brooding exterior and sported their clothes as badges of social or professional standing.

Ida was not an easy model to paint. Her moods changed quickly from exuberant joy to black depair. She would sit placidly on Romaine's covered terrace, with its inevitable black and white décor embellished with clouds of white flowers, and suddenly remark that it was an ideal place to commit suicide. Ida was a woman with 'a rather uncomfortable inner life': behind her striking and enigmatic public image was a person who was 'a great deal less than she seemed' - or so Romaine thought (Secrest, pp. 242-3).

But Ida had never pretended to be more than she was, however apparent that might seem to an outside observer. Romaine also seemed to forget that she herself was largely responsible for disorientating her in the first place. Given Ida's childhood as an orphan brought up in the house of kinsfolk and given her social detachment in a disapproving or envious world, she had achieved remarkable, tangible results in applying what talent and resources she had to an almost ideological pursuit of beauty. The moment when she evaluated its claims beside those of her love for Romaine was a dangerous one. Although Ida probably had a lesbian orientation before Romaine fixed her purposeful sights on her, the effect was no less devastating for all that. Ida was always much more ill-at-ease in the company of her own sex. Years later this was one of the first things that the dancer Keith Lester noticed about her: 'she drew herself up when talking to women, but relaxed when talking to men' (fol. 2). Paradoxically, the sex that claims the emotional attention can often be the less companionable one.

Ida managed to get herself back onto an even keel despite, rather than because of Romaine's attitude towards her. She was a passionate admirer of Ida's talent for plastic movement but she gave her no encouragement in her struggle to make a name for herself as an actress. Ida was a devoted admirer of Sarah Bernhardt. 'She would make Romaine listen for hours while she read, with a strong Russian accent, speeches as Sarah might have read them and then made Romaine choose the pitch of her voice that sounded better. Romaine, exasperated, chose the lower pitch but Ida informed her that Sarah had preferred the higher.' Meryle Secrest, Romaine's biographer, concluded that this indicated Ida's 'lack of good sense' (p. 243). One might equally conclude that it showed up Romaine as the unsympathetic and self-centred person that she undoubtedly was.

Romaine unscruplously used Ida as the object of her casual sexual desires until 1915 when she established herself firmly on Natalie Clifford Barney's rota of lovers. One of Romaine's letters to Montesquiou contains a strong hint that he once called at Romaine's house in the middle of the day and all but caught her and Ida **flagrante delicto**. It was the maid's day off, so a flustered Ida had had to explain why Romaine was still in her dressing gown: she had a cold. If so, one wonders why Romaine felt it necessary to send Montesquiou a present of 'twelve bottles of wine, one for each month of the year' (BN, 15164, fols 88-9). Clearly she thought it necessary to bribe him to keep his mouth shut.

As for the success of Romaine's revenge on d'Annunzio, that was very transitory. She herself was soon writing loving letters to him again. Ida overcame her craving for romantic solitude **à deux** and by autumn 1910 she was applying herself again to the creation of **Le Martyre de Saint Sébastien.**

For his part d'Annunzio had thought of scarcely anything else. Until 2 March 1911, when the fair copy was completed, he worked feverishly on the text. The result was a monumental drama in five acts, or 'mansions' as he called them. A young Lebanese officer, Sebastian, shoots an arrow towards Heaven and it fails to return to earth. This is enough to cause his conversion to Christianity. The Emperor Diocletian, who nurses a not-so-secret passion for the adolescent, is alternately dismayed and angered by these events and declares that Sebastian cannot abandon the cult of Apollo for the worship of Christ before he provides convincing proof of the miracle. Sebastian complies by dancing on hot, smouldering coals, which, symbolically, turn into lilies. He adds a final touch by healing a woman sick of the fevers - again a symbolic act, representing Christ's triumph over suffering. Diocletian is distraught. He calls a council of magicians and tries to bribe Sebastian to renounce his faith. His response is quite explicit: he acts out the Passion of Christ before the imperial court and looks death calmly in the face. He is bound to a laurel tree and his own companions-in-arms have the sad task of shooting him through with arrows. Finally Sebastian's soul is taken away, like his arrow, into the eternal light of Heaven.

In terms of form and content **Le Martyre** was a piece of Symbolist fantasy with its roots firmly in the decadent tradition. A woman playing the principle male part could only emphasize its faded, effete nature. It was almost exactly twenty years out of date. And yet, miraculously, with all the best ingredients of literary and linguistic expertise, lavish and original sets and magnificent music blended together, it began to display all the hall-marks of a master-work.

Montesquiou carefully sifted through the text and corrected the Italian poet's unidiomatic French. He restrained his urge to use archaic words whenever they hindered the poetic flow. He steered d'Annunzio in the direction of the Bibliothèque Nationale where Gustave Cohen, author of a major work on the history of drama, could answer all his questions about the conventions of medieval drama (Cohen, pp. 64-5, 80-1):

'Were people portrayed in the nude in the mysteries, and did women play male parts?'

'Yes, the nude did appear sometimes under some peculiarly daring conditions, but, as to the other problem, one had to invert one's terms of reference. The religious origins of drama meant that on the contrary it was men to whom women's roles were assigned...'

'That doesn't matter: Ida will be Saint Sebastian, even if the Church takes umbrage.'

(Cohen began to see his point of view:) Was it any more impious to assign the role of Saint Sebastian to a woman than to give that of the Holy Virgin to an apprentice barber, a boy hairdresser, as they had done in Metz in 1468?

The sets and costumes were designed by Bakst, inveigled away from Diaghilev by Ida's beauty and high fees. At an early point she transported him, along with theatre impresarios, maids and countless pieces of baggage, to Arcachon to discuss his work with d'Annunzio. Although his dream of creating a vast cathedral-like set had to be turned down (besides, Max Reinhardt was doing something similar for his production of **The Miracle**), Bakst did design a series of sets that count among his finest work. Montesquiou took him to the Louvre 'to inspect Sassanid fabrics, Byzantine enamels and bas-reliefs from the Eastern Roman Empire unearthed in Egypt and Syria' (Jullian, 1967, p. 225). As a result his designs stressed the overripe, almost gaudy grandeur of pagan empire that was about to fall victim to the simplicity of Christianity. The only major problem encountered by Bakst occurred when he grouped the chorus on stage according to the colour of their costumes. Sopranos found themselves isolated among the basses. Lone tenors lost their notes and their nerve and could be rescued only by the chorus master's mingling colourlessly among the crowd, singing them their correct notes.

The choice of a composer capable of supplying suitable music presented some difficulties. It was not until as late as November 1910 that Ida approached her first choice, Roger-Ducasse. He was strongly tempted but declined the commission: other commitments prevented him from accepting new work that would have to be finished so rapidly (Tosi, 1948a, p. 114). Keeping Florent Schmitt in reserve, Ida took Montesquiou up on an inspired suggestion and urged d'Annunzio to sound out Claude Debussy. And perhaps surprisingly for such a detached man, Debussy was enthusiastic. He wrote to d'Annunzio from Vienna: 'How could I not like your poetry?...the thought of working with you gives me a sort of anticipatory fever' (ibid., p. 52). On 11 December Gabriel Astruc, the impresario to whom Ida assigned the production of **Le Martyre,** entertained Debussy and his wife Emma to an intimate dinner at the Café de Paris where, with the contract signed, they were introduced to 'Saint Sebastian himself in the person of the beautiful **artiste**...Madame Ida Rubinstein' (ibid., p. 54).

According to his publisher, Jacques Durand, 'Debussy was conquered by the subject of **Saint Sébastien**...he wrote his admirable score in a state of elation. The mystical subject suited his rather personal aesthetic' (p. 21). Perhaps so, but the task of writing the music was a brutal one, if only because of the limited time available. By 29 January 1911 he still had not put pen to paper since the text was only just beginning to reach him. Composition may not even have begun before 14 February, just as Ida was hurrying back from St Petersburg excited by d'Annunzio's news that nights of working until dawn had seen the completion of the draft text. That was small consolation for Debussy as he set out to fulfil his side of the contract before rehearsals began at the beginning of April. He enlisted the help of a close friend André Caplet, who was well-known in his own right as a composer and conductor, and it was he who did the lion's share of the orchestration for Acts 2, 3 and 4. Rumour had it that he even wrote the final chorus in Act 5 but there appears to be no justification for this claim (Orledge, 1982, p. 223; 1974, p. 1035).

Debussy's task would have been difficult enough if it had been straightforward. And he was clearly upset when unforeseen problems cropped up. At times it was obvious that 'the action on the stage and the music matched badly' (Tosi, 1948a, p. 74): in the fifth act, for example, there was so little activity that the music was over exposed. He was also disturbed by Ida's specifications for her dance sequences. He wrote abruptly to d'Annunzio: 'it is impossible to do what Madame Rubinstein demands, that is to say, detach the dances from the rest so that she can regulate her movements!' (ibid., p. 70). And he wrote angrily to Astruc after a suggestion that the music for her dances should be ready by 15 April, since that would be more convenient for Fokine, who had agreed to choreograph them: 'It is intolerable that I should have to fit in with commitments taken on by Monsieur Fokine' (Astruc, 1958, p. 18).

But on the whole relations between the creators of **Le Martyre** were quite amicable. Astruc had the completed text read to them and the principal interpreters at his house the Pavillon de Hanovre on 9 March and all went well. Slowly the score began to accumulate, page by page, on the conductor's desk. The orchestra and chorus were horrified by the complexity of the music and exchanged troubled glances, but soon the enthusiasm of Debussy's friends triumphed over all difficulties. Debussy himself was very impressed once rehearsals got underway and the music and action began to gel. Indeed, as a man who 'to a very high degree was ashamed of his emotions, he was not able to maintain his usual attitude of sarcastic benevolence and, very ingenuously, wept!' (Vuillermoz, 1920, p. 157). Apparently the sight of Ida Rubinstein miming the Passion of Christ to his music was too much for him.

Meanwhile, Ida herself was having no less emotional a time. D'Annunzio was alarmed at the way in which she regarded the play as something sacred. Interpreting it was like celebrating a religious rite. Flattering? Yes, but there were unfortunate side-effects: 'She is feverish. She thinks, dreams and lives only for her new creation...She is even losing her looks, and that astounds me, for she has only two idols - her art and her body' (Antongini, p. 443).

She was so preoccupied with learning her part, having her diction supervised by a French teacher and rushing off to Monte Carlo to rehearse her dances with Fokine (who was in the middle of preparations for Diaghilev's 1911 season) that she left the task of casting to d'Annunzio and Astruc, although the poet did keep her well informed and consulted her on everything. He even went so far as to install himself in a ground floor apartment in the Hôtel des Reservoirs in Versailles, Ida's home-from-home, where she had gone during the rehearsal period. They frantically sent notes back and forward to each other, an almost farcical situation in which the page-boys had to work overtime.

There were also farcical moments at the theatre. Parisian actresses stabbed each other in the back to obtain parts in **Le Martyre** and d'Annunzio had to cope with their bitchiness: 'Don't give the part to Madame X.! The woman's a hundred years old! She can hardly stand without crutches!' (ibid., p. 444). And a colonel's widow complained that Astruc had not given her daughter a part in the Chorus of Virgins: 'I can confirm...that she is the only girl who, as a real **virgin** (she has never been out of the house except in my company), is worthy of filling the role in a work as eminently religious as yours!' (ibid., p. 445).

Another person who went through an emotional crisis as **Le Martyre** was being created was Robert de Montesquiou. He did not miss a single rehearsal nor a single performance, even though the experience left him limp with exhaustion. He regarded the work as the supreme masterpiece of two friends of genius. But he did not hestitate to make his own contribution when he felt it necessary. He made sure that the lighting made the first scene look like a medieval stained glass window. He was not above jumping up on stage 'to show the choreographer, Fokine, Saint Sebastian's gesture as he throws skywards an arrow which miraculously does not fall to earth again' (Jullian, 1967, p. 226).

Most of the time he just sat in ecstasy at the sight of Ida as the saint. Jean Cocteau came to the theatre and disturbed Montesquiou's concentration. He was told off so smartly that he could not think what to say - for once. Next day he wrote an apology: 'You reproach me for bringing my unworthy self to the theatre...I could have answered by saying that one does not forbid a believer from entering a holy place. My pain transmitted to my tongue I forget what inapt words.' Cocteau's biographer explained: he had 'stumbled into the count's psychodrama. Ida Rubinstein..., nude beneath Saint Sebastian's armour,...was the ephebus of Montesquiou's dreams, the last incarnation of Seraphita. In love with both d'Annunzio and Rubinstein, Zeus and Ganymede, the count derived tragic joy from promoting their liaison (**sic**), off stage and on. Cocteau had crashed a party of archetypes in which he seemed unpardonably **de trop**' (Brown, pp. 69-9).

Montesquiou and his heroes soon had to cope with a much more worrying intrusion than Cocteau's. On 8 May Cardinal della Volpe authorized a decree from the Congregation of the Papal Index by which all d'Annunzio's fictional and dramatic works were banned. Taking a cue from this, a society lobby, using the Bishop of Persépolis (**in partibus**) as a mouthpiece, persuaded Monseigneur Amette, Archbishop of Paris, to issue a pastoral letter in which Le **Martyre** was specifically condemned as offensive to the Christian conscience and all French Catholics were forbidden to attend performances of the work on pain of excommunication.

Ida's friends and collaborators all emitted loud howls of protest, although they might reasonably have expected the Church to be sensitive about their 'mystery'. The last diocesan conference had already urged Catholics to stay away from plays that were offensive to the faith and that had been only a minor off-shoot of the general defensive attitude adopted by the French church since the Laws of Separation of 1905 had ranged it against the 'godless state'. Nationalist and anti-semitic opinion added force to ecclesiastical fulminations. Why had this Italian come to France to sully the language with his decadent scribblings? And were not Astruc and Rubinstein, the two main organizers of this profanation, Jewish in origin? Astruc muttered half-seriously: 'I do not want to be accused of having crucified the Saviour for the second time' (Antongini, p. 440).

Montesquiou was outraged and made his feelings felt by organizing a public tribute to d'Annunzio. Readings from his works by Julia Bartet and a brilliant lecture by the count himself did a lot to mollify the affronted poet. But d'Annunzio and Debussy also made their own protest by writing to the archbishop: Le **Martyre** was a deeply religious work, a celebration of a great saint's faith. And as for the fact that he was being played by a woman, Madame Rubinstein's asexual appearance could be guaranteed not to stimulate libidinous reactions. Monseigneur Amette was not convinced: drama had long since ceased to have any mystic or religious **raison d'être.** By presenting the martyrdom of a Christian saint as mere entertainment one was committing a sacrilege and by having him impersonated by a female dancer was even worse.

Truth be told, d'Annunzio's protest was less than honest. Ida's portrayal of the saint did have an overt sexual quality: the poet even admitted his duplicity to Astruc when he remarked that, 'when Ida Rubinstein makes her appearance almost naked at the moment of supplication, it will be too late to protest. The public will have been conquered by that time' (ibid., p. 440). And, of course, in stage terms this sexual appeal was implicitly homosexual. Elisabeth de Gramont touched on this point when trying to explain the archbishop's attitude: 'there were, it appears, two archers who loved each other tenderly.' She even detected a hint of personal pique in the cleric's attitude: 'D'Annunzio had slightly irritated the archbishop my making himself too much at home in Notre Dame; pretexting an artistic urge, he used to have the organist play for him alone, threw the vestry into turmoil and with his friends, climbed the private staircase leading to the organ-loft. He even gave a garden party in the small garden that is hemmed in between the masonry and the river' (1932, p. 334).

Debussy was interviewed by René Bizet for an article in **Comoedia** on 18 May. A gentle protest, his comments did much to defuse the situation: 'the archbishop has forbidden the faithful to attend d'Annunzio's play, although he does not know the work. But let us not dwell on these annoying details...I wrote my music as though I had been asked to do it for a church...It is my faith, my own, singing in all sincerity' (Debussy, p. 3).

Meanwhile, Montesquiou adopted different tactics against another notable opponent of the play. Paul Bourget, a pillar of society and an academician, forgot his past and railed against d'Annunzio as a depraved anti-Christian. Montesquiou quietly informed him that the homosexual love-letters of his misspent youth had survived. He had kept those written to himself and d'Annunzio's devoted translator, Georges Hérelle, had some that were nothing if not explicit.

Far from being inhibited by the disapproval of the lay and clerical establishment, public interest grew as the controversy raged. A few Catholic families, glad of an excuse for economy, cancelled boxes taken for Astruc's grand season, although throughout the run of the play the less well-lit boxes in the theatre seemed to be unusually full.

But before the première on 22 May 1911 another incident occurred, as if Fate were conspiring against the project. A public dress rehearsal was arranged for 21·May. Designed as a dazzling occasion, a deliberate piece of publicity to set the seal of social approval on the work and defuse criticism, it had to be called off. That morning the Minister for War, Maurice Berteaux, had attended an international meeting at Issy-les-Molineaux and had been decapitated when a propellor accidentally fell off an aeroplane. As a mark of respect all theatrical performances were cancelled and so the throng of socialites who turned up for **Le Martyre** found the doors of the Théâtre du Châtelet barred against them. Only members of the press were allowed in to view the rehearsal.

The première next day was not an unqualified triumph. Peter Lieven felt that 'nothing but a cold success was achieved' (p. 120). Marguerite Long, worshipping Ida from afar, thought that **Le Martyre** 'suffered both from its richness and from its duality. One does not with impunity unite Adonais with a Christian Sebastian, the decadence of Rome with the mystery of the Middle Ages' (1960, p. 162). Some of the audience were bemused. Others thought the play too long. (In fact, Ida had it shortened for subsequent nights.) They had expected more music. And as time advanced into the early hours of the morning, 'they dribbled little by little out of the theatre like water from a cracked vase' (ibid., p. 163).

Some were fixated by details rather than by the work as a whole. Marcel Proust wrote to Reynaldo Hahn: 'I find the legs of Madame Rubinstein (which are like those of both Closmenil and Maurice de Rothschild) sublime' (1956, p. 206). His real pleasure seemed to be derived vicariously from Montesquiou, who perorated eloquently about the work during the first interval. The pleasure was heightened when he sat next to him during the last act: 'Connected to your enthusiasm by your wrist, as though by a metal electrode, I was convulsed as if in an electric chair' (1930, p. 231). (An echo of Proust's experience recurs in **Le Côté de Guermantes**, where Montesquiou's part is - predictably - taken by the Baron de Charlus.)

Cocteau enthused, as if to make up for his initial **faux pas**. Ida as an adolescent fascinated him: 'The very quality of her breaking voice subtly indicates the passage...from boyhood to maturity...one must recall her boyish cries to her companions to follow her...and her recital of the slave's beatitude, when her voice seems to come from out of those starry depths which Monsieur Bakst has realized for us' (1913, pp. 38-9). Elisabeth de Gramont focused on the same same points. Music and poem together were 'a symphony that makes you believe in heaven since it takes you there...I can still hear Rubinstein's hoarse voice...In her scarab-like armour, she was truly the sexless stripling that one sees in triptychs by Italian masters of the Renaissance' (1932, pp. 333-4). Others were inclined to think that her armour made her look rather too much like Joan of Arc.

Press criticism was slightly equivocal. Some concentrated on the text. Henri Ghéon called the work 'barbarity all the more dangerous as it wears the Mediterranean mask of beauty' (pp. 5-6). As for the music, some of Debussy's admirers were disappointed that it had taken second place to the text. On the other hand, that least original of composers Reynaldo Hahn commented (and was admonished by Proust for his presumption) that the music displayed 'by its native reserve, a flagrant disparity with the flamboyant eloquence and the luminous delirium of Monsieur d'Annunzio.' He was faintly shocked that the score contained some 'dissonant intonations' and that the finale was marked by a 'barbaric diatonicism' (1911, p. 4).

Ida Rubinstein's performance attracted mixed criticism. Many were disconcerted by what they saw as her transformation from a mime into an actress, whereas she regarded it as a reversion. The Russian tinge in her accent was only too obvious a target for criticism. Reviewers could not resist mentioning it. Henry Bidou remarked that she 'rolled her "r"s as if she had a mouthful of pebbles' (1911, pp. 1-2). By contrast, Louis Delluc was completely enthusiastic. Ida, playing her Sebastian before Maxime Desjardins's rather too true-to-life Diocletian, was exquisite. If she continued to play 'this beautiful **Saint Sébastien** which dazzled and astonished..., she would complete the poet's glory' (p. 115).

Adolphe Brisson confessed that he found her portrayal of the death of Christ overwhelming. He had nothing but admiration for her 'superior intuition, her extraordinary sensitivity' (pp. 2-3). And Fernand Nozière was fulsome in his praise: 'She creates...postures of an incredible beauty. She is, if one dares say so, a series of masterpieces. One is moved to the point of tears by the meaningful harmony of her poses and of her movements' (quoted Cuttoli, p. 18).

Surveying the work as a whole, Emile Vuillermoz concluded with conviction: **'Le Martyre**...is a masterpiece which is yet to be revealed. Debussy has written his **Parsifal**...But this **Parsifal** still awaits its Bayreuth!' (1920, p. 158).

But whatever the critics said, they made very little impression upon the main creators and promoters of the work. Montesquiou let letters from friends accumulate on his desk without comment. Romaine Brooks's note was scathing: 'What a pity that there aren't enough people of taste to make up an audience worthy of (Ida), an audience that would demand only the intense pleasure of admiring her' (BN, 15163, fol. 119). The painter Phillipp von Laszlo had been persuaded to see the work and did not regret it. He wrote to Montesquiou: 'I found it even more beautiful than I hoped' (BN, 15164, fol. 96).

D'Annunzio was particularly unconcerned about the critics' postmortems. He had only been interested in creating a work of art. His aim achieved, nothing else mattered. Ida Rubinstein had been his ideal saint. 'Where,' he asked rhetorically, 'could I have found an actor whose body was so incorporeal?' (Cohen, p. 81).

Ida was also strangely unconcerned about public opinion. Even the praise that Robert de Montesquiou lavished on her in an article entitled 'L'Archange d'or', she shrugged off as 'too hyperbolical'. D'Annunzio's approval was all that she wanted: 'How could I attempt to express the gratitude with which the heart and spirit of an interpreter overflows when a poet of the stature and genius of d'Annunzio most willingly avows...that she has not betrayed his ideas, that she has served his dream well?' (Rubinstein, pp. 329-30).

She was, in fact, being too self-effacing. What she had done was to inspire Debussy, d'Annunzio, Bakst and Fokine, four of the greatest creative geniuses of the day (all, except her near-contemporary Fokine, about twice her own age) to produce a unique work with all the characteristics of a masterpiece. She was not only the catalyst that activated the creative process; she had also breathed life into it by means of her interpretative skill - and her money.

And from a personal point of view, her Saint Sebastian told her a great deal: how much she had achieved; how much more she could achieve in her pursuit of perfect beauty. **Le Martyre** became a yardstick with which she measured all her subsequent stage-productions. And critics of every hue did exactly the same. Until the end of her career they looked back to her performance in May 1911 and, with almost romantic nostalgia, compared her latest work with it.

CHAPTER 4

Embodiments of Love and Death, 1911–1912

Le Martyre de Saint Sébastien was a watershed in Ida Rubinstein's career. It established her in Western Europe as an artiste in her own right, unsupported by the prestige of Diaghilev's company. Relations between these two individuals - never very warm - cooled considerably about this time, although nothing like as decisive a break as often imagined took place. After the 1911 season Ida took no formal part in his troupe's activities. But the possibility of her return was not immediately ruled out.

Nijinsky cherished a desire for her to take on the role of the first Nymph in his controversial ballet **L'Après-midi d'un faune** as he worked on it during 1911 (see Buckle, 1971, p. 179) but long before its première on 29 May 1912 the idea had been abandoned. And even as late as 1914 Ida was being talked of as the person for the role of Potiphar's wife in Richard Strauss's ballet **La Légende de Joseph.** Before he signed the contract with the composer, Diaghilev assumed that Ida had agreed to take part. Certainly Hugo von Hofmannstal and Strauss regarded this as settled - and, indeed, as a subject for congratulations (see Buckle, 1979, p. 270). However, matters turned out differently, as Romain Rolland noted in his diary after the public dress rehearsal on 14 May 1914: 'My sister and I are in two dress-circle seats...In the row in front of us is Gabriele d'Annunzio, who boos Strauss's work when the curtain falls. His girl-friend, Ida Rubinstein, must have quarrelled with Strauss; she was to have interpreted the part of Potiphar's wife and withdrew, at the last moment' (Strauss and Rolland, p. 160).

Many of Ida's former colleagues in the Ballets Russes believed that she had fallen out with Diaghilev because he refused to give her major dancing parts instead of the jewel-like mime roles in which she was such a sensation. Tamara Karsavina suggested that Diaghilev's relentless pursuit of talent had much to do with the coolness between him and Ida: 'he could not help seeing a potential gem. The search for any new manifestation of beauty accorded well with his temperament; for hardly was his task accomplished before the impetuous spirit shifted off to press forward towards a new one' (p. 157).

In Ida's case the reverse was true. She was the one who was in hot pursuit of new 'discoveries', although for her these were works of art and not stars. Her own priorities assumed an importance infinitely greater than any as an 'employee' of Diaghilev's. For example, while she was wholly engrossed in rehearsals for **Le Martyre** in 1911, Diaghilev wanted her in Monte Carlo for performances of **Schéhérazade** on 9 and 10

April. On the day of the dress rehearsal she sent a telegram excusing herself: her work in Paris prevented her from coming. Her costume was hastily refitted for Karsavina. Ida did appear for the performance on 24 April (and incidentally saved Diaghilev's skin because his contract specified that certain performers, including Ida, should appear at some point in the season.) One suspects that her belated dash to Monte Carlo was prompted more by the need to work with Fokine on the choreography for **Le Martyre** than out of any feeling of obligation to Diaghilev. His scheduling her for an appearance during the Coronation season at Covent Garden in July was something of an act of faith - an unjustified one, as it turned out.

When she induced Bakst and Fokine to work for her, Diaghilev had not concealed his annoyance. But this had not led to open antagonism between them. Instead, he let Bakst taste the bitterness of his spleen and this certainly sowered relations between them. Until his death in 1929 Diaghilev always became unreasonably angry whenever any of his creative or interpretative artists showed any inclination to work for Ida - for fees which he could not himself afford.

Another matter vitiated relations between them. Ida's semi-wild pets, to which she was genuinely attached, caused problems. Her black panther was particularly obstreperous. It seemed to be perpetually hungry (perhaps she shared her diet of champagne and biscuits with it.) It would eat simply anything. Gloves and hats would disappear down its throat and on one occasion it ate a bunch of keys. It had the habit of climbing up curtains and chewing them until they fell down, taking the bemused animal with them. Couturiers, knowing what would happen to their interior decoration if Ida arrived with her pet, would shut up shop as soon as they caught wind of its coming.

A story is told of a leopard which Ida brought back from Africa. Debussy and Bakst arrived at her apartment one day and were ushered into the salon by the maid: 'Madame will only be a few moments.' Five minutes passed in silence. Nothing happened. Suddenly they heard a crash, followed by a terrible scream. More silence. Then there was the sound of light footsteps. The door flew open and in came Ida, completely naked, dragged along by the leopard on a chain. One hand clutched her shoulder in a vain attempt to staunch the blood streaming from it. Apparently the animal had not taken kindly to being kept chained up to a chest of drawers and had taken a lunge at Ida by way of protest.

The panther could be just as dangerous. On another occasion Bakst found himself face to face with it in the same room but, after an initial twinge of fear, he became engrossed in his conversation with Ida and forgot about the beast. In the meantime it contrived to get itself

stuck inside an immense waste-paper basket and became agitated. Ida
deftly extricated it but not without cost. As Bakst later recalled,
'when she let the animal go, I was horrified to see that Madame
Rubinstein had her chest and arms literally starred with claw marks. She
hadn't said a word, and she declared that it was nothing...I was
terrified for her' (Thomas, p. 103).

But it was Diaghilev's experience that brought matters to a head. One
day he came to see Ida. He was wearing a large frock-coat, to which the
panther, waking up from a nap, took an instant dislike. It bounded in
Diaghilev's direction and he promptly leapt up onto a table with a cry
of terror. This, in turn, frightened the young animal. It took refuge in
a corner where it crouched, howling and snorting, its whiskers
bristling. Ida thought that she would die of laughter as she picked the
panther up by the scruff of the neck and threw it into the next room.
Diaghilev was saved. But Bakst added a rider to the story: 'That did not
prevent the beast from being taken away from her a few days later:
experts had declared that it was a danger to human life' (ibid.,
pp. 103-4). Ida and Diaghilev found it difficult to forgive one another
for the part each played in the episode.

Whether relations between them were strained or not was ultimately
immaterial. Ida began her career as an actress. Mime and dancing came
into her life almost incidentally. It was only a matter of time before
she resumed her original career. Although she had no intention of
letting her balletic skills atrophy, work within the confines of a
ballet company such as Diaghilev's could only prove restrictive and
frustrating.

Ida's acting ambitions soared very high. She wanted to be accepted in
the West as a great actress like Sarah Bernhardt and worked hard to
achieve her aim. Julia Bartet, the celebrated classic actress, nicknamed
'La Divine' by adoring audiences, helped her with her technique. For
some time Ida's diction continued to be marred by traces of a Russian
accent. (Parisian theatre-goers still claimed to detect it long after it
had disappeared.) She worked on the problem with several teachers. But
she was very sensitive about the subject and easily became depressed if
all did not go well (BN, 15333, fols 112, 114-15).

The person who gave Ida most help and encouragement was none other
than Sarah Bernhardt herself. At an early point Montesquiou had
introduced them. Who better to do so? He had adored Sarah since his
youth. The fact that their facial features were vaguely similar may have
had something to do with the attraction. It even tempted him to make
love to Sarah in a frenzy of narcissism. His first - and only -
heterosexual experience, it caused him to be sick for the next twenty-

four hours. But nothing dampened his admiration for her and, in a real way, Ida was the beneficiary of their friendship. Sarah was impressed by her stage-presence, even though she did not share the general enthusiasm for the Ballets Russes style. Boris Kochno painted a bizarre picture of her going to see **Schéhérazade**: 'Already lame, the great **tragédienne** had herself carried into the theatre, but scarcely had the curtain gone up than she was seen to become overwrought. Laying about her with her cane, she cried, "Let's get out of here! Quickly...I'm afraid. They are all mutes!"' (p. 46).

Sarah laboured under no such misapprehension in Ida's case. Fernand Nozière believed that she had an instinctive understanding of her nature: 'She recognized in her a woman of her own breed. In the midst of all the essentially vulgar creatures who littered the stage, these two made their way like beings of a different race' (p. 26). They treated each other as kindred spirits and Ida very consciously **tried** to model her stage-presence and delivery on Sarah's. However, it was not until the summer of 1912 that they had any serious contact at the professional level.

No sooner had the dust settled after **Le Martyre** than Ida started to think of possible projects for the following season. She temporarily turned away from d'Annunzio as her favoured author and, at least to begin with, retracted her Debussyan steps. She approached his former bosom-friend Pierre Louÿs - whose disapproval of Debussy's second marriage to Emma Bardac in 1904 had effectively destroyed their relationship. Louÿs responded with alacrity and suggested that he might write her a **mimodrame**. What he had in mind is not clear but, rather than a straight mimed play, he probably conceived of something akin to a **mélodrame**, that historic French dramatic form in which singing, dance and speech, often recited against a background of music, combine happily to make an artistic whole. **Le Martyre de Saint Sébastien** was the first notable example of this in the twentieth century and, more than anybody else, Ida Rubinstein was instrumental in reviving and perfecting it.

Louÿs wrote expressing his enthusiasm to Astruc, in his capacity as Ida's agent: 'Madame Rubinstein is the very incarnation of the character I dream of...I see a sort of identification between her and my character. But I make the suggestions and she will make the arrangements' (Astruc, 1958, p. 21). The subject of his project remains something of a mystery. He was perhaps thinking about a dramatized version of his **Chansons de Bilitis,** which would have proved a very sympathetic vehicle for her dramatic and balletic talents. Ida was attracted by his ideas at first but her attention was soon distracted by 'more interesting' proposals.

One of these proposals was a dramatized version of Théophile Gautier's novel **Mademoiselle de Maupin**. Around October 1911 Ida exhaustively discussed the idea with Montesquiou, who had planted it in her mind in the first place. And it was an excellent one, but a pit-fall loomed ahead. Judith Gautier, Wagner's 'last mistress' and an old friend of Montesquiou's, wanted to have a hand in writing the stage-play. Ida wanted to by-pass her and entrust the work to Henry Bataille, a professional dramatist who had ingratiated himself with Ida. 'He was charming to me after **Saint Sébastien**,' she freely admitted her bias, 'and said some beautiful things to me' (BN, 15239, fols 154-5). But this project too fell by the wayside, although Ida was convinced that a fine play could have been created for her.

One cannot help thinking that, for once, she might have gone too far. To play the part of the saintly ephebe Sebastian was controversial enough but the role of Mademoiselle de Maupin was not only transvestite but also unequivocally lesbian. It is difficult to imagine how Ida intended to portray her heroine being loved by a man as a man and then by a woman as a man - a woman whose love is unimpaired by her discovery of Maupin's real sex. Ida was to surmount even greater stage problems in her time, so on this occasion bourgeois convention must have been the stumbling block.

Another project considered for this season was a new play by Maurice Maeterlinck - almost certainly his **Marie Magdeleine**, completed in 1909. Ida wrote to him in October 1911 and received a discouraging answer. She told Montesquiou of her disappointment: 'Yesterday was very sad for me. I received Maeterlinck's reply. He tells me that he is very touched by my offer, but that the play has been given to Mademoiselle Leblanc, who would like to create this role in the spring' (BN, 15193, fol. 189). This was not the first time that Maeterlinck's mistress Georgette Leblanc had been given (undeserved) preferential treatment, although one does feel that, given her propensities, Ida might have persuaded Georgette to forego her option if she had brought the full force of her charm to bear upon her.

But Ida had no time to waste on such manoeuvres. On the same evening as Maeterlinck's reply arrived, she and Bakst had a long discussion and ended up by deciding to produce Emile Verhaeren's verse-play **Hélène de Sparte.** Already renowned beyond the frontiers of his native Belgium, Verhaeren would soon earn a special place in the literary pantheon as the greatest Flemish war-poet, the 'voice of Belgium' during its years of trial.

Hélène de Sparte was presented at the Théâtre du Châtelet on 4 May 1912 and ran until 10 May. Ida's second project that season was a production of **Salomé** - this time untouched by Russian censorship - and it ran from 12 to 19 June. It was an ambitious programme and all the more daring because it bounded Diaghilev's 1912 Paris season, during which he once again arrested public attention with innovatory ballets, **Le Dieu bleu, Thamar, Daphnis et Chloë** and Nijinsky's provocative brain-child **L'Après-midi d'un faune**. As if the competition for public acclaim were not enough, Ida and Diaghilev had to jostle for rehearsal-time in the same theatre and solve logistical problems that inevitably arose with the coming and going of elaborate sets and properties - each and every one of them designed by Bakst.

The plot of **Hélène de Sparte** was based on the ferocious legend of Helen's life after the sack of Troy. Having fought to avenge his honour, her husband Menelaus takes her back to the tranquility of his Spartan kingdom. But her charms are still fatal, even though by this time she has changed from a radiant blonde into a mysterious raven-haired beauty, still immortally young, as Cocteau put it, 'the embodiment of love and death' (1913, p. 42). Now two lovers pursue her, her brother Castor and Electra. Henry Bidou described the consequences (1912, p. 116):

> In the midst of these incestuous passions the idea of crime is born and grows. As Menelaus is walking in the forest guided by Electra, Castor kills him. As Castor drinks from a spring, Electra kills him, less to avenge Menelaus than to punish her incestuous rival. Helen is transfixed with horror. She longs for death. But...there is no rest for her...When she tries to drown herself in the sea, the waves bear her up...Pardon itself is denied her, because at the sight of her everything falls in love with her. Death is not strong enough to destroy this power..., nothing can. At last Zeus, her father, takes pity on her and carries her off to heaven out of divine love.

Ida, as Helen, was naturally the focus of attention but she needed a supporting cast of forty-four actors, including the colourful Edouard de Max, a troupe of dancers and a large orchestra to perform incidental music specially commissioned from Déodat de Séverac, the mildly eccentric 'regional' composer who disarmingly described himself as a 'peasant musician'. The insistent rustic effects in his score went well with the rugged, hard-coloured sets in which Bakst combined memories of Knossos and Mycenae with fantasies inspired by the disturbing plot. The costumes were brilliantly designed and lavishly executed. The overall visual effect was striking.

The public reacted very calmly to the production. For the price of the tickets some clearly expected more than was offered. In a cartoon entitled 'Les Béotiens chez **Hélène**', Abel Faivre depicted two large society women being asked for their opinion. One of them replies: 'I feel that, for the price, they ought to tell you what you are meant to think.' But G. de Pawlowski felt amply rewarded by Ida's performance: 'She is perhaps...the only mime who is capable of giving us, in real terms, the exact equivalent of a gallery of antique statues, and one could spend hours watching her simplest movements' (1912, pp. 1-2).

Montesquiou attempted to preserve the visual effect of Ida as Helen for posterity by inviting the eminent but ailing photographer Maurice Otto to Ida's studio where he photographed her in a series of poses from the play. They are remarkable works of art in their own way but they lack some of the inner vitality that Georges Tribout managed to capture when he made a set of line drawings of her in similar poses from **Hélène**. Their restrained execution succeeds so well because it emphasizes essential lines and keeps distracting detail to a minimum. These drawings were published as a slim volume, with a preface by Charles Batilliot, an unashamed paean of praise for Ida. At last she had created a complete and integrated stage-work and not just a succession of set-pieces. This innovation had provoked the critics. The ignorant, the commercially minded, the reactionaries in the world of art and literature had uttered squeals of displeasure. But Batilliot declared (pp. 5-6):

> All homage to Ida Rubinstein who has had the courage to overturn all the hallowed traditions with her personal interpretation of this tragedy; who has shown the young a new way in which love of their art can guide them; who has established as an ineluctable principle for the actor the need to be at one and the same time an image through the use of colour, a force by means of movement, a song expressed through poetry;...who sincerely serves Beauty as the first among religions.

On 12 June, just one month after the close of **Hélène de Sparte**, the public dress rehearsal for **Salomé** took place. It had a scheduled run of one week and rumour had it that each night cost half a million francs. Whatever the exact figures, the sums involved were enormous, much greater than the cost of any work appearing in Diaghilev's programme. Nijinsky's **L'Après-midi d'un faune** was still basking the the limelight of public controversy when Ida's Salomé took up from where the faun left off - only this time the fetiche upon which she threw herself was not a nymph's veil but Saint John's severed head and his bloody lips. Many were stunned into silence by the performance. Philippe Jullian attempted to describe its psychological effect: 'This Salomé hurled herself at the society of Tout-Paris, decapitated "good taste" as though it were the head of John the Baptist, and the blood from it spattered Poiret's dresses and lacquered Dunand's furniture. Naked under clusters of real jewels given her by her millionaire lovers, Rubinstein went further than Bernhardt; indeed, went too far, so far that her success was a kind of induced stupor' (1967, p. 223).

Some recovered from their stupefaction quickly enough to voice their own comments. Henry Bidou said that Edouard de Max as Herod admirably modulated his voice to the nuances of the text (despite the strain of having to personify heterosexual lasciviousness) but, as for Ida Rubinstein, her beautiful poses were what warmed the heart. Everybody was exclaiming in transports: 'What legs! What legs!' (1912, p. 125). Ida's legs certainly had a disturbing effect. One critic had strange feelings about them (Vestris, p. 2):

Mademoiselle Rubinstein makes one so afraid, tall, so tall, so long, so slender, that one would like to cut down her legs, to make her smaller. A young painter beside me, a cubist perhaps, voices this sacrilegious wish. What has happened is that he has been swept off his feet by the tragic atmosphere, created by the opulent beauty of the scene...And he forgets that Mademoiselle Rubinstein would not be able to dance without legs and that, if she did not dance, she would not obtain the coveted cut rose.

Michel Fokine, for one, would not have been pleased by that. After Diaghilev's indifferent treatment of his **Daphnis et Chloë,** they had parted company. It was a subdued Fokine who stayed behind in Paris to supervise the choreography for **Salomé.**

Cocteau passed some remarkably sober and perceptive comments on the work. Despite Bakst's elaborate and colourful sets and costumes that assailed the perceptive observer with the religious and historical symbols and forms of Judaism, the play, maintained Cocteau, was in fact a crisp black and white social satire. Wilde had meant it that way and Aubrey Beardsley's famous illustrations had confirmed his intentions, so one finds that Herod is 'delightfully snobbish in his allusions to Caesar; the princess is as preoccupied as if she were preparing a "parlour trick"; Herodias has the all-embracing eye of the really experienced hostess; and one can imagine what the smart young ambassador will say on his return to Rome' (1913, p. 51).

Despite the inevitable comparison with Beardsley, Cocteau found Bakst's scenery effective (p. 51):

The courtyard is surrounded by tortuous paths, worn unevenly by unsteady feet; the excessive size of the moon explains the exaggerated importance attached to it by all those moon-struck people; the exceptionally deep crimson ramblers cling helplessly to the walls, and the awning recalls a thundercloud, streaked with lightning. From their sordid debauch the guests stagger on to a terrace which overlooks the gutter, redolent of rotting rose-leaves, and registering, presumably, a far higher temperature than the reeking scene of revelry they have left. Can one wonder, then, at the peculiar character of the post-prandial entertainment provided?...I had hoped for the gratification of seeing Madame Rubinstein dance on her hands (like Flaubert's Salomé). She suggested many wonderful things, from an arrow to an antelope, but she did not dance on her hands! I am bound to add that that fact did not prevent her duly receiving the promised reward.

Salomé's reward was a head. Ida's reward was different. An irritated Louis Delluc exclaimed: 'At the Châtelet it was once again a case of shouts and animal cries uttered by an elegant audience who did not even have the decency to keep silent before Ida Rubinstein's admirable work' (p. 239). But the shouts that distracted Delluc so much were, in fact, expressions of approval. The enthusiasm that carried the audience away at the more exciting moments may have detracted from the dramatic tension but it was meant to be complimentary. Ida cared very little for exaggerated emotional reactions when she knew that she had succeeded in creating with her Salomé an image of 'melancholic lewdness' (Nozière, p. 29) that would remain vivid in the spectator's memory for decades to come.

CHAPTER 5

Scented Death, 1912–1914

Sarah Bernhardt was impressed by Ida's performance in **Hélène de Sparte** and **Salomé**. She saw great potential in her and decided that the time had come to give her practical help with her career. She devised a plan, which she set out in a letter to Robert de Montesquiou: 'I should like to see...your beautiful friend Ida Rubinstein play (Edmond Rostand's) **La Princesse lointaine**. Ask her to put her trust in me. I shall make her work and I alone can succeed in making of this admirable artist a complete artist...It goes without saying that I refuse all recompense. I am doing this out of love of beauty and because the young woman loves beauty as I do' (BN, 15199, fol. 30).

Ida was not too proud to accept Sarah's offer. And she accepted it gratefully, all the more so because it was a clear sign that Sarah trusted her as she had trusted no actress before. Since its première in 1895 **La Princesse lointaine** had virtually been Sarah's own property. Nobody else had dared perform it. Now she was suggesting that it would be a good practice-piece for an actress who could be a potential rival. Indeed, in September 1912, when Ida set out for Constantinople to begin an expedition to Asia Minor, she made a point of taking the play with her as 'holiday reading' (BN, 15242, fols 84-7). And by December she was studying it with a single serious object in mind. She wrote to Montesquiou with news of Sarah: 'Our Great Friend is as ever valiant, but I believe that she is really suffering...However, she is thinking about **La Princesse lointaine** and talks about its production!' (ibid., fol. 101).

And before long Sarah was talking of things that must have flattered Ida even more. She kept Montesquiou abreast of developments: '**La Princesse lointaine** is postponed until next year. It is Madame Sarah Bernhardt who would have it so; she talks about it as a definite thing. She proposes that I should play **L'Aiglon** at the same time and wants to work on the role with me immediately' (BN, 15174, fols 176-7). The suggestion was remarkable since the **travesti** part of the Duc de Reichstadt was very close to Sarah's heart. One possible explanation is that she had become so ill with her injured leg that she seriously looked to Ida as her natural successor. Montesquiou was also thinking along these lines and put his thoughts into words as subtly as possible. At the end of a little dinner party to which Sarah had invited Ida and himself, he recited a laudatory poem to his hostess. Having praised her for keeping the flame of her art burning, he ended (BN, 15165, fols 64-8):

> Et cherche, autour de nous, quelqu'un qui soit une âme
> Pour assurer le votre verbe et garder le flambeau.

Sarah seemed pleased at the hint.

In some ways Ida did put on Sarah's mantle but that was not until after her death in 1923. Indeed, the fact that she lived so long and was able to continue her career on the stage was in part thanks to Ida. She encouraged Sarah to attack the source of her physical problem and have her infected leg amputated. When she agreed, Ida paid all her clinical and surgical expenses. The wicked-tongued might say that an actress could devise no more effective a method of disposing of a stage-rival. On the contrary, like so many people who reluctantly shed diseased limbs, Sarah gained a new lease of life and was soon lurching her way again through all the roles that she had made peculiarly her own. The public loved her for it.

Ida certainly had no reason to be jealous. Sarah had helped her enormously and she had no need of her roles to further her career. When she did perform some of them in the 1920s, it was more as an act of homage (and a risky one) than anything else. Sarah was the one who was most interested in cultivating Ida as her successor-designate. Ida foresaw only the pit-falls. Besides, she seldom lacked ideas of her own. While Sarah was planning to 'give' her **La Princesse lointaine**, Ida was preparing another major project of her own, a play with the heady title of **La Pisanelle, ou la mort parfumée**, written specially for her by Gabriele d'Annunzio. Ida described its genesis: 'The activity, the work on rehearsals for **Saint Sébastien,** had reanimated in d'Annunzio's heart a child-like gaiety. He laughed at everything and at nothing. Thus the idea for **La Pisanelle** came to him, and he set out to bring out the laughing and gay side of my character' (p. 330).

D'Annunzio explained his ideas for her in a letter: 'Dear brother,' as he always called her, 'I must write a work absolutely different from **Saint Sébastien,** but with the same intensity, with a new instrumentation, with a structure total in form and movement' (ibid., p. 330). Clearly he found the effort taxing because, although he had sketched out a prototype scenario as a screen-play entitled **La Rosa di Cipro** by July 1912 and the scenario for the stage-play had been composed by the following September (in time for Ida to take it with her to Constantinople), it was not until 12 March 1913 (his fiftieth birthday) that d'Annunzio completed his three-act 'comedy' and prologue.

Ida wasted no time before collecting the proofs and delivering them to the Théâtre du Châtelet: the première was only three months away. A large cast of 212 actors had to be engaged, although this was done quickly enough. When Colette wrote to Ida asking if there might be a part for her friend Christine Mendelys, the answer came back on 1 May: 'her troupe was complete and had been a long time since' (Colette, 1961, p. 91). (Ida's cheque book worked wonders.) Wsewolod Meyerhold, a leading director from the imperial theatres, was enticed away from St Petersburg to work on the production. Bakst was encouraged to create sets and costumes more spectacular and sumptuous than ever before. And Ildebrando Pizzetti (Ildebrando da Parma, as d'Annunzio dubbed him) was commissioned to write music that would complement the colourful medieval setting of the play.

La Pisanelle was intended to be very different from **Le Martyre** but proved not to be so, since its main theme also dealt with the subject of redemption through Christian love. In the setting of the exotic Latin kingdom of Cyprus a beggar-girl (Ida dressed in rags by Worth) is discovered by the debauched Prince of Tyre (Edouard de Max) as he appears on stage, magnificently swathed in silk and riding a white horse. He gives his cloak and horse to the girl, who is unembarrassed to accept such compromising gifts. The scene shifts to a convent where a crowd of excited nuns await the predicted arrival of a saint, only to be confronted by the beggar-girl-turned-courtesan. At this point the process of her conversion begins and soon she has been metamorphosed into a nun. The prince still loves her, but chastely now. His wife fails to appreciate his finer feelings and, as Ida dances an ecstatic dance of death (choreographed by Fokine), the princess's slaves bombard the beloved with a hail of blood-red roses. She meets her martyr's death - her **mort parfumée** - as their weight and scent stifle the life out of her.

After the **répétition générale** on 10 June 1913, **La Pisanelle** ran for ten days from 11 to 21 June. The première was a glittering society occasion, attended by a host of illustrious guests, including the Italian ambassador Tommaso Tittoni. As the curtain went up, the immediate focus of attention was Bakst's sets. The audience burst into applause. They were like masterpieces of Renaissance architecture, fit for an Italian museum. The costumes were delightful creations inspired by Carpaccio's paintings. But they did not please everybody. The composer Ferruccio Busoni found the sets too Russian: 'the first scene is a hall from the Kremlin. How did it get to Cyprus?' (p. 224).

Pizzetti's music, ably conducted by Désiré-Emile Inghelbrecht, attracted critical praise: 'written in the tradition of Monteverdi,' it had an 'agonized, almost morbid charm' (Georges-Michel, 1913, p. unnumbered). The score, in fact, consisted of eleven symphonic movements, interludes and dances, along with a number of pieces designed to be played as the actors recited their lines. The music followed and emphasized the rhythms and cadences of the verse. This proved much more successful than the composer had expected. As a whole the composition remains a remarkable product for its time.

Ida's performance also came in for a deal of praise. She made a convincing transition from sinner to saint and, 'when she danced,...this enchanted an audience already conquered by the force and strange precision of her unworldly voice' (ibid.). Nobody laboured under the illusion that the play was one of d'Annunzio's best, but Debussy wrote to him after the first night and uttered words of praise (Tosi, 1948a, pp. 86-7):

> What an evening...of beauty so different from **Le Martyre**...You make use, if I dare say so, of too beautiful a subject: for the mouth of the actors, for the ears of the audience whom the motley tumult of the production almost upsets...Why occupy the eyes with so much when the ears can absorb everything? For several years now we have submitted to inflences in which the North acts in concert with Byzantium to suffocate out Latin genius, so graceful and unobscure.

An unusually gloomy Busoni confessed himself confused in a letter to his wife: 'The whole play seemed old-fashioned...full of excitable gestures, long tirades, inexplicable stabbings, deaths and screams. Melancholy, and without humour, it is like an aesthetically affected Wildenbruch play...On the other hand, it may be a masterpiece and I may be admitting myself to be unappreciative' (p. 225). Perhaps so, since he was undoubtedly out of touch with the Parisian sense of aesthetics. He was, after all, the man who had gone to see Ida Rubinstein for the first time with the preconception that 'her body was not womanly, therefore not beautiful' (p. 224).

In another sense Busoni was too much of a purist. He suspected that d'Annunzio's knowledge of his subject was superficial and this may have affected his appreciation of **La Pisanelle.** One enthusiastic critic described how the poet had descended upon the archives in Cyprus. From dusty coffers he had retrieved great armfuls of faded manuscripts, stained with blood, and brought them out into the light of day (Kraemer-Taylor, p. 805). Busoni thought he knew otherwise. He had noticed 'on d'Annunzio's bookshelves...books, old and new about Cyprus...In each volume, three or four long strips of paper were placed as markers' (p. 226). Here was his unique source-material!

For Ida the production was spoiled by the temperamental vagaries of friends and colleagues. It was with a hint of ill-will that she underwrote a deficit of 250,000 francs. Then she had to write Montesquiou a distinctly conciliatory note. Aspects of the production had offended him and it had taken an unusually tactful Romaine Brooks to persuade him to attend a performance. But he was not mollified (BN, 15333, fols 63, 65; 15164, fol. 145). Apparently d'Annunzio had behaved rather badly during rehearsals and had caused trouble over the fee he wanted. An annoyed Ida confided in Montesquiou: 'He is more terrible than ever and I think that after **La Pisanelle** I shall "commission" no more plays from him. In the midst of all this ugliness your Beautiful Friendship is more and more precious to me and I could not go on without it' (BN, 15333, fol. 115).

The fact that she had caused a minor deviation in the world of fashion helped to lighten her mood only slightly. As the designer Erté recalled, 'walking slinkily **à la léopard** was...the vogue in 1913-14. It was inspired by Ida Rubinstein who, in...**La Pisanelle**..., walked a leopard on a long chain. Such is the power of fashion, which dictates not only the colour of hair and complexion but also the shape of the body' (p. 26). A strange compliment indeed, when no other woman's body was quite the same shape as Ida's!

The effort of producing **La Pisanelle** left Ida so physically and emotionally drained that she temporized over plans to revive **Le Martyre**. Soon afterwards, on 9 July, Debussy wrote to d'Annunzio in mild panic: the conductor Inghelbrecht had just told him that Astruc wanted to give two concert performances of **Le Martyre** but he had the impression that Ida intended to mount the work again at the Théâtre des Champs-Elysées. In that case the concerts would be 'pointless, not to say dangerous' (Tosi, 1948a, p. 88). Could Madame Rubinstein see Astruc as soon as possible? But they were no further forward by 30 July when they learned that Ida 'was just about to go off to hunt lions in Africa.' Debussy was dismayed: 'It is a noble sport, one does not doubt, but what will become of so many fine projects? Is there no way of getting any assurances before her departure? If I could usefully make a personal approach, I am quite ready! If necessary I shall go to (her hotel in) Versailles with bare feet and arms in chains!' (ibid., p. 90).

Nobody took Debussy up on his offer. Ida and Walter Guinness left on their hunting expedition and did not return to France that summer. She did, however, send a series of letters to Paris regarding the drawing up of contracts. But the plan to revive **Le Martyre** advanced no further than that for the time being. Suggestions that it might be made into an opera by shortening the text and having music throughout also fell on deaf ears - not surprisingly since this would have automatically written Ida out of her part.

Nevertheless **Le Martyre** still remained in the forefront of its creators' minds. In 1911 they had been invited to perform it in Rome as part of the festivities celebrating the fiftieth anniversary of the unification of Italy. Considering the delicate nature of the relationship between the Italian state and the Vatican, it was not surprising that, when d'Annunzio's works were put on the Index, the organizing committee had tactfully cancelled the performance. D'Annunzio sued for damages and in October 1913 emerged as victor in the case.

The court hearing coincided with speculation in the Italian press that **La Pisanelle** would also be put on the Index and banned in France. Even the play's sale in bookshops - one journalist confidently predicted - would be prohibited. French journalists scoffed at his naïvety. 'Our colleague clearly does not know that censorship no longer exists in France, and that besides it never had the powers he attributed to it' (anon., 1913, p. 320).

La Pisanelle highlighted another of Ida's activities - her interest in art and artists. In order to commemorate the event (before he knew what was in store) Robert de Montesquiou commissioned an acquaintance of his, the fashionable artist Antonio de La Gandara, to paint a full-length portrait of Ida. This he did with commercial alacrity and a reproduction, entitled 'la Créatrice de **La Pisanelle**', appeared in the programme. The portrait was not an outstanding work of art and Montesquiou was slightly disappointed with it. Yet it was striking: dressed (by Worth) in a silver empire gown, with a square **décolleté,** to emphasize the line of her neck, and a small veil from which a crown of plumes springs, Ida resembled a sphinx-like Queen of Sheba. La Gandara etched her profile in hard lines to enhance the mysterious, forbidding expression of her face.

The artist submitted the portrait for exhibition at the spring Salon in 1914 and Camille Le Senne used the occasion to write at length about Ida (p. 140):

One knows how this priestess of a cult both hieratic and barbaric is discussed in the press, at the same time as she is extolled in certain chapels. To the ecstasies of thurifers the critics respond with excessive severity; however, her most arcane detractors acknowledge the real interest of her plastic art. (Now La Gandara has succeeded in representing her) with a mixture of hard haughtiness and morbid grace...In the grey harmony which envelops Mademoiselle Ida Rubinstein, the face, stern and contracted, with sharp relief, becomes tragic with its restrained anguish and ardour.

The actress in her might take that as a compliment but his concluding remark was ambiguous: 'We recognise in her the sphinx..., the empress of artificial paradises who has her Gabriele d'Annunzio but who lacks a

Jean Lorrain' (p. 140). Lorrain, who represented all that was tawrdy, evil-minded and salacious about the Belle Epoque, was the last person with whom Ida would have joined forces in her quest for beauty. Besides, Le Senne's suggestion was, quite literally, impracticable: Lorrain had died eight years before - of multiple anal fistulas, a side-effect of his passion for oversized boxers.

La Gandara's painting was far from being the first portrait-study of Ida. The nude painting of Valentine Serov had been executed soon after her sensational appearance in **Cléopâtre** in 1909. Other off-shoots of the ballet were two bronze figurines of her in the title role, sculpted by P. Phillipe. There is an off-hand note in one of Ida's letters to Montesquiou: 'Would you like us to go to the sculptor's studio to see the two things that he has done of me?' (BN, 15333, fol. 30). The truth was that just then Ida had weightier things on her mind - a new hair style which she detested.

Also in 1909 Bakst began to make plans to paint a full-length portrait of her. He had already made and would continue to make many good life-like sketches as costume studies. One of the earliest, a picture of Ida as Antigone, is very fine, an extremely dramatic, tragic figure swathed in a voluminous black cloak. The idea for the portrait formed before the end of the Paris season. On 10 July 1909 one finds him writing from the Grand Hotel in Venice to Montesquiou about 'our two interesting projects', one of which was the portrait of **la bellezza**. 'You notice how I already express myself in the Venetian manner,' Bakst added in parenthesis (BN, 15163, fol. 85). But the beautiful Ida was nowhere to be found and so work on the portrait did not begin until their return to Paris.

Bakst made many preliminary sketches of her in several poses before painting the final version: a dignified, rather girlish figure, she stands looking to the side; she is dressed engagingly in black, with a large cloak over her robe, dainty shoes, a big, elegant hat and a huge muff. Some authorities give 1913 as the portrait's date but it is almost certainly earlier: the evidence of the picture itself and the dating of Ida's letters on the subject suggest the winter of 1909-1910.

During Diaghilev's 1910 season the portrait-painter Jacques-Emile Blanche was so enchanted by the Russian dancers that he invited Nijinsky, Karsavina and Ida Rubinstein to his studio at Auteuil to sketch them and have Druet photograph them in his house and garden. Blanche was not much taken with Nijinsky off-stage. He found him conceited and ill-humoured, 'puny, featureless, and with no characteristic other than being built like a jockey' (p. 257). He did, none the less, paint a fine portrait of him - fine enough for the

Princesse Edmond de Polignac to go out of her way to acquire it. Karsavina he clearly liked and he pandered to her every whim.

Ida visited the studio on several consecutive Sundays as he worked on two portraits of her, although one does wonder how much was done 'from the life' because the finished paintings bear a remarkable resemblance to some of Druet's photographs. Both depict Ida in her Zobeïda costume. One of them, in which she is standing against the background of a gold and black lacquered screen (rather too Far-Eastern for a sultan's wife), is quite fine. The other showing Ida reclining on a cushion-covered divan, behind which a black female slave lurks in attendance, is an utterly dreadful piece. Crude in its execution, it transforms Ida's celebrated lines into a series of lumps and bumps.

What she thought of it is not recorded, but one can imagine her feelings if she knew that it would end up for all to see in the library of the Paris Opéra. In a letter, dated 13 August 1910, Blanche hinted to Ida at his own dissatisfaction with his work: 'the unforgettable hours which you did not mind spending in the studio at Auteuil...have been trivialized by the photograph and its copy' - by which he meant his own painting. All he could do was to assure her of his homage and express his regrets (BN, 15318, fols 16-17).

Montesquiou stood aloof while Blanche did his paintings of Ida because he had fallen out with him years before over what he regarded as an unforgivable sin - his desire for success as a society portrait-painter at the (inevitable) expense of artistic integrity. The count was, however, behind a scheme to have Ida painted by another fashionable painter, Phillipp von Laszlo. After seeing Ida in **Le Martyre** he was so impressed by her beauty that he wrote to Montesquiou: 'I await with impatience the date in November when I shall come to Paris specially to paint her' (BN, 15164, fol. 96). Nothing seems to have come of the project, although as late as 1921 one finds Ida passing on the news that 'Laszlo is still interested ' (BN, 15242, fol. 94).

Yet another artist who was interested and, as an artist, continued to be interested in Ida was Romaine Brooks. She did many portrait-studies of her but all the early paintings, executed while they were still emotionally involved, were in fact studies in which Ida is either painted as a nude, whose lines are all important, or appears as part of a composition with a narrative content. For example, her **Masked Archer** (subtitled **The Persecuted Woman**) of summer 1911 depicts Ida as a Saint-Sebastian-like figure being shot through with arrows by a masked dwarf who, despite his obscured face, is clearly recognisable as d'Annunzio. The picture tells one less about her models than about Romaine's conflicting feelings of love for them. She was a little apprehensive about Montesquiou's reaction to the canvas and encouraged him to come alone to see it in her studio rather than at a general viewing (BN, 15164, fol. 87). Often his comments on subjects in which he had a personal interest were best not said in front of an audience.

Romaine's only 'straight' portrait of Ida - an outstanding work - was not finished until 1917, after their affair had petered out, when Ida was no longer happy about posing for long sessions while Romaine wove her into the context of some imaginary study with uncomfortable psychological implications.

Another portrait of Ida was composed in 1913, only this time it was a verbal one and the artist wielding the pen was Montesquiou himself. He had always been fixated by the Comtesse de Castiglione, Napoleon III's mistress, who spent the last decades of her life in complete seclusion, heavily veiled to prevent anybody from seeing her faded beauty. He regarded her as an ideal of female loveliness with whom he compared all other beauties, past and present. Ida, if anything, outdid the ideal and so found herself duly celebrated when Montesquiou's biography of La Castiglione, **La Divine Comtesse**, came off the presses late in 1913 (1913, pp. 219-21). Elisabeth de Gramont, who - with rather too much fervour - shared his admiration for her beauty, commented: 'It is natural that Montesquiou should feel for this beautiful creature, the present-day sister of his Second Empire idol, an admiration verging on love' (Clermont-Tonnerre , p. 151).

When Ida received her copy, she was very flattered and sat up late reading it. Next day she rewarded the author with a few words of hyperbolic praise: 'Yesterday evening I finished by first reading of **La Divine Comtesse.** I have never read anything finer, nor more moving and the hours I passed with this book number among the most beautiful of my life' (BN, 15174, fol. 179). Then she quickly changed the subject and reminded Montesquiou of his promise to accompany her to the première of d'Annunzio's play **Le Chèvrefeuille** on 12 December.

D'Annunzio had, in fact, been persuaded to write a preface to **La Divine Comtesse,** 'a preface so full of beautiful things,' Montesquiou remarked in a sceptical moment, 'that I thought he must be speaking of himself' (Jullian, 1967, p. 228). D'Annunzio was certainly not above poking fun at Montesquiou because of his obsession with the idolized Castiglione. Reynaldo Hahn recalled an occasion in May 1914 when he was dining in a restaurant with Ida, Diaghilev, Jacques Rouché, Bakst and d'Annunzio. A ballet at the Opéra was being discussed, possibly **La Légende de Joseph.** D'Annunzio was less interested in the conversation than in persuading Hahn to write a score to a 'Renaissance' libretto provided by himself, (probably an opera based on the life of Leonardo da

Vinci, in which he had briefly interested Busoni.) The poet was clearly making no headway with Hahn because he suddenly brought the party to an end. As eleven o'clock struck he rose to go (1946, p. 213):

'Friends,...this is the hour when the ghost of the Comtesse de Castiglione descends the stair.'

'In that case,' said Hahn, 'let's stay and try to see her!'

'No!' d'Annunzio's tone was firm, '...**because she smells!**'

'How's that?' Hahn was surprised.

'Because of the emanations from her useless sex!'

Montesquiou, needless to say, was not present or d'Annunzio would not have dared open his mouth, although almost certainly the sacrilegious words were reported to him. The truth was that d'Annunzio had outstayed his welcome in France. He sensed that himself. People were beginning to find his aestheticism a little embarrassing. He was still anxious to get another major project underway but was having a singular lack of success in finding collaborators and sponsors.

For her part, Ida refused to become involved in any of his plans. The memory of her problems with **La Pisanelle** had not yet faded. In fact, during the 1913-1914 season she was a little off-hand about any new project, except perhaps a revival of **Le Martyre**. Louis Delluc tried to interest her in **Esope**, a three-act play by Théodore de Banville. He was convinced that 'it would adapt so well to her princely talent and, as a quintessentially French work, it would win over to her sympathies unjustly alienated by the exotic genius of d'Annunzio or Verhaeren' (p. 132).

Both these plans were abortive. Apart from them, Ida did seriously consider a project based on the story of David and Bathsheba. Montesquiou was the main instigator of the idea. He had been trying to drum up support for it since 1909 when Bakst, fresh from the triumph of **Cléopâtre,** gave it serious consideration. He talked of a production based on the theme of 'Bétzabée' and hoped that it would be realized in the near future. Four years later it was Ida's turn to take up the idea as a joint project with **Le Martyre**. She wrote to Montesquiou: 'By day I dream only of Saint Sebastian and of Bethsabée as my big plaything. The matter is **settled** and **must** be carried out, and you will help me with it, won't you? For I know that there will be a lot of problems' (BN, 15163, fol. 85; 15164, fols 62-3). Either the problems turned out to be insurmountable or the role of Bathsheba was considered to be too similar to that of Potiphar's wife in **La Légende de Joseph,** with which she was soon occupied, because nothing came of the matter. Perhaps this was no bad thing: the homely voluptuousness of a Bathsheba would not have suited Ida's colder, more sophisticated image.

During the late spring of 1914 Ida softened slightly towards d'Annunzio. She signed a tentative contract for an 'Indian Drama' which he planned to write. He hoped that Debussy would write incidental music for it. That fact alone might have persuaded Ida. But in the end of the day it was d'Annunzio who made difficulties. Writing to Debussy in July 1914, he complained bitterly about how little he had made from **Le Martyre** and **La Pisanelle.** 'For this third drama,' he went on, 'after that unhappy experience, I dared to ask a guarantee of fifty thousand francs while insisting that your premium should be brought up to twenty-five thousand' (Tosi, 1948a, pp. 101-2). He was basing his demand on Richard Strauss's premise that, when drawing up contracts, one should always bear in mind the luxuries that life can provide. But the imminence of war soon put paid to his artistic and financial calculations, although many years later, even after Debussy's death, the possibility of his writing an 'Indian Drama' or a 'Hindu Drama' was still being talked about in artistic circles.

Whatever Ida thought about the effect of international politics upon her cultural activities, she was scarcely less disgruntled about its disruption of her usual summer expedition to far-off places. This year Montesquiou would not receive letters from Constantinople as he had in 1912, or, the year before, one which began: 'Dear Friend, excuse the paper and the writing but I am writing to you on the deck of the boat. We are in the Red Sea and the heat is appalling'; and ended with a forwarding address in Nairobi, where the lion-hunting expedition would assemble (BN, 15164, fols 62-6). Instead, in July 1914, she went no further than Switzerland, not with Walter Guinness, whose political and military duties came before pleasure, but with Romaine Brooks.

On 28 July Austria-Hungary declared war on Serbia and that was the signal for general mobilization. Within days Germany declared war on Russia and, by 3 August, on France, the two countries dearest to Ida's heart. The two women immediately took a train back to Paris and throughout the night Ida stayed on her knees 'praying to God to avert the calamity'. Romaine's attitude was much more phlegmatic. She was 'merely exasperated. These mass suicides were inevitable...since mankind simply would not practice birth-control. The war was simply an infernal nuisance, one that interfered with her work' (Secrest, p. 252).

War certainly changed the pattern of both women's lives. It brought home the truth that they really had been living in an artificial paradise. Le Senne was right after all. Only a year before Ida had been entirely wrapped up in d'Annunzian fantasies about scented death. Now death, mass death in all its nauseating reality, was only a step away.

CHAPTER 6
Hour-Glasses and Tear-Bottles, 1914-1918

War stimulated Ida Rubinstein to almost as much activity as the arts of peace. Any idea of mounting major theatrical productions in the immediate future had to be abandoned, even though in the first six months of hostilities hope for an early peace ran high. One thing she did not do - unlike so many members of society - was to flee from Paris and then creep back a few months later when it became clear that the Germans were incapable of achieving a carbon-copy repeat of their success in the Franco-Prussian War of 1870. Apart from one trip to Italy, the furthest Ida went during the whole period was to her apartment in the Trianon Palace Hotel in Versailles. But that was no different from her usual seasonal alternation between Versailles and one or other of the grand new hotels in Paris, the Bristol, the St James and Albany or the Carlton. She also kept a small studio-apartment at 54 rue Vaneau where she worked and went through the dancer's daily practice routine. She received friends there, although this could be hazardous because the studio was on the fifth floor and the lift broke down with amazing regularity. The aged or fragile (Montesquiou was in the latter category) had to be warned about the daunting climb before accepting her invitations. For her own part she regarded the ordeal as good exercise.

Jacques-Emile Blanche spread the rumour that Ida, like the indomitable Mabel Dodge Lucan, wanted to drive an ambulance at Rheims - an unlikely ambition for somebody who employed a chauffeur to do all her driving. She left ambulance work at the Front to more robust women, such as the original of the Princesse de Bormes, or less robust men, such as Maurice Ravel, the Comte Etienne de Beaumont and Cocteau, who combined this service with that of providing showers for grateful soldiers. Ida's own contribution to the war-effort was a hospital for the wounded. She set it up in the Hôtel Carlton and ran it entirely at her own expense. This was not an act of mere cheque-book charity. She spent much of her time nursing the wounded herself. She was idolized by her patients who, even in their pain and distress, appreciated a woman with style enough to commission Bakst to design a nurse's uniform for her to wear while dressing their wounds. Her concern for the victims of war did not end there. During the war itself and for years afterwards she was heavily involved with the Association Générale des Combattants et Mutilés, contributing time and money to it and raising funds by giving regular charity performances.

Another patient who received a deal of Ida's attention - though not to the extent of having her wounds dressed by her - was Sarah Bernhardt as she lay recovering from her leg amputation in February 1915. Cosseted by luxuries provided by Ida and surrounded by messages of concern from heads of state and Queen Alexandra (the widow of a former 'admirer'), she found the ordeal bearable.

Ida's personal war-effort included her giving the occasional poetry recital, designed to boost people's morale. The poetry was almost always by Robert de Montesquiou. Abandoning the image of the effete aesthete, he sharpened his pen, brandished it like a surrogate sword and scribbled war-poems of a chauvinistic and bellicose nature. Three volumes, under the general title of **Offrandes blessées,** were published between 1915 and 1919. He described them as 'offerings...political, fairy-tale, topsy-turvy, antique, fertile, resigned, lachrymal, boreal, hereditary, sigillate, initialled, sacrificial, flagellatory, derisory, peccant, atavistic'. Others called them 'patriot doggerel' (Jullian, 1967, p. 257) but there was no denying that, recited in a grand dramatic manner, they moved war-afflicted audiences or, read privately, they provided real consolation.

When the first volume appeared in June 1915, Ida was tactful enough to compliment the author on his 'beautiful and moving' verses and to describe his private readings from them as 'sublime' (BN, 15090, fol. 38). She went further and organized a matinée recital of selected poems at the Théâtre Sarah-Bernhardt in December 1915. All went well, despite her missing a rehearsal on 17 December because of the cold and damp weather. She described this as 'being prudent for the first time in my life' (ibid., fols 176-7). Her performance was a success, not least of all because she wore as a costume Bakst's now famous nurse's uniform. And Ida was in good company. Sarah Bernhardt devoured the **Offrandes blessées** and vowed to include them in recitals during her forthcoming tour of America (BN, 15184, fols 60-1).

During the war-years several theatrical ventures claimed Ida's attention. In 1916 the Boston Opera Company was faced with the problem of replacing Pavlova and sent Max Rabinoff across a dangerous Atlantic to engage Ida as her successor. Perhaps Ida's music-hall success in the Pavlovian **Mort du cygne** had inspired the Bostonians but, however flattering the offer, a permanent contract with an American opera company was not something that she considered seriously.

Another project with an American flavour to it was the filming of **Le Martyre de Saint Sébastien.** The germ of the idea was apparently sown before the outbreak of war, possibly at the news of Ida's plans to revive the work. Around December 1913 the Comte Sylvain Bonmariage de Cerny wrote to tell her that Georgette Leblanc had introduced him to a Mr Vidal-Hult, 'the great cinema producer...who would like to make this film no matter what the cost. But he says - as everybody does - that the project is only possible with you' (BN, 15164, fol. 72). The plan was to film the work on stage at the Théâtre Sarah-Bernhardt. Ida was attracted by the idea and discussed it with d'Annunzio. His reaction was rather non-committal. (It is difficult to see why either he or Debussy would be excited by the idea since the text would be virtually lost in a silent film and the music only roughly fitted to the action.)

But it was Ida's enthusiasm that counted. She kept the idea alive during the war, though resisting pressure to begin filming before the return of peace because of the immense amount of work involved in reviving the production. She confided her ideas to Montesquiou: 'After the war I should like to play **Saint Sébastien** again at the same time as the new Hindu play and I should prefer the film not to be made before then. This is between ourselves' (BN 15199, fols 23-4; 15333, fol. 101). And she had her own way. A start was not made on the **Martyre** film until after the war - in fact, not until almost four years after it. Even then, little came of the project. After shooting the dance sequences, the producers abandoned it. The surviving fragments of the film leave one in no doubt about the reason. Ida dancing on hot coals, for example, gives one a good impression of the plasticity of her movements but the jerkiness of the film destroys any sense of dramatic intensity. It was a bold venture but one that ill-repaid the amount of thought and preparation that went into it.

Even less came of the long-awaited Hindu drama by d'Annunzio. Yet another of his unrealized dreams, he was probably wise to forget the idea after Mata Hari's execution as a spy in 1916 cast a shadow of suspicion over pastiche Hinduism.

In 1917 Ida gave serious consideration to yet another dramatic venture, a study in conflict but of a personal rather than a political nature. In 1906 the young poetess Lucie Delarue-Mardrus had written a play entitled **Sapho désespérée.** She had it performed in private and took the leading role herself. Robert de Montesquiou was fascinated by the work and, over a decade later, the memory was still fresh. In June 1917 he took Lucie to meet Ida at Bakst's house. There, as she recalled in her memoirs, 'he asked me to read through **Sapho désespérée.** His thrilling dream was to see the great artist play the piece; a fine altruistic dream of a Montesquiou who little knew of the memory that I cherish with lasting gratitude. At the end of the reading, the extravagant aesthete wept. Can I ever forget that?' (p. 219).

Ida was also clearly impressed by the play. A few days later she wrote to Montesquiou in terms that suggest a serious interest in producing it. For one thing, she thought, 'the staging for the end of **Sapho** could be very beautiful and touching' (BN, 15090, fols 38-9; 15295, fol. 220). But nothing came of their plans and one can only speculate about the possible reaction of Paris audiences to the spectacle of Ida as the despairing Sappho, the archetypal lesbian in her suicidal heterosexual phase. Perhaps it was this that gave her second thoughts about the project.

For the moment Ida was preoccupied with things of more immediate significance. As the war intensified and political unrest grew in her own homeland, she redoubled her theatrical efforts for charity. In the summer of 1917 she mounted a performance of the fourth act of Racine's **Phèdre** at the Opéra, ostensibly as part of a scheme to assist impoverished Russians. By the time she learned that the recipients of her charity would be Roumanians – those most reluctant of allies – it was too late to withdraw. She had already asked Bakst to design sets and costumes for her and was so delighted with them that she had to give the performance no matter who benefited (BN, 15184, fol. 34). To begin with she was unhappy with the role of Phèdre. But with Edouard de Max's moral support, she adapted heself to the part. And she also had encouragement from Montesquiou. He was delighted at the prospect of seeing her play Racine and went to the Opéra with Elisabeth de Gramont for the matinée gala. Unfortunately, at the most dramatic moment, the actress Berthe Bady 'rushed into the box and in her breathy voice asked Montesquiou how to find the Palais Rose where she was to recite some verses.' La Gramont only just saved the situation by steering her out into the corridor and giving her the appropriate directions to the count's house in Vésinet (Clermont-Tonnerre, p. 155).

Montesquiou's reaction to Ida's performance was predictably enthusiatic. But there was never anything predictable about André Gide's critical appraisals. And, this time, he surpassed himself with his praise (1952, p. 22):

> Those who, like me, had the good fortune to hear the fourth act of **Phèdre**...can testify that she was incomparable. I do not think that I ever heard the alexandrines recited so well as by her. Never had Racine's lines seemed to me more beautiful, more panting, richer in hidden potential. And nothing, neither in her costume nor in her acting, ran counter to that extraordinary and almost superhuman harmony.

Bakst's designs for **Phèdre** were not squandered on a single performance. The sets were later supplemented for use in another **Phèdre**, this time by d'Annunzio; and Ida continued to use her costume for a new series of poetry readings. In the spring of 1917 Montesquiou had produced a second volume of his **Offrandes blessées**, colourfully entitled

Sabliers et lacrymatoires and just slightly more hysterical than the first instalment. Ida gave dramatic readings of selected verses in various venues, including the Théâtre Français. She would have given more if some of the engagements had not been cancelled or postponed because of the German bombardment of Paris.

Sometimes enemy bombs were easier to avoid than the waspish darts of Ida's unpredictable and paranoid friend Montesquiou. She always had to be careful not to offend him inadvertently. When the anniversary of the death of his secretary-lover, Gabriel Ytturi, came round, she made a point of remembering to mark the occasion. 'Would you like to take these flowers for me to Him whom I should have loved to have known?' (BN, 15149, fol. 217). Montesquiou added them to his own bouquets as he set out for the Cimitière des Gonards at Versailles. Or in December 1916, when she received her copy of his newly published **Têtes couronnées,** her thank-you note had to stress the consolation that the book had brought her in troubled times. And she particularly urged him 'not to postpone too long the promised beautiful reading' from it. She 'awaited it with such impatience!' (BN, 15188, fols 114-15).

During the war she also acted as an intermediary between Montesquiou and d'Annunzio. The Italian poet had returned to his country before it entered the war in 1915 and, as Ida remarked, immediately fulfilled the triple destiny dreamt of by Leonardo da Vinci, that of being poet, tribune of the people and soldier. 'War in a real sense was, for d'Annunzio, what a lake is for a swan, the setting for his nobility and his beauty' (pp. 333-4). She avidly read reports of his rousing speeches and followed his progress on the battle-field until a serious wound almost destroyed his eyesight in 1916. He longed to come back to Paris but duty kept him with his regiment. Instead Ida made the dangerous journey between Paris and Venice and kept him in touch with his friends in France. And when Montesquiou's **Sabliers et lacrymatoires** appeared in May 1917, she rushed a copy to him. He instantly sent a thank-you telegram with a murmur of complaint about the absence of the author's autograph.

Montesquiou took the rebuke in good part but he did become very agitated later that year when a duly signed copy of his next work, **Majeurs et mineurs** (which contained the text of his 1911 lecture on d'Annunzio's **Forse che sì**) evoked no response from the Italian. Ida had to smooth down his ruffled feathers. What had happened was incomprehensible. She could not understand his silence. She had sent the book by registered mail to his house in Venice. 'This was at the moment of the great battle (on the Piave) and I feared that, if I sent it to the front, the precious book might be lost' (BN, 15189, fols 47-8).

Precious book indeed! Ida spent the next few days tracking down Tom Antongini (who had inconveniently changed hotels in Paris without leaving a forwarding address) only to learn the obvious: d'Annunzio had not been back to Venice for several months and his maid had hesitated to send the book-parcel to the front (ibid., fols 51-4).

Ida also made great efforts to succour d'Annunzio, although he seldom complained about his sufferings. 'After the victory,' she telegraphed to him in 1917, 'we shall build the theatre of our dreams. You will write a new play for me' (Tosi, 1948a, p. 19). Vague words but encouraging ones!

Another friend upon whom Ida lavished attention in his rare moments away from duty was Brigade-Major the Hon. Walter Guinness who, as a battalion commander and general staff officer on the Western Front, fought with signal valour throughout the war. A veteran of the South African War, he added the D.S.O. to his existing distinctions. He was mentioned in dispatches three times and, in 1918, awarded the bar to his D.S.O. But set against the backgound of mass-slaughter on the Somme and Marne, such recognition did nothing to ease the anxiety of his loved-ones.

During the war Ida continued to see a lot of another special friend, Romaine Brooks. Romaine could not ignore the conflict - much as she wanted to. The sight of Zeppelins dropping bombs round the Eiffel Tower would have distracted even the most dedicated painter. She let the tragedy of war creep into her paintings. One in particular is almost an anti-war protest: Ida, dressed in her nurse's uniform, passively surveys a dark, war-devastated landscape in which only the barbed wire seems to have life left in it.

Romaine's most important study, the formal portrait, is also from this period. One cannot better Meryle Secrest's description of this minor masterpiece (pp. 146-7):

> Romaine's portrait of Ida in black, white and grey...as she looked one day walking through the Bois de Boulogne, in a flowing black cloak with sharp lights on its white satin revers...is lit with only the suggestion of color in the clouds and the slighest highlight on the delicate nose and cheekbone. Her elaborate headdress is blown back sightly by the wind and her mouth is half open, looking as Jean Cocteau saw her, 'like the pungent perfume of some exotic essence, ethereal, otherworldly, divinely unattainable'.

Apart from this Romaine left a unique record of Ida in this period. Because she refused to continue posing for long sessions in the nude, Romaine had a series of photographs taken instead, probably in 1917 when she was finishing off the last of her nude studies. In them the Ida that one sees lying on a silk-covered divan is an elongated figure, elegant and boyishly slender but without any suggestion of gauntness. These photographs, together with some of her fully and luxuriously dressed in a magnificent fur coat and exotic headdress, show her as a much more commanding and worldly woman than the Ida of the portrait. Meryle Secrest criticizes Romaine for failing to capture the commanding authority of Ida's image but the portrait is surely intended to depict the withdrawn, pensive side of the sitter. One does agree with Meryle Secrest's comment that 'one can see from these photographs...what intuitive grace gave such authority to her slightest gesture and why all...Paris was in awe of her.' What the photographs show is 'the reality of this command; the sinuous, almost tigerish, sense of movement' (p. 247).

Leon Bakst also worked on a portrait of Ida during the war years and she seems to have borne the sittings with a greater degree of patience. The picture had to be as perfect as possible because it was destined for the walls of Montesquiou's Palais Rose. In May 1917 a rather hesitant Ida wrote to the count: 'The portrait is finished. I think it beautiful. I hope that it will please you. Bakst himself is satisfied with it and told me how happy he is to think that it will be in your house. Myself, I have had the joy of posing for you!' (BN, 15199, fol. 24).

Montesquiou was more than just pleased. In a state of elation he dashed off a flowery poem inspired by the work and sent it to the artist. Not to be outdone, Bakst replied in just as grand - if rather less measured - a fashion: 'Dear Master and Friend, I am so happy and so proud to receive your beautiful and remarkable verses, inspired by the portrait of Madame Rubinstein! Your friendship and kindly lance broken on my behalf touches me still and I am so pleased to think that my portrait is among your fine collection of art' (BN, 15163, fol. 151).

A fellow Russian, another creative genius, with whom Ida had dealings at this time was Igor Stravinsky. In the late spring of 1917 she began to plan a grand production of Shakespeare's **Antony and Cleopatra** for the 1917-1918 season, if circumstances permitted. She approached a friend, that well-known lover of English literature, André Gide, to make the translation for her and he responded with enthusiasm. For a work of Shakespearean proportions and profundity a substantial score was needed and Bakst suggested that Stravinsky was the man for the job: he was capable of producing music striking enough to match the text and interesting in its own right; and he could be relied upon to complete the work in the relatively short time available. Informal contact was made with him at Morges in Switzerland and on 26 June 1917 Charles Pequin, Ida's agent, formally asked him to accept the commission.

Stravinsky showed great interest and was eager to start work. But from the beginning things went wrong.

Ida wanted the work to be completed in six months but, as Stravinsky complained to Bakst, Gide was not prepared to come to Switzerland to discuss the project until the beginning of August, by which time he and his family would be on holiday at Diablerets, in the Vaud. Gide would have to meet him there. The encounter duly took place and they jointly worked out a scheme for incidental music consisting of ten more or less substantial pieces.

But during those summer months the pressure Ida was putting on her collaborators apparently relaxed. She did not get round to arranging the terms of Gide's contract until late September. It was, in fact, not signed until 12 February 1918 and work on the translation was not completed until later in the spring of that year. Time also slipped by for Stravinsky. As late as 18 November 1917 nothing definite had been settled. He telegraphed to Paris: 'I have started the music; should I continue?' And he hinted at the real problem in his concluding sentence when he added: 'Ask Bakst to send the advance to the Banque Cantonale' (Stravinsky, Vera, and Craft, p. 161). In a word, he was forcing the issue. Ida and her business advisor were still studying his terms carefully. They suggested modifications. Stravinsky made some concessions but by the middle of December their negotiations had broken down and the colaboration was abandoned.

If the plan had gone ahead, Stravinsky's music would - as always - have proved interesting because he clearly had distinct ideas of his own about Shakespearean productions. He later recalled his discussions with Gide on the subject (Stravinsky, Igor, and Craft, 1960, p. 145):

The musical style would depend on the style of the whole production, but he did not understand what I meant. Later, when I suggested that the production be in modern dress, he was shocked - and deaf to my arguments that we would be nearer Shakespeare by inventing something new, and nearer to him in every way than he was, veristically, to Antony and Cleopatra. I still believe...that the music in Shakespeare's play should be Shakespearean, i.e., period music...'modern music' is only justified in 'modern' versions of the plays.

Whether Stravinsky had formulated very specific ideas on a 'modern version' or not is open to doubt but Gide did record in his journal, admittedly more than five years later, that Stravinsky 'would gladly collaborate on **Antony and Cleopatra**, but only if Antony were given the uniform of an Italian Bersagliere' (1951, p. 754).

Gide did not record how Stravinsky expected Ida to react to such a suggestion when both knew perfectly well that only a period production would allow her scope for the lavish and exotic spectacle envisaged by her. Perhaps Stravinsky was not happy about having Shakespeare as a 'collaborator'. At no other point in his entire career did he find inspiration in his work nor, indeed, in the work of any other established literary genius. It was as though he deliberately shied away from anything that might overshadow his own genius. What is surprising is that negotiations with Ida should have broken down because of financial considerations since his economic position in 1917 gave him very little room for manoeuvre. Besides, there is no other example of a contract with Ida failing to materialize because of a disagreement over money – however inclement the prevailing economic and political climate.

For both Stravinsky and Ida the events of 1917 were troubled. The abdication of the tsar on 13 March and the creation of a provisional government may not have been too disturbing. But as communist agitation grew throughout the summer and rumours that Russia would make a separate agreement with Germany began to circulate, their uneasiness grew. And Diaghilev did nothing to dispel the anxiety of Russian expatriates and Frenchmen alike when, after a performance of **L'Oiseau de feu** on 11 May, at the opening of his solitary wartime season in Paris, he had a **moujik** in red parade a red flag on stage.

The 'October Revolution' on 6 November decisively closed the door on Ida's old world. She was cut off from her native land. She became stateless and, in a sense, homeless. Her property was sequestrated and all income from Russian sources dried up. Sentiment apart, this did not cause her too much hardship. By far the largest proportion of her vast fortune had already been invested outside Russia. Her aunt had not married into the Cahen d'Anvers banking family for nothing. Ida certainly made no effort to change her life-style. If anything, her material possessions increased because she put her mind to buying a large house in Paris and a private aeroplane was soon added to her yacht and limousines as a symbol of her economic survival.

But none of this compensated for the loss of friends and homeland. It did not relieve worries about the future of her adopted country, France, as the Bolsheviks signed an armistice and opened peace negotiations with Germany at Brest-Litovsk on 3 December 1917: the arch-foe, free of his embroilment on the Eastern Front, might have his armies at the gates of Paris within weeks. Even Trotsky's delaying tactics, which skilfully postponed the signing of a peace agreement until 3 March 1918, only increased uncertainty in the minds of Russian exiles. There is very little that somebody in Ida's position cold do, except make the token gesture of signing an anti-Bolshevik petition at the time of the Brest-

Litovsk negotiations and more tangible, redouble her efforts to help Russians cut off in France or fleeing there for sanctuary.

One Russian whom Ida was not pleased to see appear in Paris was her husband. She was even less pleased when he asked her for a divorce. She refused. Witnesses testifying to the adultery of the guilty party would have to be produced in public and she had no desire for that sort of publicity. She was even more determined not to let a breath of scandal harm Walter Guinness's budding career in politics. Horwitz was furious: everybody in Paris knew about their liaison, so what had she to lose? He set a private detective on their trail but soon discovered that they were so discreet about their friendship that no substantive evidence could be produced. The divorce proceedings were dropped and, once his underhand tactics came to light, the frustrated husband had the grace to fade from the scene.

Meanwhile, the tide had turned in the fortunes of war. In July 1918 Foch began a decisive counter-offensive on the Western Front and hope revived in the allies' camp. This also gave a boost to Ida's morale. In the dark spring of 1918 Gide had chosen the obvious title of **Antoine et Cléopâtre** to complete Shakespeare's metamorphosis into French. If only a suitable composer could be found to write the incidental music, the project might be ready in time to celebrate the return of peace when the theme of the warrior vanquished by love would have significant implications for more than just herself.

When the Armistice was signed on 11 November 1918, it found Ida in the same position as when war broke out – on her knees. She made straight for Notre Dame to hear a **Te Deum** sung in thanksgiving for the restoration of peace.

CHAPTER 7
Asps, Orchids and Frozen Tears, 1919-1921

While he lay convalescing in Venice in 1916, Gabriele d'Annunzio wrote to Ida Rubinstein with proposals for a new play: 'Tell me what you want for this new piece. I think that, after the war, it would be advisable to avoid subjects alluding to war. People will want to be spared blood and abandon themselves to the purest fantasy' (Rubinstein, p. 334). Ida agreed: much of her work in the immediate post-war era contained a strong element of escapism. And she was not exactly out of line with the new generation's thinking on the subject. Surrealism was in fashion. Men disavowed the creeds of the major powers and international organizations to cultivate the banal, the simple or the primitive. Frivolity became a ruling passion for some. Experiments with a range of opiates brought oblivion to others.

Ida's expression of these aims differed radically from theirs. If simplicity ever entered into her reckoning, it was only in the substance of some of the literary works interpreted by her. Otherwise, the bigger, the more elaborate, the more extravagant the production she mounted, the better pleased she was. As a result she often found herself rather out of sympathy with the cynical and self-centred philosophy of hedonism that motivated sections of Western society in the 'twenties. In turn, many questioned the **means** of expression employed by her and, in consequence, questioned **her** motives.

However, if her first post-war production was escapist and fantastic, it did not avoid violence. The subject chosen was the life of the Arabian king Imroulcaïs. The critic Charles Tenroc described him as 'a kind of Arab Homer,...a popular poet and fierce warrior; this distant figure of a conqueror enjoyed as much fame in an Arabia before Mahomet in an era when the Koran had not invented veils for women, an Arabia embroiled in struggles between tribes' (1919a, p. 86). The adventures and poems of Imroulcaïs were translated by Edmond Doutté, the sociologist and orientalist, a specialist in North African studies, and Ida asked Fernand Nozière to make them into a grand drama. He succeeded very well. As Tenroc remarked, 'the murders alternate with frenetic loves in the glowing deserts, to finish with Imroulcaïs, like Hercules, poisoned by his cloak' (ibid., p. 86).

The man Ida turned to for incidental music was the veteran composer Camille Erlanger. The summit of his career had been reached a decade or more earlier with his sensational opera based on Pierre Louÿs's erotic novel **Aphrodite.** By the time he came to tackle the **Imroulcaïs** commission, he was at the end of his career. In fact, the score was his last work, since he died on 24 April 1919, just six weeks after the production. The music was designed to reflect the action of the play to the point of being subservient to it. Erlanger took particular care over a dance for Ida in her role as Ocem Djoundab, Imroulcaïs's wife. His work attracted warm critical comment: 'Erlanger has written stylish music - and with style...It has a picturesque restraint in which the bric-à-brac of the Cairo street is totally absent. Some preludes and motifs, a sensual dance, make up the score, a picture painted from a skilful and unobtrusive palette, evoking the streets of Damascus' (ibid., p. 86).

When **Imroulcaïs, le roi errant** reached the stage of the Théâtre des Alliés at the beginning of March 1919, it attracted a deal of interest. M. Joubé, who played the Arabian king, gave a fiery performance but found that attention focused more on his boots and spurs than on his acting. As for Ida, the critics simply exclaimed about her 'fairy-tale' elegance. She was tall and beautiful, like a 'palm-shoot' (ibid., p. 86). But what attracted (or distracted) most attention was something that happened off-stage. One of the actresses, a Mademoiselle Sida-ben-Said, was forbidden by her Islamic faith to appear on stage but so convinced was she of her vocation that she promptly converted to Christianity.

There was certainly nothing escapist or unbloody about the production in which Ida took part a few weeks later. On 1 April the Syndicat de la Presse Parisienne presented a gala matinée at the Opéra in aid of the departments liberated from German rule and at the top of a bill including Sarah Bernhardt, giving a dramatic recitation of Fernand Gregh's poem **Triomphe,** and Luisa Tetrazzini, singing arias by Ambroise Thomas and Rossini, came Ida Rubinstein as the familiar character of Salomé but in a different work, **La Tragédie de Salomé,** a ballet after a poem by Robert d'Humières with music by Florent Schmitt. She was in good company with a Herodias played by Christine Kerf and a Herod in the form of Georges Wague, Colette's former actor-colleague.

Ida was not the first to dance the part of Salomé to Schmitt's powerful and exotic music: Loie Fuller had created it in 1907 and Diaghilev had presented Karsavina in it in 1913. But Ida performed it with new choreography by Nicola Guerra and achieved a resounding success. The audience was amazed by her remaining on points throughout the entire piece. Jacques Durand felt 'giddy with the choreographic virtuosity. The spectacle was extremely beautiful, the general impression was intense, the success considerable' (p. 110). Certainly the Paris public relished another chance to see a Herod stretch out lecherous hands towards the young princess's adolescent nudity. But, as

Tenroc remarked, Ida's spectacular performance in a spectacular production did not unbalance the action by claiming all the attention: 'The heavy truculence of the drama unfolded itself in a series of effects which achieved a neat balance with the choreographic interpretation' (1919b, p. 118).

The gala performance (at which Durand noted with mock surprise the august presence of Ignaz Paderewski, veteran pianist and head of the newly constituted Polish state) was such a success that **La Tragédie de Salomé** was incorporated into the Opéra's repertoire. And until almost the end of the season on 27 June Ida continued to dance in it as a double-bill feature with either **Rigoletto** or **Samson et Dalila**. After that she gave up the role. Perhaps she thought it too close in spirit to her interpretation of the Wilde-Glazunov **Salomé**. She was content to see another ballerina dance the part when **La Tragédie** appeared in the same programme in which she premièred her **Artémis troublée** in 1922.

In 1919 **La Tragédie de Salomé** came up in a context quite different from a charity gala. At the end of August Ida collected two copies of Montesquiou's latest volume of poems, **Un Moment du pleur eternel**, one for herself, the other for Gabriele d'Annunzio. This time she did not send it by registered post but took it in person to Venice in her new aeroplane. D'Annunzio received the present with suitably poetic exclamations and on 1 September sent the count congratulatory messages, borne on 'the mystic wings of Sebastian' (Montesquiou, 1923, p. 181) - Ida's aeroplane, 'which had been "baptized" by the poet and (whose fuselage) bore Saint Sebastian's words, **Je viens, je monte, j'ai des ailes!**' (BN, 15164, fol. 68). Montesquiou was so touched by the fervour of the Italian's love and admiration for him that he took a sheet of violet writing-paper and scribbled down a quatrain to commemorate the event (ibid., fol. 34):

Le messager céleste annoncé par vous-même
Dans mon jardin fermé paraît brillant et beau
Et, de partir, certain que toujours je vous aime
Lui fait rouvrir son aile en portant un flambeau!

A few days later Ida was back in Venice to be with d'Annunzio at the start of his much publicized flight from Rome to Tokyo. Instead she arrived to witness a historic event. He and a band of fanatical followers refused to accept a condition of the Paris Peace Conference whereby the northern Adriatic port of Fiume, wrested from defeated Hungary, should go to Serbia instead of Italy. D'Annunzio's little army decided to defy the Western allies. They seized the town and, to everybody's surprise, succeeded in holding it until 1921. Just before the expedition set out, d'Annunzio took Ida out onto the balcony of her hotel, the Danieli. Gazing out over the lagoon, he told her about his secret plan to capture the town. 'I am feverish for mortal adventure,' he confessed (Rubinstein, p. 334). According to Tom Antongini, who heard the story from the poet's own lips, Ida's response was equally feverish. She embraced him with the words 'I love you.' But, he explained, 'the origin of that rare effusion was certainly heroic, for she added: "Throw all the English into the sea for my sake!"' (p. 443) - rather unlikely words for somebody whose lover would soon occupy the position of Under-Secretary of State for War in the British Government.

On the evening of 9 September d'Annunzio gave a dinner in Ida's honour at his house the Casetta Rosa: 'She will dance for us to the music of Florent Schmitt,' he exclaimed beforehand. 'I have asked her to come...in the silver jacket and white and black shawl...Inside me there is such sadness but hope. And I constantly hear the beautiful fervent voice that sings: "Italia! Italia!"' (quoted Gatti, p. 342). In fact, Ida as Salomé figured as one element in ambiguous fluctuations of orientation that affected him at that time: the warrior in him wrestled with the peace-loving poet; the Don Juan, then so wrapped up with his mistress Luisa Bàccara, came alive in the all-but-explicit homosexual ambience of his company. It affected him enough to write: 'A well-trained greyhound or race-horse, the legs of Ida Rubinstein, the body of a true Ardito returning from the fords of the Piave, are among the most expressive beauties in the world' (quoted Jullian, 1972, p. 289).

During the campaign the problem of the conflict between war and the arts of peace again troubled d'Annunzio. He turned to Ida for an answer: 'Dear brother,...at Fiume, in the strife, in the tumult, in the frenzy, in the blood, I thought of you and of our leave-taking...I confided my heroic secret to you, and at Fiume, sometimes, I sought you in my dreams. Will Sebastian indeed live again? But you must also think of **Fedra**, which is yours. France must finally get to know that **Fedra**' (Rubinstein, pp. 334-5). His words had the suggestive force of prophecy. **Le Martyre** did live again and his **Phaedre** did breathe French air - but not until a few years had elapsed.

While d'Annunzio was fighting his battles and dreaming of a civilized future, Ida was involved in plans for two different projects. The first came to very little. The second underwent an even longer period of gestation than **Phaedre**.

About mid-summer 1919 the director of the Opéra, Jacques Rouché, received an exuberant letter from that weather-worn dramatist Georges de Porto-Riche. His friend René Blum had met Gabriel Fauré at the home of Alfred Cortot (at the time when they were working on Fauré's **Fantaisie** for piano and orchestra) and Fauré had apparently expressed a strong desire to work on a project with Porto-Riche. He gave Rouché a few details: 'It is a tragedy-ballet in two scenes from the Byzantine period...I have read it to Madame Ida Rubinstein and Monsieur Bakst, who were delighted by it and want to mount it' (AN, AJ 13. 1208: Porto-Riche). Porto-Riche begged Rouché to let him read him the libretto before Fauré left on a working holiday at the end of the week. It would only take three-quarters of an hour. He was sure that Rouché would be impressed: 'the venture is dramatic enough to charm you with its plot and its rapid picturesque action' (ibid.).

Rouché showed some interest. Porto-Riche enlisted the help of his art-historian friend Paul Léon but then discovered that communication with Fauré in his retreat in the idyllic but remote Annecy-le-Vieux in Haute Savoie was virtually impossible. The project eventually came to nothing despite the apparent enthusiasm of all concerned. It is difficult to know if Ida really took it seriously. How successful it would have been is another matter altogether: a 'Byzantine tragedy', however well produced, smacked too much of **fin-de-siècle** decadence for the taste of post-war Paris. But Porto-Riche did not abandon the idea of using Ida as a vehicle for his work. He tried to interest her in another venture in 1924 and again in 1925 but met with a much more guarded response.

The second projected production of 1919 brought Ida for the first time in contact with the great Catholic poet and distinguished diplomat Paul Claudel. He and his young colleague and friend Darius Milhaud had collaborated to produce a French text and the music for a classical masterpiece, Aeschylus's **Choephori,** or **Les Choéphores** as it became. They had designed the work so that the parts of Electra and Orestes were sung and the others recited by actors.

Milhaud's music was performed by an orchestra, chorus and soloists at a Delgrange concert on 15 June 1919. But both poet and composer were anxious to realize a full-stage version of the work and set out to interest Ida, whom they saw in the part of Clytemnestra, partnered by Edouard de Max. Preliminary discussions began in July 1919 and, on 3 September, while Ida was winging her way back to Italy, Claudel wrote to Milhaud from Copenhagen and instructed him to work out their ideas with her and with Edouard de Max and José-Maria Sert, whom they wanted to design sets (Claudel, 1961, pp. 51, 55). Claudel visualized a performance of **Les Choéphores** taking place in Monte Carlo, if possible, before March of the following year. But clearly a lot depended upon Ida. On 16 November one finds him writing (still from Copenhagen) to Milhaud: 'For **Les Choéphores,** why don't you go to see Ida Rubinstein at 54 rue Vaneau? It's she above all whom we must interest in the project' (ibid.,

p. 59).

However, Claudel's hopes were disappointed. Ida's interest was not strong enough to give the scheme the necessary impetus. But she did not forget the idea because sixteen years later she put her mind to a production of the play in Brussels in 1935 - when she was more of an age to play the part of Clytemnestra!

During the 1919-1920 season Ida's time was almost entirely taken up with **Antoine et Cléopâtre,** which finally reached the stage of the Paris Opéra on 14 June 1920. Before that moment there were several set-backs and innumerable delays. Ida had thought about the idea of herself in a Shakespearean role for some time before definite plans began to take shape in 1917 when she recruited her first collaborators, Gide and Stravinsky. Only Gide stayed with the project, translating the play in moments snatched from writing his tell-all autobiography **Si le grain ne meurt.** But as his translation neared completion in the early months of 1918, both he and Ida were disconcerted to hear the news that Firmin Gémier was mounting a production of the same play (translated by Lucien Népoty) at the Théâtre Antoine in Paris. Although Gide knew that his translation was better, more poetic, nearer the spirit of the original, and Ida knew that her production would be grander, more lavish and more controversial than Gémier's, it was foolish to follow too closely on its heels. Commonsense suggested a tactiçal delay.

The extra time gained allowed Ida to tackle the problem of the incidental music with more care. Instead of the rush-job expected of Stravinsky, a score was commissioned from Florent Schmitt, the colourful, if rather irritable composer of **La Tragédie de Salomé.** Ida had known him for some time and had considered asking him to write the music for **Le Martyre** in the event of Debussy's refusal. Schmitt responded to the challenge of Ida's idea of a monumental production of **Antoine et Cléopâtre** by writing six symphonic episodes for full orchestra, each intended to evoke the particular atmosphere of key-points in the play, such as the love of Antony and Cleopatra, the battle of Actium, the orgy in Cleopatra's palace and, finally, her burial. One of the more striking moments in the score was a lush and colourful oriental dance during the orgy scene, specially designed to give scope to Ida's talent for voluptuous dance-sequences and, in dramatic terms, to justify Antony's submission to the Dionysian allure of the East. But as Schmitt's biographer, Pierre-Octave Ferroud, has pointed out, just as **La Tragédie de Salomé** can be seen as representing the conflict between two religions, so his music for **Antoine et Cléopâtre** highlights the Shakespearean theme of conflict between two civilizations, with the semitic East finally ceding victory to the Latin

West (p. 93).

Schmitt took great care with the score and continued working on it until within a few months of the première. After that he made sure that his music did not sink into oblivion by arranging it into two substantial suites, which took their place in the orchestral repertoire after a successful Lamoureux concert in Paris on 17 October 1920.

In the end of the day Gide proved to be a more difficult, demanding and opinionated collaborator than either of the (very irascible) composers involved. Ida's relationship with him was more that of a friend than of a patron. This is not surprising when one considers their respective standing in the French artistic world. The tone of their conversation was highflown and the substance of their letters more often than not about one of Ida's current literary fads. Late in 1919 she was absorbed in Baudelaire, and Gide made sure that she read everything written by himself on the subject of **Les Fleurs du mal** (BN, 15164, fols 75-6; 15165, fols 85-6). Montesquiou hovered in the background vicariously sharing in Ida's pleasure. But when it came to the business of producing **Antoine et Cléopâtre**, Gide proved less amenable, less amiable.

When the stage rehearsals began on 11 May 1920, Gide decided that nothing had gone right and he came to the staggering conclusion that it was impossible to make a work of art of a play (1951, p. 681):

> The monotonous delivery of the actors evens out the text and, so to speak, sandpapers it. None of them seems sensitive to the beauty of the words themselves. It is like the roller that one runs over lumps of earth after ploughing. I am surrounded by twenty-five men, who would be my enemies, if it were **my** play that I had to defend...I shall attend all these rehearsals for my personal instruction; but...I am not interested in this 'realization'.

Only the charm of the actors and their obvious commitment to their work helped to mollify him a little.

Gide took his display of indifference further. A misunderstanding occurred between Ida and Jacques Drésa, the designer commissioned because of his unique style that contrived to blend orientalism with eighteenth-century elegance. Ida was delighted with the costumes, all except her own, so, she decided, Drésa would only choose the colour-schemes and Worth would design and make her gowns. Gide intervened tentatively: 'I made diplomatic efforts between them, while not giving a damn about the result.' He then took Ida off to her agent to let him work out the problem. Gide's only comment was cantankerous: 'All this takes a terrible amount of time. Without any doubt I should have been better to go off on a trip' (ibid. p. 681). Few would have disagreed with him.

Ida also had to cope with the job of casting and put up with the eternal problem of artistic temperament. The major roles were filled without too much trouble. Edouard de Max would be a flamboyant Antony, but a reliable one - as reliable as his surprisingly virile growth of beard. (He always shaved immediately before a performance but always died in the last scene with a five-o'clock shadow.) Armand Bour, Georges Wague and their colleagues in the leading parts were all established actors and trusted friends. Casting the minor parts caused more trouble. Madeleine Giraud (wife of Victor Margueritte, author of the sensational novel **La Garçonne**) was determined to play the role of Charmian. Her approach was indirect, if obvious. She bombarded Robert de Montesquiou with letters praising Ida in the most extravagant terms: 'The masterpiece of grace, of harmony, of noble and perfect art who is Madame Rubinstein' or 'that soul of a goddess' or 'a single being in whom so much grace is allied to so much intelligence.' Then finally the request: 'Would you ask Madame Rubinstein if she would not object to entrusting me with the part of Charmian in **Cléopâtre**? - I have all the right qualities for it and should consider it an incomparable joy to work at her side' (BN, 15163, fols 125, 126, 129, 130). Poor Madeleine Giraud! When the offer came at last, she was smitten with such a fever that she was incapable of replying.

But, Ida confessed, this was only a minor crisis compared with that of having 'to struggle in the midst of a thousand difficulties'. Yet before long she could say: 'I believe that I have now overcome a good part of them and I hope that all will go well for my Cleopatra' - so, she informed Montesquiou, she was taking a trip to Avignon to see an exhibition. Her only regret was that he could not come with her (BN, 15165, fols 47-9).

Even more remarkable, on 4 May 1920, within a few weeks of this major production, she took time off to appear at the Opéra in a grand gala in aid of Russian refugees in France. There were six substantial items on the programme and fourth on the bill came a dramatized recitation of Alfred de Musset's **La Nuit de mai,** in which Sarah Bernhardt played the Poet and Ida the Muse. Diaghilev's company danced two ballets: **Les Sylphides** and, as the **pièce de résistance, Schéhérazade.** Ida donned her old costume for Zobeïda and made a unique return to the ranks of her former colleagues, although Nijinsky was no longer her lover as the Golden Slave: Massine, as in everything, had stepped into his shoes; and a venerable Enrico Cecchetti paced the boards in the inappropriate role of the Chief Eunuch.

The opening night of **Antoine et Cléopâtre** on 14 June was a spectacular affair. Friends and foes alike flocked to see the latest episode in the career of Ida Rubinstein. A dedicated opponent, P. Saegal, critic of **Le Ménestrel**, made a cowardly jibe (1920, p. 253):

> The show dragged on in length and, towards one o'clock, the orchestra, following the audience's example, discreetly improvised a variation on the Farewell Symphony. For it was only towards two o'clock in the morning that Cleopatra at last decided to die, before an irreducible squad of intrepid noctambulists! But - and this was the heart of the matter - Madame Ida Rubinstein had had the satisfaction of asserting herself as a tragic actress.

Critics constantly complained about the length of productions in the French theatre but **Antoine**'s staging was so elaborate that the action must, indeed, have seemed slower than usual.

Marcel Proust ranked himself among Ida's admirers, although he too left before the last act - but not out of boredom. As he sat in the Princesse Soutzo's box with Henri Bardac, news arrived that a close friend, the great actress Réjane, had just died. He rushed off to her house to offer the comfort of his silent presence to her grief-stricken son Jacques Porel. The light of a great star had just been extinguished but, as far as Proust was concerned, a new one was in the ascendant. A few days later, when Bardac accused Proust of paying no attention to the play because he had chattered throughout the performance, he quickly realized how mistaken he was: 'Raising his hand in protest, with a falsely indignant voice but sincerely mocking, Proust accused me of insensitivity, and, by delivering a lecture...on Shakespeare, on the acting of Madame Rubinstein, on the intonation of Monsieur de Max, on the lighting in the banquet scene..., he gave me proof that he had taken in even the minutest details of that evening' (p. 105). Even the conversations in the neighbouring boxes and the antics of the spectators below in the stalls had etched themselves clearly on his mind.

In **Le Gaulois** Louis Schneider wrote a balanced review (1920, p. 4):

> Ida Rubinstein...lent to the character of Cleopatra all the seductiveness required by the English poet...She has already gained so many victories for herself and here again she triumphed...We are indebted to her for an evening of art of the most meritorious kind; she justly deserved a major share of the applause which throughout the evening greeted this very difficult and complex reconstruction of **Antoine et Cléopâtre.**

André Germain - not the gentlest of social commentators - had high praise for her. Her **Antoine et Cléopâtre** would 'remain one of the most beautiful spectacles of his life...Ida Rubinstein's genius sets out across the ages to rejoin...that of Shakespeare. This woman, princess and serpent,...has at one moment the reptile's sinuousness with which the rhythm of the eternal temptation is entwined and at the next an empress's gestures that set their seal on the splendour of the World' (1924, pp. 63-4).

Montesquiou paid Ida a special tribute by writing a laudatory article about her performance for **Le Théâtre.** Impressive and lavishly illustrated, the piece was sent round to friends for their admiring comments. Ida herself was suitably gratified: 'Thank you with all my heart for your beautiful article. I am proud and overjoyed by the words you have written' (BN, 15165, fols 52-3).

However, Ida was not bowled over by her success. She certainly thought twice before tackling major productions in the future. Two years were to pass before she staged anything on such a grand scale. In the meantime a number of other distractions claimed her attention. After **Antoine** she rested at her favourite hotel the Trianon Palace in Versailles. But before long she was **en route** for Venice to make a film of d'Annunzio's tragedy **La Nave** for the film company run by Arturo Ambrosio and Armando Zanotto. The plot was highly dramatic, not to say blood-thirsty: the Venetian **condottiero** Marco Gratico loves the beautiful Basiliola (Ida). Unfortunately, his brother Sergio also loves her. The fact that he is a bishop does not inhibit his passion nor does it inhibit his brother from killing him. Marco leaves the scene of his fratricide on a new mercenary enterprise and the unhappy Basiliola commits suicide by burning herself to death.

Apparently d'Annunzio's opinions on the production were remarkable, all the more so since he had seen very few films of any significance. None the less, he left responsibility for the interpretation almost entirely in Ida's hands. His son Gabriellino acted as a capable artistic director and producer. As a silent film it gave d'Annunzio's exotic text little scope for expression. The music that Pizzetti had written for its stage production could not be used to any great effect. But somehow this placed all the more emphasis on Ida's beauty and the plasticity of her movements and gestures. Elisabeth de Gramont was enchanted: 'Madame Rubinstein's face, free of the fixed colours which she is forced to employ in the theatre, never appeared to me more perfect than in the grey film of **La Nave**...The structure of her cartileges (since after all they talk about nothing but her legs!), linked with perfect art to the arch of her eyebrows and to the sinuousness of the mouth, relates her directly to Luini da Milano's most beautiful figures' (Clermont-Tonnerre, p. 151).

Ida made another film the following year, this time with Giulio

Aristide Sartorio, the poet and Raphaelesque painter. Under the title of **San Giorgio**, it provided Ida with an opportunity to indulge in a sumptuous extravaganza of aestheticism, a kind of inverted homage to Donatello. The film did not claim much serious critical attention.

Meanwhile, during much of 1920 and 1921 Ida was preoccupied with a venture that had all the characteristics of a stage project. For so long she had lived in hotels in Paris and Versailles and kept only her small studio on the fifth floor of 54 rue Vaneau. Now she decided to buy a large house at 7 place des Etats-Unis, directly facing the Paris residence of the Duc de La Rochefoucauld and his vivacious and intellectual wife, Edmée. Ida set about creating a work of art by arranging the interior decoration and the garden as a kind of domestic stage-set for herself. And until the bulk of the work had been finished, she refused even her closest friends a glance at it. Montesquiou was firmly kept away: 'The little house into which I have moved is still not worthy of receiving you. But,' she added in an attempt to compensate, 'the new motorcar is here and, if you wish, on a Sunday or a Thursday, we could go on an outing together. That would give me great joy' (BN, 15333, fols 80-1).

Meanwhile, Bakst was busily working on the house's décor. And the result was impressive. On his first visit the journalist Pierre Lagarde was overwhelmed by the sight of the place: 'The house was vast and silent. The work-studio with a sloping floor like a theatre platform..., a décor by Bakst with blue friezes, a décor so large, so high, that at first it seems bare.' The grand drawing-room, hung with heavy curtains kept back by weighty gold tassels as in a theatre, was partly lined with wall-mirrors. This gave the room a mysterious quality, elongating it like 'a window to the impossible and to truth'. The **objets d'art** decorating the room were strange, even disturbing: draperies from Abyssinia, a Senegalese instrument of torture, stark and simple, gleaming ominously in a shady corner, from ancient Athens a statuette with the pure lines of a frozen gesture, on a Japanese occasional table a book bearing the unmistakable writing of Gabriele d'Annunzio (p. 1).

The garden was just as much a work of art and Ida used it for **al fresco** dinner parties. Marguerite Long left an enchanting picture of one of them: 'It was a summer evening of long, clear hours. The table was set on a veranda surrounded by white hydrangeas and trellises garnished with white lilies. It gave on to a fairy garden designed by Bakst and covered with red roses' (1971, p. 40).

But there was nothing static about the garden's colour-scheme. Stravinsky revealed that Ida had 'commissioned Bakst to arrange the flower beds...so that all the flowers were in trays and the whole garden could be changed every few weeks' (Stravinsky, Igor, and Craft, 1960, p. 146) (The Queen of Hearts' gardeners could have learned a lesson or two from that.) This enabled Ida to match her dress with the flowers - or vice versa. Nozière described her artful manipulations of nature: 'The paths of the little garden are of blue mosaic. There is a fountain. There is a column. There is a pergola. Suddenly, there are only mauve hyacinths, then red azaleas, then the uniform whiteness of lilies. Rapid transformations, total, magical! Ida Rubinstein, whose dresses harmonize with these efflorescences, passes by, mysterious - and smiles' (p. 31).

This house - and garden - served as her Paris home, the headquarters where she planned her life and career for the next two decades and more.

However, during the immediate post-war years Ida spent a great deal of time away from Paris and travelled far and wide, as if to make up for lost time. At one moment she was camped in a tent at the top of a mountain in Sardinia. Next she would be off hunting bears and deer in the forests of Norway or back again in Africa pursuing lions. Sometimes Walter Guinness accompanied her. Often she would set out on her own with a retinue of native bearers. At night they kept fires burning round her tent to frighten off wild beasts. During the day they would carry her on a palanquin within shooting-range of her prey. Although she often set out on her strange expeditions at a moment's notice, she always made sure to take a sumptuous wardrobe with her - 'pyjamas of gold lamé, boleros covered with precious stones, turbans with plumes like those of a sultana, magnificent hunting attire, dainty lingerie' (Long, 1971, p. 40). Michel Georges-Michel told the story of how she was travelling alone with her entourage in the south of Abyssinia when the richest planter in the district espied her from afar (1944, pp. 138)

> astride the traditional mule and dressed completely in brown buffalo hide, her legs encased in saffron-red boots and her fine fingers twirling above her head a parasol in white Veronese kid. The planter approached and paid his respects. He offered her the hospitality of his house and his table. But Madame Rubinstein was faintly amused because she had with her...on her pack-mules her tents that made into bathrooms, kitchens and reception rooms. And she countered by inviting him to dinner...That evening he was literally stunned when the huntress received him wearing on her head a turban, upon which a diamond brooch sparkled, a low-cut silver-lamé gown, on her feet little gold slippers and from head to toe she was dripping with brilliants and precious stones.

Her yacht, the **Istar**, was always kept ready to sail and her monkeys and a pet panther lived on board, waiting to welcome her in their own inimitable way. Sometimes, when on overland expeditions, she would leave her yacht behind and travel by passenger liner. On 1 September 1921 Paul Claudel embarked on the **André–Lebon** at Marseilles and was surprised to find Ida - or Madame Guinness as he called her - already on board. She and Walter Guinness aimed to reach Djibouti in French Somaliland but they were quite happy to sit on deck while the ship meandered across the Mediterranean, past Corsica and Sicily (and 'Etna's cone in the evening with the sun setting at its foot'), then round the coast of Greece. 'The conversation on board was like the dialogue of the dead...each one talking about his past life' (1968, p. 516).

Ida and Guinness left ship and continued their trip on land. And Robert de Montesquiou received brief letters from exotic points **en route.** From Hajin, 'a really strange and really beautiful land', she assured him: 'I have regained all my strength and shall happily resume my work' (BN, 15333, fol. 79). A note arrived from 'a little oasis of oleanders, far from anywhere, in the middle of the desert' (ibid., fol. 82). Another letter followed it: 'I am now on the shores of the lake at Bangwuolo, which I believe is the most beautiful place in the world' (ibid., fol. 83). Montesquiou welcomed news from her because he was becoming isolated from a society that was increasingly foreign to his way of thinking. He was also isolated because almost constant ill-health kept him indoors and often compelled him to make convalescent trips to the south of France.

In October 1921, without managing to see him first, Ida left on yet another journey, after being reassured by the count's physician Dr Couchaud that he was in better health. On 2 November she penned a long letter to him: 'I am writing to you here right at the source of the Blue Nile, in a mysterious forest full of orchids and violets, leopards and apes' (BN, 15093, fols 223-4). But her thoughts were still preoccupied with his health. Her mind was also on her plans for the following year. She explained them to him (ibid., fols 222-3):

before I left, I agreed to dance, in April, a new ballet at the Opéra **Diane troublée.** This will be an eighteenth-century Diana and she will dance in pink slippers. Bakst will do a libretto for it and Fokine will come from America to compose the dances. The music for it is very beautiful and I believe that it will please you. In June I am giving **Saint Sébastien** again at the Opéra; I know that you are opposed to this project, but my soul craves to play it again. The Poet was delighted when I told him of it, and I know also that you will be happy with this work, which you love and which you have so nobly championed.

On 3 December Montesquiou took up a pencil and wrote a reply. His doctor had been too kind-hearted to say how ill he really was and now his chronic illness was complicated by lung congestion. He assured Ida of his support for her work and told her that, when she arrived back in Paris on 12 December, she would find a lot of letters full of news of all his doings that autumn. Also waiting for her was an advance copy of a volume of essays, **Elus et appelés**, which he had dedicated to her. He ended on a sad, reflective note: 'What wounded me cruelly was not playing my part in the ravishing Shakespeare which you staged so worthily' (ibid., fols 248-50). Montesquiou added no signature and put his pencil down at that point. The letter lay unfinished on his desk. He never wrote another word again.

For the next week he lay seriously ill at the Pavillon de l'Amirauté, a rented villa surrounded by palms and tubs of orange bushes overlooking the old town of Menton. On 11 December, the day before Ida's return to France, he died as a result of renal failure. On 19 December Ida attended a service for the repose of his soul at Saint-Pierre-de-Chaillot. And two days later she was by his graveside in the Cimitière des Gonards at Versailles, where his beloved Gabriel Yturri waited to be reunited with him in death. Only a handful of friends accompanied the body on its final journey. No members of his family nor any of the society hostesses who used to fawn on him appeared. Elisabeth de Gramont, Natalie Barney and the painters Frédéric de Madrazo and Louise Breslau stood by. Dr Couchaud said a few gentle words over the coffin and Lucie Delarue-Mardrus recited a poem. Swathed in black veils to hide her tears, Ida stood alone 'as erect as a yew-tree among the graves' (Jullian, 1967, p. 271). She had brought a sheath of orchids as a last gift for her friend. As the party left, a first flurry of snow fell, melting on the exotic flowers and glistening like tear-drops.

Montesquiou had been a difficult friend, but a faithful one. Ida always cherished his memory and acknowledged her debt of gratitude for all his help and unfailing championship of her work. To commemorate his death she gave several recitals of his poems from the three volumes of his **Offrandes blessées** inspired by the tragedy of war. Years later she still kept a portrait of him in her drawing-room as a reminder of their unique friendship. For unique it was in both their lives, exalted and at the same time curiously intimate - despite the discrepancy in their ages and despite the fact that they never addressed each other in the second person singular!

However, by 1921 the time was ripe - indeed, overripe - for Ida to break away from his intellectual tutelage, which, had he lived any longer, would have become a shackle inhibiting the free range of her thought and the individual expression of her art.

CHAPTER 8

Forbidden Loves, 1922-1923

The ballet that proccupied Ida Rubinstein's thoughts at the source of the Blue Nile reached the stage of the Opéra on 1 May 1922 with a Greek form of its title, **Artémis troublée**. But, Diana or Artemis, the chaste goddess of classical antiquity was upset. Why? Trying his hand as a librettist, Bakst created an interesting, almost cynical variation on the theme of the Acteon legend. The handsome young hunter Acteon stumbles upon Artemis and her entourage of possessive amazons. With the most ferocious of them, Alkippé in the lead, they surround Acteon and seize him. But before they can tie him to a tree and tear him to pieces, he steals their thunder temporarily by turning to Artemis and pleading that, if he must die, she should kill him with one of her arrows. She is moved by his passion, frees him and draws him into her tent. The amazons are outraged by this betrayal of their misanthropic principles. Alkippé envokes the aid of Jupiter (strangely Latin beside the Greek Artemis!) He brings her to her senses and sends Acteon off into the forest metamorphosed into a stag. Artemis resumes her vocation as a huntress only to find that the next stag she kills sheds its skin to reveal a dead Acteon. After a momentary pang of desolation, she recovers her divine dignity and is carried off by her band of amazons, delighted to see her cured of her double-damned love - for a mortal and for a man.

Bakst's attempt to 'doctor' the story of Acteon by highlighting an unexpected side of Artemis's nature, far from making it into a tale of heterosexual love, only served to emphasize its essentially lesbian undertones. As if to avert moralistic criticism, he divised a deliberately artificial setting for the ballet. He conceived it as a mythological court-entertainment such as was performed before Louis XIV in the late seventeenth century. All the décors and costumes were of the period. White wigs, powder and patch, stiff bodices, antique jewellery and crinolined tutus, though suitably diaphanous and transparent, they were all designed to emphasize the 'unreal' nature of the piece. And the music chosen for the ballet also underlined this divorce from reality.

Ida, Bakst and the choreographer Nicola Guerra were impressed by a symphonic poem written by the young composer Paul Paray, a Prix de Rome winner and currently conductor with the Lamoureux Orchestra. The work was his **envoi de Rome,** the product of his stay at the Villa Medici, and had been written without any thought of accompanying a choreographic composition. However deliberately contrived, this almost automatically attracted some rather obvious criticism: 'This music is excellent, clear, elegant, orchestrated with a perfect sense of sound-values...a work of a remarkable artist...who is certainly a symphonist but is he sufficiently gifted for the theatre?' (Bertrand, Paul, 1922, pp. 202-3).

The reaction to Ida's interpretation of the role of Artemis was much more vocal. Although the ballet was only one of the four items on a programme devised by the Opéra's director, Jacques Rouché, it easily outshone the others. **La Tragédie de Salomé** and Ravel's comic opera **L'Heure espagnole** were old favourites and evoked only passing murmurs of approval. The final item, another new ballet entitled **Frivolant**, a nebulous piece to music by Jean Poueigh, inspired little serious comment. It was a very different case with **Artémis troublée**. Ida was the moving genius behind its creation, despite it being an official Opéra production, and so criticism centred upon her rather than upon the theatre's direction. Yet, as Emile Vuillermoz pointed out, Ida was prepared for any criticism. She had 'taken up again the ungrateful and magnificent role of benefactor of the arts. She was not unaware that this vocation was perilous and that it demanded as much in the way of sacrifice as of philosophy. She exposes herself to harsh comment and personal spitefulness. For such is the law of the Jungle' (1922, p. 4).

But, in fact, he - and most of the critics - did have nothing spiteful to say about her. She had captured the atmosphere of Louis XIV's court. She was 'an aristocratic goddess, a great lady in disguise, chosen for the unusual slimness of her immaterial body; she dances on fragile points and effortlessly assumes a series of poses of a precious beauty, rich in pictorial and literary erudition' (ibid., p. 4). The critic of **Le Journal** continued the theme. Ida Rubinstein was 'an incomparable mime whose most profoundly original qualities were developing still' (anon., 1922a, p. 2).

Charles Bert added his views: her 'interpretation of the role of Artemis...is interesting; one is conscious of all her intelligence in it and applauds her talent' (p. 3). Jane Catulle-Mendès exclaimed about 'Ida Rubinstein, long, long, elongated even more by a plume that touched the ceiling of the theatre, with angular grace, at times of an almost pure sculptural beauty, recalling an Egyptian or neo-Greek fresco' (1922, p. 2). Robert Dézarnaux was fascinated by the same vision: 'She is long like Houdon's Diana...even more so! Her arms have the slimness of arrows, and her legs the fragility of a doe's legs...she still has her fine and mysterious face, her Assyrian profile' (p. 2).

The veteran ballet critic André Levinson remarked upon the 'supreme paradox' of Ida's appearance as a classical dancer (1922, p. 1):

> I have no idea how to express my admiration for the intelligent
> and haughty dilettantism of that remarkable artist...And now today
> she copies traditional technique with stupefying ease. Tall,

'unnaturally' so, slender enough to make a perverse ephebe by Aubrey Beardsley look stocky, wearing the heavy tutu of brocade satin like a light loin-cloth - she defies nature and raises herself upon her points...And see those static poses, with elongated and tapering lines, impeccably self-assured, giving the appearance of contour captivating in its very exaggeration; those **port de bras** framing her little cameo-like head, her pale face of an implacable empress, affecting the slender form of a lyre.

Ida must have revelled in such a gush of praise and been amused by the exclamations of surprise at her commanding display of classical technique: she had gone through the traditional practice routine for at least two hours every day for the last decade and a half.

But after **Artémis troublée** Ida had scarcely a spare moment to reflect upon her reviews. She immediately plunged into rehearsals for the long-awaited revival of **Le Martyre de Saint Sébastien**. A **répétition générale** took place on 15 June 1922 and was followed on Saturday 17 June by a charity performance to raise funds for a monument to those who had fallen on the Somme. Lucien Corpechot noticed how passers-by stopped in surprise to see the great doors of the Opéra wide open at 10 o'clock on a Saturday morning and flocks of people crowding into the auditorium but, he reflected, if it had not been for the soldiers of the Somme, there would be no performances or galas at the Opéra (1922, p. 1).

A fellow critic, writing anonymously in **Petit Bleu**, focused upon the political implications of Ida's production and expressed a radical point of view. In default of Gabriele d'Annunzio's Hindu drama, she was giving Paris audiences a second dose of **Le Martyre**. It was all very well for her to pay out large sums to have her work mounted at the Châtelet, but for Jacques Rouché to allow her to rent the Opéra, a state-subsidized theatre and a national institution, was nothing short of a scandal.

As the writer went on, it became clear that he did not object to the work as such. The Opéra (whose correct title was, after all, the Académie **Nationale** de Musique) received a grant of 800,000 francs, 'so it is enough - even too much - that international stars are welcomed there, without permitting into the bargain a rich foreign actress...to come and make propaganda for an enemy of France. For Monsieur Gabriele d'Annunzio is not our friend' (anon., 1922b, p. 3). Ida Rubinstein, he went on, seemed to forget that she had signed an anti-Bolshevik manifesto after the Revolution but she was the same woman who had recently welcomed to her Paris mansion the Soviet commissar for Foreign Affairs, Gheorghi Chicherin. In the late spring of 1922 no journalist needed to explain that Chicherin was the man largely responsible for the signing of the second Treaty of Rapallo, on 16 April, by which Germany and the Soviet Union unexpectedly established diplomatic relations and agreed to a system of economic co-operation. The victorious powers, particularly Britain and France, regarded the pact with amazement and horror, not least because it aimed a deliberate blow at the allies' plans for war reparations. Why Ida wanted to meet Chicherin is not clear. Perhaps she had hopes of recovering her property sequestrated in the Soviet state. But that seems unlikely. Perhaps she saw him simply as a fellow Russian, a man of brilliant intellect and a kinsman of the great nineteenth-century philosopher and sociologist Boris Chicherin. But Ida's 'misdemeanour' was insignificant beside d'Annunzio's.

He was the man who, in January 1919, had written the **Letter to the Dalmatians**, in which he attacked the French (officially Italy's allies), threatening to confront them with 'a grenade in each hand and a knife between the teeth'. The writer may have forgiven d'Annunzio his impulsive Irredentism that had caused the allies almost two years of trouble, but he was in no mood to forget his offensive behaviour nor to be taken in by his present avowals of friendship: 'Let us wipe the sponge over this escapade; let us not hound...d'Annunzio with our hate - agreed! But don't inflict us (and to the thud of bank-notes on our national stage) with the interminable tirades of his plays' (ibid., p. 3).

Robert de Flers took a much more philosophical view of the matter (p. 2):

> The exigencies and fluctuations of our diplomacy can, at certain times cause...conflict with decisions taken on the other side of the Alps...one has only to think of d'Annunzio. This is not a good enough reason to forget that he is a great French poet...His finest homage to France is his having written some of his works, **Le Martyre**...among others, in the French language.

Flers's words did something to soften the blow dealt by the **Petit Bleu** critic.

Emile Vuillermoz - and whose views were more respected? - made a crushing retort to the chauvinist critic. Debussy and d'Annunzio were personalities who had a right to exceptional treatment. And yet Jacques Rouché (1922, p. 162),

> who is a master in the art of composing theoretically fine programmes, decided not to include Debussy's masterpiece in the Opéra's repertoire but, according to his usual dilettante formula, to give some 'one-off' performances with the assistance of...Ida Rubinstein. Of course,...this sublime score would have profited from being put into the hands of some committee of honour, crammed with marshals, ministers and academicians, to work out the budget

for a patriotic work.

The plain fact was that Ida had had to finance virtually the whole project and Rouché had allotted her a wholly inadequate rehearsal time with the result that 'yet again the Opéra has ruined a masterpiece for us!' (ibid., p. 163).

Vuillermoz was, in fact, referring to a general problem that had caused an eruption with a very specific epicentre. On Friday 16 June, the day after the dress rehearsal, the conductor, André Caplet, whose help in orchestrating **Le Martyre** in 1911 had been so invaluable, wrote a curt note to Rouché: 'Given the pitiful conditions under which the dress rehearsal of **Le Martyre**...took place, it is impossible for me to agree to conduct the performance tomorrow. My admiration and fondness for Debussy's music is too great to allow me to present his work with such a state of disorder on stage. Consequently, I ask you not to count on me tomorrow, Saturday' (BN Opéra, **Le Martyre**, dossier).

And Caplet refused to be mollified. A young conductor, Henry Defosse, stepped into his shoes and earned universal praise for his courage, although there was little he could do about the quality of the production. Meanwhile, Caplet was not be found anywhere. Instead, reporters on his trail were confronted by the composer and critic Louis Vuillemin. He vehemently defended him: 'Caplet's action does him honour and I think that this precedent should warrant all musicians' categoric opposition to the doings of certain directors.' Vuillemin became very agitated - 'the fiery and spirited image of a blond Viking' - and declared they they ought to form 'a league of discontented musicians' (Scize, p. 3).

Many agreed with Vuillemin but it was too late to do anything to save the production from almost inevitable criticism. By contrast with Bakst's striking décors and costumes, which even after eleven years bowled over blasé post-war audiences, the acting left a little to be desired: the cast had clearly not had a chance to warm up. One of **Le Martyre**'s greatest drawbacks, in the eyes of a new generation used to the cultivated simplicity of **Les Six**, was its massive proportions. Gaston Carraud muttered something about Debussy's music being 'chained to a terrible literary cannon-ball...Its dismembered parts appearing... like the splendid débris of antique marbles emerging into the light of day' (quoted Cuttoli, p. 17).

However, reactions to Ida's efforts - and to the performance as a whole - were quite favourable. Those new to the work were fascinated by the androgynous image of Saint Sebastian and by the 'fetichistic, sadistic and unchaste text', by the limpid voluptuousness of the saint's dancing and by the 'distracted eroticism' of the emperor (Tenroc, 1922,

p. 1). Even the waspish Jean Poueigh had a compliment to pay: Ida Rubinstein as the 'slim, graceful and proud...androgyne is the incarnation of a Sebastian whose plastic beauty corresponds to that of the music. The poses are of supreme distinction, perhaps a little affected, but which are controlled by the instinctive intelligence of the interpreter' (p. 2).

On 23 June, when the play completed its run (against all odds), Ida could feel satisfied, despite the disappointing outcome of the long-awaited project to film the work. But her efforts did have one long-term result since **Le Martyre** was subsequently made part of the Opéra's official repertoire. However, then or later, she had little time for self-congratulation. The very next day, Saturday 24 June, she appeared on stage again at the Opéra in an entirely different, though much less exacting role. As a charity event on the eve of the Grand Prix, a Venetian ball was held in the auditorium of the theatre. The theme was Venice in the eighteenth century and guests, who came in their thousands, were entertained by a series of tableaux. The **Times** correspondent described everything in detail (anon, 1922c, p. 9):

> The first (tableau) showed the marriage of the Doge (Edouard de Max) with the Adriatic (Ida Rubinstein). Then followed the reception of the Persian Embassy by the Doge...Prince Karer...son of the Maharajah of Kapurthala impersonated one of the Persian princes, and other notabilities in French society were recognised in the procession...The incarnation of Venice was equally splendid, with...Cécile Sorel as 'Venice' sitting on a throne, with her courtiers prostrated at her feet as they paid homage to her beauty.

The actors' costumes were sumptuous, two in particular: 'Monsieur de Max as the Doge wore robes of pale gold brocade; Madame Ida Rubinstein as the Adriatic glittered in diamonds and gold waves as she rose to meet her lover' (ibid., p. 9).

The audience was equally glittering and illustrious. 'The Princesse Murat..., the Marquise de Ganay..., Madame Jean Hennessy and the Princesse Edmond de Polignac were recognised behind their masks' - though with a physiognomy like Madame de Polignac's that was no difficult task. Outside in the Place de l'Opéra crowds of people watched the guests come and go: 'No such fête had been seen in Paris for many years. There was nothing of the carnival about it, no wild scenes of merriment, but soft laughter, gay smiles and murmured gallanteries marked it as a true revival of eighteenth-century modes and manners' (ibid., p. 9). Whatever the writer meant by that!

No sooner had Ida shed her role as the Adriatic, repudiating, so to speak, her marriage to the Doge, Edouard de Max (indeed, this was their last public appearance together), she turned her full attention to another major project, d'Annunzio's **Phaedre**. Until it reached the stage almost a year later, she tried not to be distracted by anything else, although some tried hard to interest her in other works. For example, in December 1922, the doyen of the French theatre Aurélien Lugné-Poe wrote to Jacques Rouché wondering 'if Mme I.R. (**sic**) might not find a very fine use for her talents in Manfred (the role itself.)' He then added a postscript: '**An extremely beautiful thing for her**' - he heavily underlined the words - 'would be **Dionysos** by Gasquet with music by Léon Moreau' (AN, AJ 13. 1208: Lugné-Poe).

These ideas were not new. Lugné-Poe had been urging Rouché to let him produce these works - along with Ibsen's **Peer Gynt** - for at least two years before he set his sights on Ida. But nothing came of his proposals, interesting though they were. The **Manfred** he planned was to be based on Lord Byron's poem and the music - it went without saying - would be the overture and fifteen numbers specially composed by Schumann as a background for a dramatic recitation of the work. The revival of **Le Martyre** had clearly impressed him with Ida's skill in transvestite parts. But what he had in mind when suggesting Joachim Gasquet's **Dionysos** as a suitable vehicle for her talent is not quite clear, except that he could scarcely have thought of casting her in the role of the god of wine.

Ida seems to have given more serious thought to a project devised for her by the American dancer Hubert Stowitts, a colleague of Pavlova's between 1915 and 1921. He sketched out plans for a Shinto style ballet entitled **Kagura or the Laughter of the Gods** with music by Prokofiev. Prokofiev certainly never considered writing a score specially for the ballet and it is hard to image which of his extant works might have adapted most suitably to an oriental scenario. All that the public ever saw of the project was a set of five designs for the production which Stowitts exhibited at the Knoedler Galleries in New York in 1923. One can only speculate about what Ida would have made of the possibilities of a work in the classical Japanese style but, given its traditional emphasis upon mime and static poses, it might have proved a most successful vehicle for her unique combination of talents. But the amount of thought that Ida could give to any of these suggestions was severely limited by her preoccupation with the problems of mounting **Phaedre**.

As early as March 1913 d'Annunzio had approached Gabriel Astruc with the idea of producing his monumental play **Fedra** in France. Nothing came of the suggestion. But he was still dreaming of the idea six years later during the Fiume campaign. Despite her earlier resolution not to have anything to do with any new d'Annunzian venture, Ida was apparently so mesmerized by the soldier-poet's heroic exploits that she had a change of heart. As soon as the last curtain came down on **Antoine et Cléopâtre,** she put her mind to the play and commissioned a translation from a young admirer of d'Annunzio's, André Doderet. (Indeed, so fervent was his admiration that once, when Ida told him that Eleanora Duse, legendary as an actress and just as legendary as the poet's mistress, lay seriously ill in the Hôtel Regina in Paris, he rushed off with a bouquet of flowers for her, although he had never met her.)

Doderet completed his translation in the late spring of 1922 and, as soon as **Le Martyre** was over, he found himself invited to an intimate working-lunch at Ida's house. Bakst also came because he was working on the sets, his last major enterprise as it turned out. Natalie Barney and Romaine Brooks made an impressive entrance: they had come more to spectate than to assist at the birth of a new work amid the roses and hortensias of Ida's garden. Two evening meetings followed when Doderet read through his text, at the same time keeping an eye on his beautiful hostess, dressed in a shimmering robe with a corsage of rare flowers.

In August Ida sent a slightly bewildered Doderet to see d'Annunzio at Gardone. He arrived in Italy to find the newspapers full of a great speech which the poet had just made from the balcony of the Palazzo Marino in Milan to a crowd seething with discontent. Nobody will ever know how much credit is due to d'Annunzio for preventing civil war in Italy during those summer months. In the short term his influence was probably greater than any other single factor because of the respect he commanded from every section of the community. By the end of October Mussolini had provided a more partisan solution to the problem of national unity with the 'March on Rome' that set Italy on the road to fascism. It was against this background that Doderet finalized details of his translation with the author.

The political situation was just as disturbing early the following year, 1923, when Ida once again sent Doderet to Italy, this time to Florence to sort out problems with the incidental music. Ildebrando Pizzetti had already written a three-act opera based on d'Annunzio's **Fedra** and it had been performed at La Scala, Milan, in March 1915. When Ida suggested that his score might be adapted as incidental music for her production, he was not entirely pleased and it took strenuous efforts on the part of Jacques Rouché and Doderet to settle their differences. Even then the result was not exactly satifactory. As one reviewer remarked, 'Pizzetti's music, though certainly interesting, is not up to the competition from the text; it is reduced to the state of vapour, like an April shower falling on a torrent of lava' (Heugel, pp. 266-7). Ida was to find a more exciting and original solution to this problem when she revived the production in 1926.

A **répétition générale** in aid of charity took place on the afternoon of Wednesday, 6 June 1923, and the Opéra was crowded with celebrities. Anatole France had insisted on having a box. Cécile Sorel, Jean Cocteau and Edouard de Max were conspicuously present in the auditorium. Paul Valéry, Henri de Régnier, Henri de Montherlant and Paul Morand with the Princesse Soutzo mingled with a host of other personalities in the wings during the intervals. The one person who did not appear was d'Annunzio himself. Everything was prepared for his arrival but all that came - very late in the day - were sad telegrams to Rouché and Ida: the old war-wound in his eye had flared up and he had to have complete rest. Rouché took care to avoid conjecture by having his telegram published in **Le Figaro.** There, for all to see, were the poet's flowery words vowing eternal friendship for France: 'Before the war, during the war, after the war, I was and I am still faithful to my second fatherland' (quoted Doderet, p. 111). His telegram to Ida was more poignant and more revealing: 'To my tribulations is added an eye complaint that lingers with me. In the painful darkness, I see your radiant image and my miserable defect is compensated for by the vibrant perfection of your art' (ibid., p. 113). Truth be told, though the eye trouble was genuine, d'Annunzio was being kept on a very short rein by Mussolini: he was too dangerously charismatic a figure to be allowed out of sight.

As for **Phaedre**, the production and the performance were equally impressive. Bakst's sets, which returned in spirit to the Mycenean splendour of **Hélène de Sparte,** were grand and barbaric, their colours hard and threatening, the product of the artist's manic depressive state but entirely apt for a drama as intense and violent as **Phaedre.** In fact, sections of the audience found it a little too much of a visual and intellectual onslaught. The heroine's burning passion for her step-son and her internal turmoil may have represented a fascinating recurrence of primitive humanity's struggle between the animal and the divine in its nature but act after act of 'perpetual tension and continual paroxysm from which one demanded in vain a moment of repose' was almost too cathartic an experience (Heugel, p. 266).

Bakst's sets too had an equally overwhelming psychological effect. Jacques Heugel, the critic of **Le Ménestrel,** commented: 'related to all the conventional images of that nightmare of archaism to which the Ballets Russes inured us, like the viscous anatomy of the octopus..., they correspond much less to our physical world than to the lower regions which the psychic call the astral world' (p. 267).

It is idle to speculate as to what Bakst made of Heugel's pronouncements on his work because, by now, his tortured mind was completely concentrated upon the task of refurbishing his sets for a revival of **Le Martyre** later than month. Designed by Ida as the finale of her 'd'Annunzio Season', it was a much more satisfactory production than the previous year's one: this time she had the full co-operation of the Opéra's management and the music was under the strict control of Philippe Gaubert.

But having toyed with the forbidden loves of an Artemis and a Phaedra and celebrated the sacred and profane attractions of a Sebastian, Ida was now ready to go on to explore conflicts of passion much closer to her own world.

CHAPTER 9

Two Courtesans and the Idiot, 1923-1926

Sarah Bernhardt's death on 26 March 1923 left a considerable gap in French theatre-life. Anybody who tried to fill it would automatically invite dangerous comparisons between herself and that legendary figure, all the more formidable now that she was dead. Though a devoted pupil, Ida made no attempt to step into Sarah's shoes. She had no need to since her own talents were very different, unique in their own way. Ida's style of delivery only vaguely resembled hers and their appearance was not in the least similar. Yet critics - and sometimes friends with misplaced enthusiasm - found themselves comparing the stage-presence of the two women. Sarah inadvertantly played into their hands by morally obliging Ida to live up to the standard set by her in the role of Marguerite Gautier in Dumas's **La Dame aux camélias.** In the year before her death Sarah coached Ida in the part and late in 1922 saw her perform the last act of the play at a charity gala in aid of destitute Russians. The death of Marguerite is the most dangerous moment for any actress tempted to substitute sentimentality and melodrama for the black despair and false hope characteristic of a consumptive's death agony. Ida resisted the temptation. As a result, Sarah made her promise to take over the role and make it her own, and so the production that opened on 27 November 1923 with a gala performance (appropriately) at the Théâtre Sarah Bernhardt was almost an act of filial piety on Ida's part.

Paris society was there in force because, apart from the attraction of a glamorous new production, the proceeds would go to the war-wounded, and the Minister of War and Pensions, André Maginot, assisted with his presence. And what they did see when the curtain rose certainly satisfied their curiosity and stimulated their critical faculties. The décors and costumes by Alexandre Benois riveted their attention: he had created an opulent set recapturing the atmosphere of a Louis-Philippe drawing-room, 'extracting a real charm from the florid forms of excessive ornamentation' (anon., 1931e, p. 12). H. de Sombreuil remarked that, if the sets were new and astonishing, 'the costumes were dazzling, spendid and superb,...something that surprised no one.' Ida appeared wearing an ermine robe but it 'did not make us forget the golden locks and sweet smile...of the Immortal Sarah.' Yet, Sombreuil added, when one remembered the war-wounded, Madame Rubinstein's bold venture seemed completely worthwhile (p. 7).

René Bruyez made another kind of comparison. He had wondered apprehensively what the hieratic creator of Saint Sebastian would do with the character of a nineteenth-century courtesan but 'her incomparable individuality caused a new personality to emerge...Ida Rubinstein truly recreated a role which was never written for her and in which she discovered, none the less, strains of the most undeniable emotion' (p. 16). Lucien Corpechot waxed lyrical: 'Madame Rubinstein achieved, in each of her poses and in her ornamental melancholy, an image of romantic passion, of that passion that George Sand, Musset, Gautier, Berlioz, Hortense de Méritans, all these men and women who chose love as the sole god of life!' (1923, programme). And Bakst noticed with some satisfaction that Ida 'does not...die like a little slut; she dies like a princess, or perhaps like Marguerite Gautier in person...It is too beautiful...She has a superior sense of beauty which causes her never to be satisfied with second best; she searches for an exciting perfection' (Thomas, pp. 90, 99). Paul Souday went further and pronounced on the question avoided by the others: 'Since the death of Sarah Bernhardt, Madame Rubinstein is the greatest plastic actress of the day' (ibid., p. 98).

Ida's **Dame aux camélias** was so successful that she gave fifty performances of it over the next two years. By the end of the decade the total had topped one hundred. When would-be detractors realized that she had triumphed against all odds, they moderated their language. Always quick to criticize her, Diaghilev confined himself to one rather underhand jibe. He was jealous of Benois's collaboration with Ida and turned on him petulantly. 'Why do you do it?' he demanded. 'Come now, do (Gounod's opera) **Philémon and Baucis,** and show that you **can do** better for me than for Ida' (Lieven, p. 346).

If audiences were anxious about Ida's gear-change from a male saint to a very female courtesan, they were even more uneasy about her next role. In February 1924 she appeared at the Théâtre Sarah-Bernhardt in Maurice Rostand's play **Le Secret du Sphinx** in the unlikely part of the spirit of the Sphinx. The plot bordered on the absurd but maintained some kind of dignity because of its verse form. An Italian poet Paris Egliano, with his mistress and brother, set out for Egypt to discover the Sphinx's secret. The brother approaches the beast first but promptly falls dead. Paris tries his hand; receives a whispered message from the Sphinx but, unlike his brother, survives the experience. He returns to Italy; writes a play about the Sphinx and achieves great success. At that point the spirit of the Sphinx reappears and confesses that she did not tell the poet the truth in the desert: 'The secret of the world is too sad; a poet who exists to sing of love and life must not know it' (Ouvray, p. 92). All very enigmatic! But Paris accepts this verdict and ends up in his mistress's arms.

Critics commented on the sumptuous presentation of the play: the sets were magnificent, clever and tasteful. The costumes were designed by an increasingly well-known compatriot of Ida's, Romain de Tirtoff, otherwise known as Erté. He was delighted with his task: 'It gave me the greatest pleasure to be permitted to design the costume of the Sphinx, explaining all the mystery of the fabulous monster' (quoted Spencer, p. 188). In a word, it was striking: Ida wearing an elaborate headdress in gold and green with mauve decorations.

And the care lavished upon the staging successfully diverted attention from the curious plot. Only Maurice Rostand was discontented. He had written the play just after the discovery of Tutankhamun's tomb in November 1922, probably hoping to cash in on interest in that fascinating and slightly sinister event, and he had had Sarah Bernhardt in mind for the Sphinx's part. Instead, he grumbled, 'I only had Ida, dear to d'Annunzio' (p. 250). But Rostand had another shock coming to him. Everybody criticized or (worse) ignored the play and commended the acting. Pierre d'Ouvray's comment was typical: 'The interpretation is excellent...The Sphinx is Madame Ida Rubinstein: she was mysterious and as strange as you could wish for' (p. 92). And all the more so because half the time she had to cope with a considerable impediment in the form of a yashmak!

Later in February 1924 Ida shed her sphinx-like image and reverted to being Saint Sebastian for a further revival of **Le Martyre** at the Opéra. It was even more of a success than before because another technical problem had been ironed out: the choirs of Paradise were now placed on stage, though still remaining invisible. This made life easier for singers and conductor alike. The production was also mounted at the Théâtre de la Monnaie in Brussels a few months later in May.

At the end of the season Ida reverted to her profession as a dancer when she mounted the short ballet **Istar** at the Opéra on 10 July 1924. The work was not new, since it had been created at the Opéra by the choreographer Ivan Clustine for Natasha Trouhanova in 1912, and the score by Vincent d'Indy had been written even earlier, in 1896, as a set of variations in search of a theme, a musical commentary on a passage from the sixth song of the **Epic of Izbudar**. But it seemed to be a suitable vehicle for Ida's talents: Istar, the daughter of Sin, directs her steps towards the land of the dead and, confronted by seven doors at its entrance, she dances before them, shedding at each one part of her clothing or one of her ornaments until, as the music reaches the goal of its unadorned theme, she raises the final veil and enters the forbidden land to drink the waters of life. By doing so she sets free her young lover. Dramatic and exotic, a kind of well-intentioned Salomé, Ida drew to her charity gala summer crowds eager to help the victims of the

Madagascar disaster - and to catch a glimpse of her in the nude.

Sadly the production itself had a casualty. Ida commissioned Bakst to design the sets and costumes. The choice was an obvious one since the story lent itself to the colourful orientalism at which he excelled. But Bakst was a sick man, physically unwell and low in morale. A glance at the letters written in his last years clearly show how the strain of overwork, sickness and nervous tension was wearing him down inexorably. He vented his feelings on his fellow collaborators. In 1921 it was Fokine who was the **bête noir,** as he changed his mind ten times about choreographing **Artémis troublée** (AN, AJ 13. 1207: Bakst, fols 5, 9). Then, Bakst complained to Jacques Rouché, he was not being paid enough for his work. As he put it, 'unfortunately one must live, as they say, and also let one's dependants live.' Even Diaghilev was paying him more for his work on **The Sleeping Princess.** And with the première of **Artémis troublée** only three weeks away, he was still haggling with Rouché about the fee for individual costumes (ibid., fols 10, 11, 19 21, 23). In the middle of 1922 he vowed never to do any more work for the Opéra or for Ida. 'I wish she would choose another painter!' he exclaimed (ibid., fol. 27).

But, the immediate crisis over, he was soon talking about a new season, convinced that it would be 'as brilliant and glorious for her as that of 1922!' (ibid., fol. 36). However, his work for **Phaedre** in 1923 put him in a state of agitation. Then, faced with the problem of providing sets and costumes for **La Dame aux camélias,** he was plunged into despair. But no sooner had Ida passed on the task to Benois than Bakst started to complain again: she was so preoccupied with **La Dame** that she was giving the **Istar** project scant attention. He was having to bear all the burdens. The work on Ida's costume alone was 'terribly complicated'. He poured his woes out on Rouché: 'I shall spend all my time supervising the least details, because Madame Rubinstein always orders from couturiers, not from theatrical costumiers, and couturiers have to be **told about each stitch of the needle!**' (ibid., fol. 31).

That was the last straw. Bakst could not cope with work for her while Diaghilev was bullying him to design five sets plus a hundred or more costumes. He had a breakdown. One day, after climbing the endless steps to the rehearsal and property rooms right at the top of the Opéra, 'he suddenly lashed himself into a state of great excitement, without any justification, and, bursting into wild and abusive shrieks, he ran out of the theatre...From that day none of his friends saw him again' (Lieven, p. 307). He shut himself in his room, allowing only a nurse near him, until he was moved to a clinic outside Paris at Rueil-Malmaison, where he died on 27 December 1924.

The official cause of death was renal failure precipitated by pulmonary complications, but the real cause of his trouble was arteriosclerosis, which was the root-cause of his irrational and manic-depressive behaviour in the period before his final collapse. It was a terrible experience for Ida to see the deterioration of a man whose work had been so closely linked, physically and spiritually, with hers since the inception of her stage career. He had also loved her so devotedly that many had speculated - though without any real justification - on the nature of their relationship.

In the meantime, another close collaborator of Ida's died. Edouard de Max ended a colourful career by insisting, against his doctor's orders, on appearing in a performance of **L'Ami Fritz** on 6 September 1924, to celebrate the victory on the Marne. The strain was too much for him and he died on 28 October at the age of fifty-nine - still too young to play the part planned for him by Colette, who visualized him as an aged misogynist Don Juan surrounded by young women to whom he neither wanted to nor could make love (1971, pp. 45-7). Ida had known and worked with him for the best part of a decade and had found him a remarkably rewarding stage partner.

But at this point in her life no set-back or personal loss could inhibit Ida's pursuit of her professional ambitions. In mid-1924 she was already working on a project that had half-formed in her mind while still a girl in St Petersburg. Dostoyevsky was then - and remained - her favourite author. Of all his characters the one with whom she most closely identified herself was the anti-heroine of **The Idiot**, Nastasya Filippovna Barashkov, the unworldly beauty forced at an early age into a life as a courtesan by a rich old roué. Why she should have felt some empathy with this half-demented, erratic woman is not entirely clear. Perhaps her style and appearance struck a familiar chord: she was 'an extraordinarily beautiful woman...in a black silk dress of an extremely simple and elegant cut; her hair, which appeared to be dark brown in colour, was done up in a simple, homely style; her eyes were dark and deep, her forehead pensive; her expression was passionate and...haughty. She was rather thin in the face and...pale, too' (Dostoyevsky, p. 56). It might have been a description of Ida herself.

She commissioned Wladimir Bienstock and Fernand Nozière to make a stage-play out of the monumental novel. An almost impossible task, one would have thought, but they succeeded remarkably well by concentrating largely upon the passionate fixation of the reckless, rather sinister Parfyon Semyonovich Rogozhin with the constantly vacillating Nastasya. The 'idiot' himself, Prince Leo Nicolayevich Myshkin, the Christ-like figure, the holy fool with an infinite capacity for forgiveness because he believed that 'the world would be saved by beauty' (ibid., pp. 419-20), around whom the action really revolved, was relegated to a distinctly secondary position. The result, however, was amazingly successful, a perfect vessel for the full range of Ida's dramatic talents - even in the last scene, in which her murdered body formed the centre-piece: her pale, emaciated beauty riveted the audience's attention, just as the absolute stillness of her set-poses in **Schéhérazade** had electrified them years before.

When the curtain rose on the drama at the Théâtre de Vaudeville on 1 April 1925, the critics were struck by the rich sets created by Benois. They were instantly transported back in time to mid-nineteenth-century Russia. They marvelled at the wardrobe of sumptuous robes and jewellery worn by Ida. But even more, it was the series of visual images created by her as the play unfolded that fascinated and sometimes disconcerted them. Gabriel Boissy posed a question (p. 2):

> From what fairy-tale world does she come? Is it a dead princess, a Carpaccio, a Gustave Moreau with hieratic gestures who walks among the living? One gazes, stupified, as if hallucinating before this miracle of unreality, on that bloodless, mummy-like face, those swooning gazelle's eyes, with the frenzy of an injured cat...Ida Rubinstein offers a glass of liqueur like the Archangel Gabriel offering a lily to Mary. Where does she come from down to this earth?

And M. Armory described her as 'pale and phantom-like...a mirage of aestheticism, a hallucination on the stage,...milk-white from a wax museum...pathetic, sad, encompassing in the sweep of her gesture the hysteria of fatalism' (p. 2). M. Feyran commented on the 'unreal' image she presented, an otherworldliness emphasized by her far-off voice and her intonation like a divine chant of a Pythian prophetess. By contrast, Pierre Blanchar as Myshkin was so simple, so perfect as to be almost irritating (p. 171). But that was what the director, Armand Bour, intended. How else could he achieve the necessary dramatic contrast with the wild Rogozhin and the manic Nastasya? Perhaps Myshkin was meant to be the reincarnation of Ida's Saint Sebastian, 'the knight of the ideal chastity of the only divine love' (Legrand-Chabrier, pp. 1-2). Whatever they concluded about the deeper significance of **L'Idiot**, all agreed that Armand Bour's carefully worked-out production was excellent.

After **L'Idiot**'s relatively long run throughout April 1925, Ida made no further stage appearances that year. But she did not fade from public view. Off stage, as on stage, she always presented a ravishing sight of opulence and richness. Rumours circulated that she had her dresses made from the rarest, most costly materials and never wore them more than once. This was not done for purely visual effect: even the most sceptical believed that each month thirty complete sets of the costliest lingerie were delivered to her house - extravagant perhaps, but it did save a fortune in laundry bills! And as for her diet, many were still convinced that what she saved by living on biscuits she spent on champagne.

Ida also continued to attract the attention of creative and executant artists eager to interest her in their work and talents. For example, in September 1925 one finds her business manager Monsieur Gardieur writing to Jacques Rouché about Georges de Porto-Riche: he had used Léon Blum's brother René to intercede with her about a play in which he had tried to interest her the previous year. Ida's reply had been slightly crisp: he should address himself directly to Rouché (BN Opéra, **Le Martyre,** dossier). One wonders why her attitude to Porto-Riche had changed. Was she hesitant about associating with the man who would go down in history for having warned the Prince Antoine Bibesco against gaining a bad reputation from letting his name be too closely linked with that of his friend Marcel Proust? More likely she had no wish to take on fresh commitments as she prepared to set off on a long trip abroad on 1 October. Besides, she had already made plans for the coming year - and they were ambitious ones.

In March 1926 she realized her dream of performing **Le Martyre** before an Italian audience and in the presence of Gabriele d'Annunzio. This took place at La Scala, Milan, and none other than Arturo Toscanini conducted the orchestra. The evening was a triumph, the work's apotheosis.

Afterwards, the poet, dressed in uniform and followed by a young adjutant, came on stage. The audience, packed with his wartime colleagues, applauded tumultuously. But, as Guy Tosi speculated, how much of the enthusiasm was for the man, how much for the work? (1948a, p. 42). Man or work, Ida was delighted with the reception, although she was a little perturbed when d'Annunzio began to make a speech and was more than a little disconcerted by the time the harangue ended more than half an hour later. As she later remarked, 'I, poor Saint Sebastian, forgotten on the stage, I remained tied to the tree of my martyrdom' (Moustiers, p. 3). But once released from her tight bonds, she too was carried away by the waves of emotion washing round the poet and by the palpable love that the crowd felt for their national hero. 'When he left the theatre, the crowd hedged him round or followed him, like the archers surrounding Sebastian' (Rubinstein, p. 335). Ida's pleasure was complete when a note arrived from d'Annunzio: 'Little sister, this evening you have yet again surpassed yourself. You were more beautiful than ever, more melodious, more ardent. I am going, with my heart beating in time with yours, to the great Toscanini's house. Rest peacefully, sleep soundly in the arms of poetry' (ibid., pp. 329-30).

But despite his bravado, d'Annunzio's world had, in reality, collapsed. Since his withdrawal from Fiume in January 1921 he had been something of an embarrassment to the Italian authorities. The archetypal patriot, possibly the most popular person in the whole country, as soon as Mussolini came to power, he had to be relegated to the status of a 'national monument', almost a tourist attraction, in case he became a focal point of opposition to the régime. Honours were heaped upon him and in 1924 Victor Emmanuel III conferred on him the suitably romantic-sounding title of Principe di Montenevoso. But that did not conceal the fact that he was a prisoner in all but name in his villa, Il Vittoriale, at Gardone on the shores of Lake Garda. Under the pretext of providing him with protection, Mussolini had him kept under constant surveillance. His visit to Milan in 1926 was something of an exception. Certainly it was the first time he had been in Milan (or any major city) since October 1922. And after the scenes at La Scala his admirers were never again allowed to gather en masse to adulate him.

The following month Ida arrived in Rome to mount her current repertoire of plays. With the best intentions in the world she planned to open at the Teatro Constanzi with a performance of Le Martyre. Hopefully the triumph of Milan would be repeated and Rome, at last, would come to know d'Annunzio's masterpiece. But at very little notice the gala performance was cancelled. The acoustics in the theatre were defective and would be especially bad for a work containing long passages of recitation in a foreign language - at least that was the official excuse. The theatre management had, in fact, decided that it would be inadvisable to perform a play that was still on the Index within a stone's throw of the Vatican. Nothing had changed since its removal from the list of events celebrating the fiftieth anniversary of the unification of Italy in 1911! But this time the situation was even more delicate because Mussolini was eager to conciliate Pope Pius XI in the hope that the quarrel between the Vatican and the Italian state could be ended to their mutual advantage. Ida, to whom the work was quintessentially an expression of Christian faith, was the unwitting victim of ecclesiastical and political pressures that meant little to her. However, she accepted the situation with good grace and on 9 April mounted La Dame aux camélias as a gala performance in aid of charities organized in memory of the king's mother, Queen Margherita, who had died at the beginning of the year.

A glittering audience numbered, so it seemed, all the Roman nobility and a good number of foreign dignitaries, including the French ambassador, Camille Barrère. Backstage the atmosphere was slightly tense because Roman theatre-goers were notoriously blasé about the romantic repertoire and usually dismissed it with an affected shrug. But Ida's artistry quickly warmed them to her performance. None the less, she found the experience nerve-racking and until admirers, led by the Principessa Borghese, flocked to her dressing-room during the interval and showered compliments on her, she refused to believe in her success.

A second performance of **La Dame** was given some days later, followed by two performances of **L'Idiot**. But it was for one final item in her repertoire that Roman audiences waited with most impatience. Ida had decided to mount **Phaedre** as a tribute to d'Annunzio. That fact alone caused considerable excitement but there was also a deal of speculation about new incidental music which she had commissioned from Arthur Honegger. Three performances of his dramatic cantata **Le Roi David** had just been given in Rome during the Easter period and it had caught the Romans' imagination. He had suddenly been revealed as a serious composer of international stature and not just a sixth part of a Cocteauesque 'happening'.

Pizzetti's music had not been entirely satisfactory, so Ida's thoughts had turned to Honegger. Apparently d'Annunzio influenced her decision: he knew and liked Honegger's **Roi David**. He fancied himself as a musical connoisseur and unashamedly told Honegger so: 'You know perhaps that I have the keenest and most loving ear in the world for listening to good music; and that I owe this quality, quite rare among writers, to my close friendship with Claude (Debussy)' (Delannoy, p. 122).

Ida's association with Honegger was a new departure in her career as a patron. Hitherto all the composers with whom she worked were either well-established figures or reliable, conventional craftsmen. Honegger was not the most exaggeratedly avant-garde of composers. By 1926 his work was widely acclaimed. But he was still young and very much associated with the new generation of post-war composers eager to reflect the new spirit of the age in their works. Ida's faith in Honegger was so amply rewarded that she continued to work with him to the end of her career, commissioning in all six major scores from him, more than from any other composer. He also inspired her to commission works from his contemporaries - and with worthwhile results - although one must stress that, however much she loved music for its own sake, she almost always thought of it as having a supporting function in a stage production, a play, a **mélodrame** or a ballet. The one possible exception was Honegger's own dramatic oratorio **Jeanne d'Arc au bûcher**.

Honegger's score for **Phaedre** (which amounted to a substantial symphonic suite suitable for concert performance) was extremely powerful: it expressed in unequivocal terms the violent emotions of the drama, Phaedra's burning passion for her step-son Hippolyte, his magnetic and disturbing beauty, and his father Theseus's jealousy; and it ended by depicting Phaedra's death in the moving tones of an impressionist employing the musical palette of the twentieth century.

But a disappointment was in store for Honegger. When he conducted the music on the first night of **Phaedre** at the Teatro Constanzi on 19 April, the audience heard little of his work. Crowds of young people who still regarded d'Annunzio as a more charismatic leader than Mussolini came to the theatre in the hope that the poet-hero would appear and repeat his Milan 'performance'. They carried banners and were in a very boisterous mood. But when it became clear that no d'Annunzio was coming, they began to hoot and boo. And nothing could be done about it: their idol was far away in the north of Italy, a virtual prisoner in his Vittoriale. As if to commiserate with each other, Honegger paid a visit to d'Annunzio at his villa immediately after the Rome season. The composer was disconcerted at first by the poet's attempt to pay him a compliment by firing a seven-gun salvo from a cruiser 'beached' in the grounds of the villa: the shots climbed the seven notes of the scale, leaving them in suspense on the leading note. But Honegger soon warmed to his host: 'His conversation was a display of fireworks, and one understood how this man of a predominantly unattractive physique had such a success with women' (1966, p. 107).

On her way back to Paris Ida also stayed at Gardone but her visit was longer. This gave rise to some talk. On the surface the letter that d'Annunzio received from her afterwards might seem to confirm rumours about their relationship: 'After these fifteen days passed close to you, brother, I really cannot live without you' (Tosi, 1948b, p. 2). But since their friendship had already lasted for sixteen years without a breath of scandal, one can only conclude that Ida was simply using d'Annunzio's own hyperbolic language to express her concern about the circumstances in which she found him. The word 'brother' provides the main clue to the nature of their intimacy. The only man who was ever emotionally close to her was Walter Guinness and he continued to see as much of her as his duties as a married man and as Minister of Agriculture and Fisheries permitted.

CHAPTER 10
Orpheus and the Empress, 1926–1927

Ida Rubinstein's effort to bring d'Annunzio to the Italians during her 1926 tour was remarkable. But, interestingly, despite her closeness to the poet, it was the last time that she performed any of his works in public, with the single exception of a very brief revival of **Le Martyre** in London in 1931. She made no attempt to mount **Phaedre** in the version with Honegger's music in Paris. French critics who heard some of the music in its concert version asked petulantly: 'Perhaps Madame Rubinstein...will one day provide us with the opportunity of giving it a proper appraisal?' (Petit, p. 296). The truth was that Ida had come to a turning point in her career. From the late spring of 1926 through to the summer of 1927 she wrestled with the problem of how her artistic ideals could best be expressed. Would she succeed better as an actress or as a dancer? Her immediate decision was to concentrate upon dance as the ideal medium. But as she worked out her ideas in the period between 1928 and 1934, the final result almost inevitably had to be a synthetic one, a combination of dramatic technique and dance form - a solution that realized itself in some unique and completely modern stage works.

In 1926, at the beginning of Ida's 'transitional period', one of her most fervent admirers, Fernand Nozière, published a slight biographical sketch of her. He used its twenty-seven pages to praise everything she had ever done. And, ironically, he bent over backwards to stress that she was, first and foremost, an actress. She had set out to be one in Russia at the start of her career and 'in France she had pursued her intention of being a **tragédienne** at the service of poets' (p. 25). Her efforts had not always been greeted with undiluted public rapture. But she was a sincere artist. She thrived on constructive criticism. She persisted and she succeeded. This combination of patience and tenacity, of sweetness and savagery, was reflected in her range of dramatic expression: she could portray a young girl one moment and a she-wolf the next (pp. 25-6).

Ida unwittingly caused some offence because of the simple fact that she was able to finance the productions of her dreams. She hated tawdry sets that suggested nothing more than the painted cardboard they were made of. Only materials with rich textures could create real dramatic illusion. And, Nozière continued (pp. 7-8),

> she does not seek to show us the banality of our times...She does not take the elements for her productions from everyday life...Two schools of thought are at odds with one another and, in the struggle,...Ida Rubinstein is treated without indulgence, without

consideration. She is very far from the realists...They declare that she does not accept their rules. Most certainly she is not a realistic actress. She does not believe that art follows in the footsteps of photography.

What Nozière did not add was that Ida's suspicion of realism and her use of historical themes and settings were not intended as a form of romantic escapism but as a means of releasing the human spirit from the bonds of transitory material considerations. Beauty is timeless. By discovering it in the past one can project into the future. An obsession with the reality of the particular can obscure that truth.

The past and the future were very much present in Ida's first 'transitional' work. She decided to mount Roger-Ducasse's **Orphée** at the Opéra. By September 1925 all the preliminary arrangements had been made. The première was scheduled for the following spring. **Orphée** could technically be described as a **mimodrame** since it employed a combination of mime, dance and music to unfold the plot. The idea was not new nor, indeed, was the work itself: it had been composed just before the war at the request of the celebrated Russian pianist and conductor Alexander Ziloti, Bakst's brother-in-law. Ziloti liked Roger-Ducasse's music and made a trip to Paris specially to persuade him to compose the ballet for presentation at the imperial opera house in St Petersburg.

The work was completed in 1913 and, on 31 January 1914, Ziloti gave it a concert performance, mainly to introduce the music to those involved in a stage version planned for later that season. Ida may well have heard it at this point when on one of her last visits to Russia. One thing is certain: the newly appointed director of the Paris Opéra, Jacques Rouché, was in St Petersburg at the time and heard the work. He was impressed and made a mental note of it. But war intervened and put paid to any idea of a stage production either in Russia or in France. Everybody, except the aggrieved composer, forgot about **Orphée's** existence until more than a decade later when he reminded Rouché of the work and persuaded Ida to take an interest in it. But, sadly, after such a lapse of time, the work, so much the product of the pre-war Fauréan 'school', seemed slightly dated compared with the music of the post-war period. But it suited Ida's purpose. There was great dramatic potential in the Orpheus legend: his love for Eurydice, her death, his unsuccessful attempt to retrieve her from Hades and his own death quite literally at the hands of the bacchantes. The transvestite role of Orpheus gave her an ideal opportunity to highlight the basic ambiguity of the character in a way scarcely attempted in a work of art and literature since classical times until Cocteau's explicit development of the theme. His **Orphée**, in its first theatrical form, dates from about the same period. The suggestion of a connection between Ida's asexual Orpheus and Cocteau's one, however distinctive their own individual characteristics, is an interesting one and not improbable.

The form of the **mimodrame** also lent itself to Ida's purpose. With **Orphée** she had an opportunity to reassert herself as a mime and ease herself gradually into full-scale choreographical work. Unfortunately, however well-planned in advance, a last-minute rush to mount the production meant that the results were not as perfect as she would have liked. The première was fixed for 31 May 1926, to be preceded by a **répétition générale** on 29 May. But if one examines the correspondence between Ida's agent and Rouché during the April of that year, while she was still in Italy, it is quite clear that chaos reigned. A telegram, dated 10 April, came from Ida: she was worried about the costumes. Benois was the man for the job: 'he alone can do designs that go with the sets.' At the same time her agent was trying to arrange for the costumes to be made up. She had the Opéra's costumier, Allegri, in mind but he could not produce the finished product before 15 June (BN Opéra, Ida Rubinstein, dossier II, fols 7-10). The situation was so serious that she contemplated returning to Paris immediately. Instead, she decided to write to Rouché and ask him to postpone the production until October. But on 30 April she received a very unequivocal answer from him (ibid., fol. 11):

> It is absolutely impossible to postpone the performance until October for musical reasons: two months of work with the chorus and with the dancing would be lost, and I should be obliged to have the rehearsals...continued thoughout the vacation...As for the question of the costumes, it is too late to dream of obtaining designs from Monsieur Golovine or even to ask another artist to make them. So you would be well advised to choose costumes by Bakst, or by other artists, that are in the stock of pieces already mounted by you, or select some Greek tunics from the Opéra's stock.

Rouché ended by insisting that, 'after all the procrastinations of the last month', she must give him immediate and exact answers to all his questions: work in progress would have to be halted unless, of course, she thought of taking **Orphée** abroad and wanted Golovine's costumes for that (ibid., fol. 11).

Rouché was perhaps a little too pessimistic because the costumes and even sets by Golovine did arrive in time and the opening night of **Orphée** was, in fact, able to be postponed - but by weeks rather than months. A **répétition générale** took place on 11 June.

Ida had taken the astonishing risk of appearing the previous evening in a gala performance of **La Dame aux camélias** at the Odéon. But she considered the charitable cause worth it - the Association des Ecrivains Combattants. The audience, laced with ministers and government officials, was brilliant; the amount of money raised impressive; and the performance an undisputed triumph. And on 12 June, the day after **Orphée**'s public dress rehearsal, Ida returned to the Odéon to give another performance of **La Dame,** a touching, if daring thing to do because it followed on from the official unveiling in the Place Malesherbes of François Sicard's memorial statue of Sarah Bernhardt, who had made the role of Marguerite Gautier so much her own. Next day, 13 June, the première of **Orphée** took place at the Opéra and finally its run had begun in earnest.

Considering the production difficulties, the critical response was generally good: the work itself came in for some adverse comment while the production was praised. Louis Schneider recalled how the work had been conceived in 1912 and heard in concert form in St Petersburg in 1914 and in Paris in 1922 before adding: 'The young musician, doubtlessly not wishing his work to be buried under the dust of oblivion, had made cuts for its performance at symphony concerts. Scores have this in common with flowers: they fade when theatres impose too long a delay on them' (1926, p. 3).

Jean Chantavoine was not very happy about the **mimodrame**'s suitability as a veheicle for Ida's talent - quite apart from the fact that the protagonists were mute throughout the work and Orpheus was legendary for his singing! In portraying him Ida 'began by displaying extremely beautiful legs, admirably tapered; in the last scene, under the red veils with which she draped herself, she reminded one of Sarah Bernhardt in (Racine's) **Phèdre.** But...the undulating profile of her bust did not allow her to portray an ephebe with the least verisimilitude, an ephebe who would not necessarily be a hermaphrodite' (pp. 277-8).

A different view was expressed by Jane Catulle-Mendès. She would have preferred another subject since the Orpheus myth had worn itself out. (How wrong can one be?) Yet she had to admit that Ida as Orpheus was 'both delightful and magnificent. The pure line of her immaterial and perfect body, the style of her poses calls to mind the most sublime **bas-reliefs**...She represents all the wondering idealism that Orpheus now represents for us. It is an unforgettable vision' (1926, p. 2). Possibly Jane Catulle-Mendès was letting her personal emotions run away with her.

Louis Laloy was even more enthusiastic (p. 2):

I do not believe that any artist apart from...Ida Rubinstein is capable of holding our attention for so long with the dumb language of the pose and restrained movement. Everything in her tells us: 'I want to be beautiful.' And what she wishes, she obtains. Each of her poses seems to be made for the painter's brush or the photographer's lens...If there existed an academy of gesture, Madame Rubinstein would by right be its president...in perpetuity.

Ida learned many lessons from **Orphée.** In particular, it helped her to plan her future activities with a greater degree of certainty about the kind of production best suited to her talents.

While she put her mind to long-term projects, she made just one more appearance on stage in 1926. On 11 November, the anniversary of the Armistice, she figured at the top of the bill in a gala performance for holders of the Croix de Guerre. Vincent d'Indy's **poème dansé, Istar,** was revived and preformed with the costumes and sets that caused Bakst so much mental stress in his last days - a fitting tribute to him as well as to those national heros whose war experiences did not prevent from appreciating Ida's high-class striptease act. **Istar** was given another airing a few months later, on 28 April 1927, in a charity concert organized by **Paris-Midi.** A choreographed version of a concerto by Martini and Strauss's stunning **Salomé** ceded pride of place to Ida's performance as Istar. The receipts were considerable.

But during the 1926-1927 season she was largely preoccupied with a major enterprise which she had started to plan as early as 1924 and which, by the time it came to the Opéra's stage on 18 February 1927, was giving her cause for doubt. She had dreamt of creating another mystery-play in the style of **Le Martyre** and, like it, centred on 'a subject of faith and beauty'. As Gaston Rageot put it, 'her instinct took her quite naturally to Saint-Georges de Bouhélier, who resembles a sorcerer with the magic power to make poetry spring forth from reality, since reality is poetry itself.' Rageot concluded by asking the question: 'Why should the progress of poetry in the theatre not be the same as that of music over the ages?' (1926, p. 5).

Did Rageot really imagine that poets of Bouhélier's ilk with their conventional verse could change poetry's status as the ugly duckling of the theatre? Certainly the transformation was not going to be effected by the long-winded work that he foisted upon Ida - **L'Impératice aux rochers.** The action takes place in Italy. The Emperor Aurelian is wounded by an arrow while out hunting and is only saved from death by a miracle granted in response to his wife Victoria's prayers. Once recovered, Aurelian sets out to fulfil a vow to visit the Holy Land as a beggar, leaving his wife in the care of his brother Otho (who had, in fact, shot the mysterious arrow and blamed an innocent man for his own crime). But soon he shows himself up in his true colours by lusting

1. I.R. as Salomé, 1908

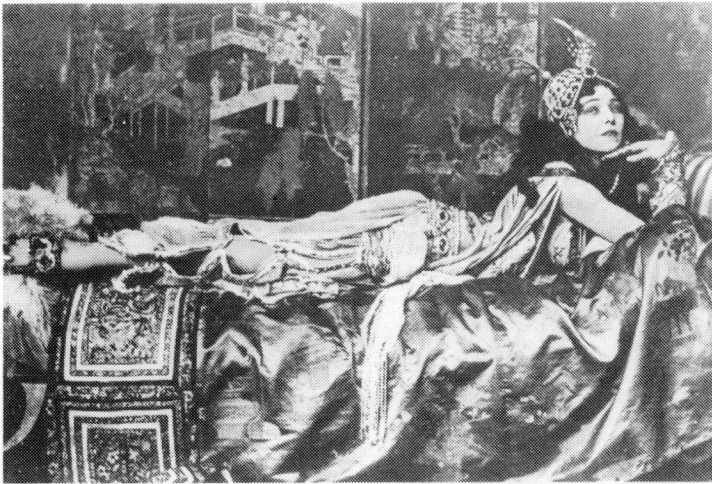

2. I.R. as Zobeïda in
   Schéhérazade, 1910

3. Leon Bakst, Costume design
   for **Salomé**, 1909

4. 'Larry', Cartoon of I.R.
   and Nijinsky in
   Schéhérazade, 1910

5. I.R. in Le **Martyre** de
   Saint Sébastien, 1911

6. Romaine Brooks,
   Self-Portrait, 1923

7. Comte Robert de
   Montesquiou

8. Valentine Serov, Portrait
    of I.R., 1909

9. I.R. at the Lido in
    Venice, with the
    Squadriglia di San Marco
    and Gabriele d'Annunzio
    and Walter Guinness, 1920.

10. I.R. as Cléopâtre, 'La Dame bleue', 1909

11. I.R. in **Antoine et Cléopâtre**, 1920

12. Portrait Study of I.R.

13. I.R. in **La Dame aux camélia**s, 1923

14. I.R. in **L'Idiot**, 1925

15.   I.R. in **Boléro,** 1928

16.   I.R. in La Princesse
      Cygne, 1928

MADAME IDA RUBINSTEIN

17.   Programme Cover for 1929
      Season

18. I.R. in Norway, 1922

19. I.R. in the garden of h
     house in Paris, c.1934

after his sister-in-law. She retaliates by trapping him and imprisoning him in a tower - at least until her womanly heart softens and she imprudently releases him at the very moment of her husband's return. The ungrateful Otho promptly accuses her of infidelity and she, hurt by her husband's doubts, refuses to defend herself. As a result she is condemned to die in a rocky wilderness. But all that is needed is a prayer to the Blessed Virgin, who not only rescues her immediately but also endows her with the power to perform miracles - with a specialty in curing leprosy. Incognito, she works numerous cures. Her reputation spreads. The emperor calls her to Rome to cure none other than Otho who, by a kind of counter-miracle, has contracted leprosy. The empress, sensibly, obliges him to confess his guilt before curing him. Husband and wife are reunited amid general rejoicing.

In order to make such a plot plausible on stage, Ida had to commission Benois to create a series of magnificent and elaborate sets - so elaborate that they took an interminably long time to change between scenes, much to the annoyance of audiences already wearied by the length of the play itself. (The whole evening lasted a solid five hours!) It was not hard to predict that 'these splendid sets would soon go off to decay in some warehouse in the suburbs' (Delannoy, p. 120).

The other 'prop' for the play was a substantial amount of incidental music which Ida commissioned from Arthur Honegger in 1925. Composed in the same year, between 6 August and 13 November, this work was, in fact, the first of Ida's Honegger commissions since she did not approach him for a score for **Phaedre** until late 1925. This was completed in March 1926 and first performed the following month, long before the première of **L'Impératrice aux rochers.** At the time Honegger himself expressed surprise at Ida's faith in him because he felt that his music for **L'Impératrice** was not a success. With some justification he implied that Bouhélier was partly to blame. Honegger had deliberately tried to give his music an archaic feeling. This took the audiences off-guard. And music-lovers who had come primarily to hear the première of a new score were disappointed to find it 'chopped up into little fragments and lost in the midst of...the spectacle' (Prunières, 1927, p. 247). Or, as Rageot put it, 'at the Opéra we are accustomed to hearing music. We are astonished to hear so little, all the more so since the programme bears the name of a musician of whom one has great hopes...Ida declaims...Why does Honegger's orchestra remain mute?' (1927, p. 153). Even before the performance Honegger was discouraged. As far as Saint-Georges de Bouhélier was concerned, the music was entirely ancillary to the play and to the general stage spectacle: 'Nevertheless, he was not entirely satisfied.' Honegger later recalled one incident. 'He complained that the orgy scene was lacking in nude women. We tried to persuade him to accept the usual tradition of the subsidized theatre, but he was obstinate: "I demand nude women!"' (1966, p. 106).

And as if that were not bad enough, the poor composer had to suffer another indignity. The director, Sanine, decided 'to bring the actors into the atmosphere of the orgy and forced poor Mlle Atoch to play all the music on a wretched rehearsal piano, battered by generations of ballet performers. This was done amid the greatest consternation. Then, calling off the whole thing, Sanine exclaimed: "You have heard that horrible music: it's a disaster, a real disaster!"' (p. 106). Honegger was inclined to agree, and so was all the more surprised when, immediately after this episode, Ida gave him the job of writing music for **Phaedre.**

Ida at least could distinguish the wood from the trees. She must have found Honegger one of the sanest persons engaged in the production. When Sanine was not shouting scathing comments, Bouhélier was sitting in the Opéra auditorium supervising rehearsals like 'a sort of god presiding over the genesis of a world' (Rageot, 1926, p. 5). The director of the Opéra, Jacques Rouché, was not always helpful. Clearly exasperated by the length of time **L'Impératrice** was taking to gestate, he kept sending Ida letters demanding advance payments and requiring her to sign commitments for costumes being made by the Maison Muelle. On 23 December 1926 he wrote her a fairly rude letter. He had read in the newspapers that she intended to present **La Dame aux camélias** at the Odéon at the end of January. Good! That meant that he would not have to interrupt his run of **La Traviata.** (Indeed, what an awkward coincidence!) And she would, of course, be moving her sets to the Odéon. Rouché either thought better of the matter or subsequently heard a different version of the story because he stopped the letter before it was posted (BN Opéra, Ida Rubinstein, dossier II, fol. 12).

Predictably enough, after the public dress rehearsal on 17 February 1927 and the première the following day, some adverse comment appeared in the press. P. Saegel went straight to the point: 'The form of the Mystery which, in the Middle Ages, represented the living expression of an outburst of collective faith where the audience took part directly in the action, nowadays only possesses a superficial, as it were archaeological interest' (1927, pp. 85-6). Medieval turns of phrase and the use of an octosyllabic line did not fit very well with the anachronisms of modern language.

On the other hand, Maxime Girard had nothing but praise for the production and for Ida in particular (p. 1):

Ida Rubinstein has just presented **L'Impératice aux rochers** on the stage of the Opéra, with the brilliancy and perfection with which she customarily endows each of the spectacles that she mounts...Just homage should be paid to her artistic efforts...The creator of **L'Impératrice**...can pride herself today on the results obtained...

She is reproached with the flexibility of her talent. Dancer, dramatic mime, tragic actress! What genre will she tackle next? Her friends know her aesthetic and that she does not consciously single out one talent from the others...They converge for her on the same end...She considers that dance, music and tragedy are three sisters and that they are appropriately represented intimately interlaced.

For...Ida Rubinstein...our constant objective should be to give...a little of the charm of illusion to the harsh reality of everyday life.

Maxime Girard certainly numbered himself among the friends who understood Ida's aesthetic and told her to ignore the criticism of the malicious or jealous. They were proved wrong by the public who came in droves to see the play. Even the President of the Republic, Gaston Doumergue, made a point of attending her performance on 1 March - but then he did have rather **recherché** tastes!

But, success or failure, **L'Impératrice** marked the end of a phase in Ida's life. Had the production not been so long in the making, the phase would have ended sooner because, by 1927, her thoughts were beginning to run along different artistic lines. And for the rest of the year she appeared in no new stage productions - unless one counts a lecture on the subject of d'Annunzio that she gave to an enthusiastic audience of women at a Université des Annales meeting on 15 March. She used the occasion to describe in some detail the whole of her artistic collaboration with the poet. The audience reacted as though it were being let into a series of fascinating secrets and showed its appreciation with frequent bursts of warm applause. And when Ida finished speaking, she was recalled to the platform, in true theatrical fashion, and given a rousing ovation. The lecture was subsequently published in both French and Italian and remains a glowing tribute to a good, if somewhat wayward friend whom she admired as a poet and as an Italian patriot. As for his effect upon her own life, Ida paid him a generous compliment: 'I danced and I mimed when I first made the acquaintance of Gabriele d'Annunzio. I can say that he gave me a voice. He contributed a verbal expression to the great lyric impulse that animated me' (p. 325). She was being too modest: her career as an actress had already begun by the time of their first meeting in 1910 and her preoccupation with dance was, in any case, only a temporary one. Ironically, as she was giving the lecture, she was contemplating returning to a full-time career as a dancer.

This casts a tantalizing side-light upon a moment in literary and musical history that occurred at the end of 1927. Two old friends Paul Claudel and Darius Milhaud were planning to collaborate on a new work entitled **Christophe Colomb.** Claudel had already written an epic script. He now had to decided whether to make it into a play with music or into a libretto for an opera. Max Reinhardt was showing an interest in producing it as a play or even as a film. Another possibility was that Ida Rubinstein might consider mounting it. On 2 December Milhaud wrote to ask Claudel if he should speak to her, since he was seeing a lot of her at the time. Milhaud was clearly thinking in terms of her creating the part of Columbus as a **travesti** role. Claudel was less happy about this: he visualized his Columbus as 'a man alone with all the voices of the sea, the sky and nature around him' (1961, p. 85). Ida was not quite his idea of the intrepid explorer braving the elements to make his momentous voyage of discovery, so he halted Milhaud in his tracks. By this time Max Reinhardt's interest had waned. Milhaud fell out with him. But all turned out for the best: almost immediately the work was accepted by the Berlin Staatsoper, where it was produced very lavishly as a full-scale opera. It was extremely successful and had a long run.

Claudel's instinct about Ida was probably right and one suspects that she would have shared his reaction, even if she had not been so preoccupied at the time - and she was very preoccupied, as the events of the following year soon made clear. She even resisted attempts to draw her into a project to film **La Pisanelle.** Despite her regard for d'Annunzio, she refused to be diverted from her chosen path. Fortunately she was saved much embarrassment because the producers, the Casa Italiana, soon abandoned their plans when they learned of d'Annunzio's extravagant scheme for the realization of a dream that had begun as a sketch for **La Rosa di Cipro** in 1912. In 1928 Ida intended to realize her own dreams.

CHAPTER 11

Cupid and the Spanish Dancer, 1928

After the disbanding of Rolf de Maré's Ballets Suédois in 1925 only one major company dominated the world of dance in France, Diaghilev's Ballets Russes. In 1928 Ida challenged this monopoly by forming another troupe with the name of Les Ballets Ida Rubinstein - not Les Ballets Juifs, as Diaghilev sneeringly suggested. Her enterprise differed from the others in one significant way: she was not only the directing force behind the venture but also the principle star of the company. Many were taken aback by her boldness, especially when the scope of her plans became clear. They were even more amazed when they managed to work out - despite the secrecy that surrounded the subject - that she would be forty-three years old by the scheduled opening date in November 1928.

But why did she embark upon what was by any standard such a risky venture? Quite simply she had become a little dissatisfied with drama as a means of artistic expression. Ballet provided a more obvious framework for the achievement of her main aim in life - the creation of absolute beauty. From the practical point of view she had to launch herself upon this new phase of her career at this juncture or not at all. She knew that her technique as a dancer had reached a high point in its development. To delay any longer was impossible: at her age most ballerinas would be thinking of retiring from the stage. As it was, she could only look forward to five or six years more in the strenuous world of the dancer.

Ida lost no time in building up a substantial repertoire for her company by commissioning a series of ballets, generally from a much younger set of writers and composers than previously. Rumours about the extent of her activities circulated in artistic circles but it was not until late in the day that all the details became known. In the meantime, public attention was distracted by the way in which she set about assembling a company of dancers and choreographers without any apparent concern for cost. She engaged Bronislava Nijinska as chief choreographer and ballet mistress and Leonide Massine agreed to interrupt his work in New York to choreograph two of the ballets.

Nijinska also had the task of auditioning recruits for the troupe - or, as some thought, plundering talent from companies throughout Europe. Anatole Vilzak was appointed as **premier danseur.** His wife Ludmilla Schollar would take second place to Ida. Among many others, dancers such as David Lichine, Alexis Dolinoff and Nina Verchinina signed contracts with the company. Rupert Doone, Joyce Berry and Frederick Ashton were attracted over from London. A little later, on his way back to England from a holiday, William Chappell broke his journey in Paris. He auditioned for Nijinska and was given a contract. Diaghilev was worried by this recruitment-drive and kept a suspicious eye of Ida's build-up of talent, 'a veritable conservatoire of ballet' (Haskell, 1972, p. 66). He wrote to Serge Lifar: 'Madame Nijinska has taken on four (of our) men for the **corps de ballet** but,' he added as if to discount the loss to his company, 'they tell me, not the best' (Lifar, 1940, p. 335).

On 1 August the company began rehearsals. Each day Nijinska made the young dancers undergo a gruelling routine of practice and rehearsal. It frequently lasted from 9 a.m. until 11 p.m. with only two extended breaks for luncheon and dinner. Nijinska made few exception to the rule: the younger dancers or those, such as Ashton , who had come to ballet 'late in life', were told that they would soon harden to the régime. And this continued unrelentingly for the next four months. As a joke the dancers used to refer to the troupe as 'La Compagnie des répétitions de Madame Ida Rubinstein' since the countless rehearsals seemed to get them no nearer the stage. But the experience was invaluable for some of them, particularly Lichine and Ashton, who learned a great deal about the craft of choreography from watching Nijinska at work.

The one major exception to Nijinska's rule was Ida herself. Ashton later recalled the impression she made on her troupe (p. 15):

> She was an enigmatic personality of compelling appearance. Though we were all remote from her in the company, we were constantly being reminded that Madame Rubinstein was **très distinguée.** She did all her rehearsing privately...When she appeared among us, we were ordered to put on clean shirts, and bottles of eau-de-cologne were provided for our use. She would walk through her parts, white-gloved and richly clad in furs, while her mystified company looked on...We had the feeling of being in a company run by an Electress of some Palatinate for her own amusement. Only the very best collaborators would do to produce her concept of beauty.

In his relatively humble position Ashton felt that Ida made peripheral economies in an otherwise lavish enterprise, since his own salary was only 1,000 francs a month during rehearsals and 1,300 francs once performances started. And when Sophie Fedorovitch told him, 'You won't be able to have a bath every day on that salary,' he burst into tears (Vaughan, p. 26). But that might say more about the cost of baths in France than about Ida's salary-levels, which were certainly not below average. Perhaps it really was cheaper to distribute bottles of eau-de-cologne to hide the smell of male sweat, which she hated so much.

As for the creative artists involved, Ashton did not exaggerate when he said that Ida employed 'only the very best collaborators'. A glance at the works commissioned quickly demonstrates that: Ravel's **Boléro**, Honegger's **Les Noces de Psyché et de l'Amour**, Milhaud's **La Bien-Aimée**, Stravinsky's **Le Baiser de la fée** and Henri Sauguet's **David**. She also commissioned Georges Auric to write **Les Enchantements d'Alcine**, although it was not produced until the end of the season in May 1929. In addition Ida staged Ravel's ballet **La Valse** for the first time in its definitive version (also in May 1929), although she did not commission the work. A ballet entitled **La Princesse Cygne** was created with music taken from Rimsky-Korsakov's opera **Tsar Saltan**. And Nicolas Tcherepnine arranged music by Borodin for a confection called **Nocturne.** Nine new ballets in all, the list was very impressive and the work of composition or arrangement and choreographing was long and complicated. But, predictably, it was the background to the composition of works by living composers of established reputation that attracted most attention. On the opening night of Ida's season, 22 November 1928, it was the far from straightforward birth of Ravel's **Boléro** that was the main source of rumour and anecdote.

In the spring of 1928 Ida asked Ravel to orchestrate some piano pieces from Albéniz's **Iberia** as the basis for an impressionistic ballet with a Spanish flavour. Ravel was enthusiastic about the idea: everything Spanish fascinated him. But his excitement was short-lived. One evening, at the end of June, his friend, the concert-pianist Joachin Nin, relaxing with an after-dinner cigarette, casually asked Ravel what he was working on. Ravel told him about the commission. But, Nin hastened to explain, the project was impossible because, unfortunately, these pieces by Albéniz had just been orchestrated by the conductor Enrique Arbós as a ballet for La Argentina, who planned to mount it next season. Nin was amazed at Ravel's apparent lack of concern. His comments were direct and to the point: 'Damn me. Who is this Arbós in any case?' This Arbós, Nin pointed out, just happened to have a contract with the music publishers Max Eschig, who had secured exclusive rights over the work. Nobody could infringe their copyright. Next day a telephone call to Eschig only served to confirm Nin's devastating news. Ravel was disconsolate: he had enjoyed orchestrating **Iberia**. But his first thoughts were: 'What could one say to Ida? She will be furious' (Nin, pp. 211-12). Two days later a nervous Ravel set off for Paris to see her - and, incidentally, take part in the 14 July celebrations, which he loved so much. As it turned out, Ida was not annoyed. She adopted a positive approach to the problem and simply encouraged him to go straight ahead and compose some other 'Spanish' piece for her.

New ideas came soon. Sir Francis Rose, the painter and impressionistic memoirist, recalled Ravel's coming to see Jean Cocteau at the Hôtel

Welcome in Villefranche, where he 'played on the badly tuned upright piano in the drawing-room...several ideas for a Spanish movement which he later called **Boléro**' (Rose, p. 110). By early August Joachin Nin had gleaned a more precise idea of what Ravel had in mind. He received a short note from him saying that he was working on a pretty unusual piece: 'no form properly speaking, no development, no or nearly no modulation; a theme in the style of Padilla (the "popular" composer of **Valencia**), rhythm and orchestration' (Nin, p. 213).

His friend Gustave Samazeuilh gathered some more information: Ravel had composed a double melody, each section eighteen bars in length. What he intended to do was to repeat the fascinating, syncopated melody over and over again, enriching and varying the orchestration to achieve the effect of a gradual crescendo. As the shattering climax came, the internal repeats in the melody would be eliminated to heighten the effect. Ravel worked out his ideas on paper and by mid-October **Boléro** (replacing the original title of **Fandango**) was completed.

The plot, woven together with the music, was slight but atmospheric: in an ill-lit tavern men sit drinking. A dancer tries out some steps on a large table in the centre of the room. The men pay no attention at first. But as the slow stately dance gradually begins to evolve and the rhythm becomes more insistent and the dance becomes more frenetic, they start to take an animated interest in her. Their excitement reaches fever-pitch as the dancer brings her improvisation to an abrupt climactic end.

Originally Ravel had envisaged a different interpretation of his work. According to René Chalput (pp. 237-8),

> he visualized **Boléro** not between four walls but in the open air; he wished to stress that there was something Arabic in the obstinate repetition of the same two themes. Then - and this is pretty subtle - he detected an analogy between the alternation of the two themes riveted to one another and the links of a chain and a factory assembly line (**chaîne**). Well, for that one had to have a group of male and female workers, coming out of their work-shops, to join in the general dancing. Finally, he wanted to suggest the bullfight by introducing a clandestine dalliance between Marilena and a toreador whom the jealous, deceived husband happens on unexpectedly, and stabs on the unfaithful woman's balcony.

One can only speculate about Paris audiences' reaction to this Carmenesque piece of melodrama. Perhaps it was just as well that lack of time prevented Ravel from indulging in his romantic flights of fantasy.

Boléro was placed last on the programme for the official opening night on 22 November and this only increased the general tension as public interest grew in anticipation of witnessing some spectacular - or disastrous - event. As Sir Francis Rose recalled, 'this new venture was the talk of Paris...Everyone was excited and it was whispered that the money would run out before the extravagant curtain for the stage had been made' (p. 110). But the money did not run out, although the final bill for the venture was reputed to be in the region of nine million francs. Some would have happily seen it fail from lack of funds - Diaghilev in particular.

He rushed back from Manchester with the sole purpose of assessing for himself how serious a threat Ida posed. And it was a far from wasted journey because his opinions were very influential. Most people were gullible enough to take them at face value, although they tell one only about the state of Diaghilev's mind and nothing about the quality of Ida's work. He poured out his feelings in a letter to Serge Lifar (Lifar, 1950, pp. 198-9):

> The house was full, but in the audience there was a number of people with free seats from the management. However, not one of us was given a seat, neither myself nor Boris (Kochno), Nouvel, Sert nor Picasso...We managed to get in only with great difficulty. **All our people were there**, Misia (Sert), Juliet (Duff, Etienne de) Beaumont, (the Princesse Edmond de) Polignac, Igor (Stravinsky) and other musicians, Mayakovsky etc. The whole show was boringly provincial. Everything was too long-drawn out...even the Ravel which takes only fourteen minutes.

The first ballet of the evening must have stirred up emotional memories for Diaghilev. **Les Noces de Psyché et de l'Amour** was planned and designed by Alexandre Benois, according to him, as the fulfilment of an old ambition. Apparently the idea of basing a ballet on the music of J.S. Bach had been the subject of serious discussion between Nijinsky and himself in 1913 on their fateful voyage to South America, during which the dancer abandoned his life with Diaghilev to marry Romola de Pulszky. Needless to say, on their return to Europe the scheme was shelved. 'Nevertheless,' Benois recorded, 'I did not give up the idea of a Bach ballet and succeeded in achieving it in 1928 in an elaborate production created for Ida Rubinstein' (1941, p. 352).

According to his biographer Louis Delannoy, Honegger was not very excited about being asked to compose the score for this Bach ballet. He was suspicious of the current neo-classical fashion for spicing up the music of the Masters à la Stravinsky and serving it up as fodder to the public. Honegger disagreed with the comment made by Stravinsky on his creation of **Pulcinella**: 'one is allowed to rape provided that one begets a child' (Delannoy, p. 126). He had no intention of engaging in an archaeological exercise. He used the full range of modern orchestral effects and was not afraid of employing a saxophone or a celeste. The result was successful: the music remained engagingly close to the spirit of Bach. The critic Pierre-Barthélemy Gheusi noted with some relish that 'this congenial sacrilege enchanted the snobs and rubbed the reactionaries up the wrong way' (p. 2). Charles Tenroc made a brief, pithy comment: 'Bach, modernized by Monsieur Honegger, is something like Napoleon rigged out in an opera-hat and Shakespeare dressed by Monsieur Cocteau' (1928, p. 744).

But it was not so much the music as the spectacle on stage that claimed attention. The audience was confronted with a kind of (ibid., p. 744)

> mythological court ballet where one expects to see the Sun-King playing Jupiter among the nymphs and the divinities of Olympus, dancing to Lully. Solemn balletic entrances by Apollo and the Muses, a bearded Pluto and his three-headed Cerberus, a jealous Venus, Neptune and his tritons, Mercury and his caduceus circling round Psyché who, thanks to the intervention of the king of the gods, falls finally into the arms of Cupid played by Madame Rubinstein.

Diaghilev's account of the ballet was totally lacking in balance or charity. Admittedly he was enchanted by 'a really wonderful sight: a young man wearing a pink blouse with blue trimmings and a red velvet cape covering his back, on his head a red wig with a dazzling green crown; his handsome boy's face was artistically powdered. He was triumphantly brought on the stage by his companions, and he danced a kind of classical variation' (Lifar, 1950, p. 239). This Apollo, Diaghilev suddenly realized, was Unger, a defector from his own ranks.

Benois's décors were dismissed in a crushing phrase: 'dull and colourless, the same as thirty years ago, only worse' (ibid., p. 239). Nijinska's work he described as 'showing no sign of originality: just a nameless mess, and a choreography that one does not even notice' (ibid., p. 239). Her husband, Singayevsky, shared in the condemnation. He appeared as Pluto, 'naked with a beard down to his waist and an extraordinarily funny cap on his head. He was completely unsuccessful, like everybody else' (ibid., p. 239). But for his description of Ida Diaghilev tapped a source of undiluted venom (ibid., p. 238):

> The worse thing we saw was Ida...When she appeared with Vilzak, **nobody,** not even I, recognised her. All bent, her red hair dishevelled, without any style, wearing ballet shoes (all the others had helmets, feathers and heels), - this was to make her appear less tall...She is incapable of dancing anything; she goes

on her points, her knees bent...Her face appears to consist of nothing but an enormous gaping mouth with close-set teeth attempting to grimace a smile. It was frightful. She wore a pistachio-coloured toga (no doubt costing 1,000 francs a metre), and her figure is thicker than before, whereas her legs have grown thinner. She is as old as the devil.

No other passage, out of reams of critical appraisal, has done more to tarnish Ida Rubinstein's image. Its impartiality is totally suspect. How, for example, can it be reconciled with the view of Gheusi, the **Figaro** critic and no sycophant? 'Ida Rubinstein...charmed us in **Les Noces de Psyché**...by giving us once again (a display of) her sovereign poses and gestures' (p. 2).

Honegger's work was followed by another ballet to a score by a fellow member of **Les Six**, Darius Milhaud. His autobiography gives some valuable insight into his work and the problems involved in its composition (p. 213):

In 1928 (Ida Rubinstein) commissioned me to orchestrate some waltzes by Schubert and Liszt for a ballet called **La Bien-Aimée**, with décors by Benois. Although the subject was a simple one, it involved some ticklish problems in the situation arising when a young pianist throws a spell on those around him through his playing. What I had to do was to try to exceed the virtuosity of Schubert's waltzes, those adorable short pieces only a few bars long already made difficult in all conscience by Liszt's variations. I was only able to do this by means of the Pleyela. This was for me an amusing experience from every point of view, for the mechanical rigidity of the Pleyela compelled the conductor to follow it as if it had been the most implacable soloist imaginable.

Critical reaction to the gimmick of an orchestral score written round a pre-recorded part for mechanical piano divided predictably into two camps: it was either ridiculous or ingenious. Diaghilev, needless to say, was more interested in Ida's performance than in the work itself. He described his version of the scene for Lifar's benefit: 'She wore a very short tutu, well up above the knees, white, with silver spangles. Vilzak, in grey trousers, was supposed to represent a poet who never stops playing the piano; Ida was the Muse. It was disgraceful. Long classical passages, an adagio, a variation, after which she went into the wings, sheepish and hunched-up' (Lifar, 1950, p. 238). Diaghilev's view was so obviously prejudiced as to be worthless in itself but clearly the first performance of **La Bien-Aimée** misfired. However, nobody could agree on what was the problem: the music, the choreography or the dancing - or, indeed, a combination of them all. Gheusi also inclined to the view that the ballet was too classical in texture, although he presented his case only in the form of a mild rebuke to Ida: 'In **La Bien–Aimée** Madame Rubinstein...preferred to dance like a ballerina, to increase her point-work, to be lifted up, in...Vilzak's robust arms, in soaring flights in the style of the Second Empire school, to convince us finally that she is a true ballerina' (p. 2).

Ravel's ballet **Boléro** ran no danger of falling between two stools. Predictably, Diaghilev voiced a strong opinion, again singling out Ida for special criticism: 'Still with the inevitable red coiffure, she spent a quarter of an hour clumsily turning on a table as large as the whole stage of the Monte Carlo Opera' (Lifar, 1950, pp. 238-9).

Henry Prunières's reaction was very different. One only had to hear the first few bars of Ravel's score to be captivated by its magic. As for Ida Rubinstein, she 'understood that the power of the score was such that the dancing had to seem like a sort of visual projection of this radiant music. She therefore created in collaboration with the great Russian painter Alexandre Benois, a picture in the manner of Goya...This ballet is, from all points of view, the one that achieved the most enthusiastic success' (1929, pp. 243-4).

But then that all depends upon how one defines success. An elderly woman in the audience cried out: 'Crazy! crazy!' When Ravel heard the story, he uttered a laconic comment: 'She understood it!' (Long, 1971, p. 172).

Variations in opinion are even harder to judge in cases where those involved were obviously biased or bent on saying the right thing to the right person at the right moment. Stravinsky was to be seen in Ida's dressing room after the performance. He whispered: 'Charming, from the bottom of my heart I tell you, it's delightful.' Diaghilev put around a different story: 'The following morning Igor telephoned me to express his regrets as well as his indignation at what we had seen the previous evening' (Lifar, 1950, p. 239). It is not difficult to tell why Stravinsky was so defensive: Diaghilev had yet to appraise his own contribution to Ida's list of novelties. That opportunity came the following Tuesday, 27 November.

CHAPTER 12

The Kiss and the Boy David, 1928

The genesis of Stravinsky's ballet **Le Baiser de la fée** was almost as eventful as that of Ravel's **Boléro**, although it was a very different kind of work and took much longer to compose.

While Ida was planning her programme in the autumn of 1927, Stravinsky was just finishing work on his score for the ballet **Apollon musagète.** She heard of this and made enquiries of Gavril Païchadze, Stravinsky's editor at Editions Russes de Musique, only to learn that Diaghilev had an option on it. Undaunted, she wrote directly to Stravinsky in Switzerland on 5 December and asked him to come to Paris to discuss a project that she and Benois had in mind. Stravinsky replied that he could not come until February, so both Ida and Benois wrote to him and explained their ideas. One of their suggestions seemed deliberately designed as a bait for him. He later explained: 'The idea was that I should compose something inspired by the music of Tchaikovsky. My well-known fondness for this composer, and still more, the fact that November, the time fixed for the performance, would mark the thirty-fifth anniversary of his death, induced me to accept the offer. It would give me an opportunity of paying my heartfelt homage to Tchaikovsky's wonderful talent' (1975, p. 146). By 15 January 1928 Ida and Stravinsky had agreed terms: his fee was fixed at $6,000 (although she eventually seems to have paid him $7,500); he would choose a suitably Tchaikovskian subject; and the manuscript would be delivered by the end of summer.

Stravinsky searched around in the tales of Hans Christian Andersen and came upon a story that he had completely forgotten, **The Ice Maiden:** 'A fairy imprints her magic kiss on a child at birth and parts it from its mother. Twenty years later, when the youth has attained the very zenith of his good fortune, she repeats the fatal kiss and carries him off to live in supreme happiness with her for ever afterwards' (ibid., pp. 146-7). Stravinsky thought that, as a work designed to honour Tchaikovsky, it was appropriately allegorical, 'the muse having similarly branded (him) with her fatal kiss, and the magic imprint made itself felt in all the musical creations of this great artist' (ibid., p. 147). To emphasize the point he changed the original title to **Le Baiser de la fée.**

Stravinsky did not begin work until the beginning of July 1928 and, as a result, he had to write the substantial score at breakneck speed over a period of four months. During the summer he remained at Echarvines on the Lac d'Annecy and in the autumn moved to Nice to work on the orchestration. Echarvines was an idyllic spot, ideal for composing - so he thought. Unfortunately he rented a workroom in a mason's cottage that was not the most tranquil place in the world. The odour of cooking, 'an acrid and nauseating smell of garlic and rancid oil', penetrated the thin partition wall separating him from the workman's family. Moreover, the mason, with clock-work regularity, quarrelled with his wife every day. Shouts, screams and sobs distracted him from his work and made him apprehensive about the safety of the mason's wife and child. He realized too late that, strange though it seemed, this was a kind of **modus vivendi**: he had the village mayor remonstrate with the mason about his cruelty, 'whereupon,' as Stravinsky put it, 'the famous scene from Molière's **Médecin malgré lui** was repeated. Like Martine, the woman resolutely took her husband's part and declared that she had no reason to complain of him' (ibid., p. 145).

Eventually Stravinsky was under such pressure to finish the work that he found himself putting every available moment to good use. One day he had to pass through Paris on his way back to Nice from an engagement and woke up in the train expecting to find himself in the suburbs of Paris. But not so. He was in a totally unfamiliar place. Apparently, during the night, his coach had been shunted into a siding at Nevers and he would be four hours late in reaching Paris. But the will triumphed: 'Far from a station and on an empty stomach - not even a scrap of bread was available - I was nevertheless unperturbed by this mishap, and turned it to profit by working in my compartment during these four hours' (ibid., pp. 147-8).

Stravinsky had to cope with another hazard - Diaghilev. He was not only jealous of the composer's collaboration with Ida but also generally worried about the scope and quality of her whole enterprise. Added to that he learned, rather late in the day, that she had put out feelers for **Apollon musagète**. On 8 August 1928 he wrote to Stravinsky: 'But what is this I hear about **Apollon** with Ida Rubinstein?' - an odd question since, eight week before, the ballet had gained considerable acclaim at its Ballets Russes première in Paris. Ida was scarcely likely to compete with that, even if she could secure rights over the work. Stravinsky's reply to Diaghilev was dry and factual (Stravinsky, Vera, and Craft, p. 286):

> You ask about 'this business of my offer of **Apollon** to Ida Rubinstein.' It is a question neither of 'business' nor of 'an offer', unless you are referring to inquiries addressed to my publisher concerning my ballets. But since you seem to be particualrly interested in this case, I can tell you that Rubinstein, like many other theatrical entrepreneurs, has inquired from Païchadze about **Apollon**. I myself never offer my works to

anyone, either directly or indirectly.

The **Apollon** incident only served to worsen relations between Diaghilev and Stravinsky when they were already strained to breaking-point over **Le Baiser.**

But Stravinsky's problems were not over - and some of them were of his own making. On 17 October he wrote to Païchadze telling him that he had just completed the piano score (ibid., p. 285):

> I hasten to share with you the joy of finishing the music for the **Fée**...I am sending the whole end of the piano score to you in a few days for engraving, not for familiarizing Ida with it, or Nijinskaya or Benois...It is necessary for people such as they are - not particularly initiated - that I play the music for them myself. Therefore I ask you not to let anyone look at it before my arrival. Nijinskaya will howl, but do not pay any attention to that.

By 'people...not particularly initiated' Stravinsky meant anybody who, thumbing his way through a completely new manuscipt, might not immediately understand every nuance of his works, in other words, everybody. If Bronsilava Nijinska did howl, it was because of the way in which he sent her the orchestral score in dribs and drabs, covering it with elaborate stage directions and even changing the action in the final scene. While he stayed at Echarvines finishing his work, Nijinska choreographed the ballet bit by bit with the result that he did not see it as a whole until very near the opening night. Some of it he liked; but he added, 'there was...a great deal of which I could not approve, and which, had I been present at the moment of their composition, I should have tried to get altered...It is hardly surprising in these circumstances that the choreography...left me cold' (1975, p. 148). What Stravinsky did not add was that the reason why he could not assist at the creation of the ballet was that he had taken so long to begin writing the music and was more than a month behind the agreed delivery date. Did he really, one wonders, expect Nijinska to wait until 30 October, when he finished the work - just twenty-seven days before the première? His attitude seems all the more ungracious when one learns how glad he was to have Nijinska as choreographer, since he fully expected Ida to give the job to Fokine, whom he loathed. He would bristle whenever he had dealings with him over **L'Oiseau de feu** because Fokine insisted on referring to it as Stravinsky's 'musical accompaniment' to **his** 'choreographic poem' (Stravinsky, Igor, and Craft, 1960, p. 35).

But in his role as conductor, Stravinsky confessed himself well enough pleased at his generous allotment of four full orchestral rehearsals but was soon complaining bitterly about having 'to contend with the dreadful system of deputizing - so fatal to the music when at each rehearsal musicians, without warning, send others to take their place' (1975, p. 148), as if that were something new among French orchestral players! Yet, despite these problems, **Le Baiser** was ready in time to figure as the main attraction on the programme for 27 November.

The evening began with **Les Noces de Psyché et de l'Amour** - to which, on second viewing, Diaghilev warmed slightly: 'I noticed a little **pas de deux** danced by (Nadejda) Nikolaeva and Unger, which I missed the first time, and it is really worth seeing!' (Lifar, 1950, p. 239). But there was no doubt that what Diaghilev had come to see was Stravinsky's ballet. At the earliest opportunity he committed his thoughts to paper (ibid., pp. 239-40):

> I came back from the theatre with a terrible headache, caused by everything and particularly by Igor('s ballet)...It is difficult to say precisely what it is. In my opinion, it is more than anything else like a bad suite by Tchaikovsky, tearful and tedious, apparently orchestrated 'in masterly fashion' by Igor. (I say 'apparently' because I find the sonority dull and the workmanship quite lifeless). The **pas de deux** is good, based on a superb theme by Tchaikovsky...This is the only clear passage (with a coda in the style of **Apollon**) in the whole thing (and even here the theme is melancholy!) I find it impossible to describe what happens on stage...the first scene takes place in the Swiss mountains, the second in a Swiss village - a fête with **Swiss** national dances; the third scene represents a Swiss mill, the last some more mountains and glaciers. The heroine of the ballet is Schollar. She dances a **pas de deux** with Vilzak which, if not exactly Pepita, is at least an honest imitation...Benois called to mind the décors of the Théâtre de Monte Carlo.

Diaghilev did not confine himself to expressing his own feelings. He attempted to convey something of the audience's reaction (ibid., p. 240):

> The theatre, though full, made one think of a drawing-room in which some respectable person has just farted. Everybody pretended not to notice anything and Stravinsky was called back for two curtain calls. His ballet is still-born. **All our set** simply shrugged their shoulders, apparently except for (Walter Nouvel), who could find nothing musical about **L'Oiseau de feu** at the time of its composition, but finds this piece musical and extremely interesting. He confided this opinion to Sauguet safely enough since Sauguet is working for the Ballets Juifs.

Not a word about Ida! But then, in the case of **Le Baiser**, Stravinsky's 'crime' - not to mention Nijinska's and Benois's - was that of treason or, at the very least, desertion, whereas Ida's offence was one of competition and by this point he was pretending to himself that he had nothing to fear on that score.

What is surprising is how some serious, presumably unbiased critics joined in the attack on Stravinsky's work, though one of the most charming scores he ever wrote - too charming perhaps. Boris de Schloezer recognized it as one of his most substantial works - it did, after all, last fifty minutes (1929, p. 279):

It is perhaps also the prettiest, the most pleasant: the ear is satiated. It would be ridiculaous on our part to sulk about our pleasure and reproach Stravinsky for having made extensive use of...Tchaikovsky's piano music: the composer of **Le Sacre** has right enough to take a rest from exercises in virtuosity; one can even understand his wish to let us recover our breath for a moment and amuse himself by entertaining us...I hope however...that the next time he will want to do something else.

The **Times** correspondent in Paris wagged an even sterner finger at Stravinsky: 'This curious score, with its deliberate borrowings from Tchaikovsky, its telling orchestration, and its harmonic devices..., presents problems which alone justify its existence. It suffers from a persistent dryness, Tchaikovsky's tunes being in sudden contrast to the surrounding matter' (anon., 1928, p. 14).

But these comments sound mild beside those of Benois's old enemy Leonid Sabaneev, who launched a blistering attack on the work (pp. 405-6):

We are confronted with a new type of innovation - innovation by expropriation. I cannot blame Stravinsky for this. In the first place it is quite modern, and therefore must be good. Secondly, I see clearly the 'revolutionary necessity' for such a step. These expropriations, this recourse to the fairy's kiss of Pergolesi, of Tchaikovsky, are dictated by the instinct of self-preservation. A decaying talent, a talent which has lost its power of invention, is obliged to fall back on rejuvenating resources; it compounds for itself a musical **elixir vitae**...But all this...undoubtedly proves one thing - the ageing of the creative power...It began long ago, but, dazzled by the brilliance of the previous pyrotechnical achievements, we hardly noticed it. After **The Rite of Spring** it became perceptible in those senile dodderings from side to side. **Œdipus Rex,** and even the Pianoforte Sonata, are typically senile compositions. Now we are eventually witnessing the final act of the drama - the sunset of Stravinsky.

Time, needless to say, has damned Sabaneev with his own words but how strange they must have seemed to contemporaries who compared them with the views of Henry Prunières, the doyen of music critics (1929, p. 243):

> **Le Baiser de la fée**...is an admirably made pastiche...which far surpasses the model. Tchaikovsky never developed his ideas with this ingenuity and this concision, never did he orchestrate with so much care, avoiding padding and trivialities. Stravinsky shows us here how Tchaikovsky ought to have written and strives to avoid the habitual faults of the master. With that difference, he succeeds in giving us the illusion of hearing an unknown ballet by him.

Though gratified by his compliments, Stravinsky would not have liked Prunières's criticism of Tchaikovsky, the man whom he had set out to honour with his work.

While the ballet which Ida had been instrumental in delivering into the world was being fought over, she herself emerged unscathed. The **Times** correspondent was almost effusive: 'The dancing showed up excellently. The chorus work...was informed with an altogether commendable vitality...The solo dancing was unequal, and Madame Rubinstein easily stood out from among the other executants. The beauty of her movements, her graceful form, and the dignity of her appearance, the whole enhanced by her seemingly great height, all these were undeniably worth coming to see' (anon., 1928, p. 14).

Jean Proudhomme's comment was brief but no less complimentary: 'There are some excellent artists with...Ida Rubinstein, who, expressive, impassioned, triumphant, mimes and dances the role of the fairy' (p. 4).

However, having spent one evening trying 'to penetrate the mystery of this nebulous and libidinous symbol' (1929, p. 744), as Charles Tenroc described the fairy's kiss, the audience that gathered for the third evening of ballet on Thusrday, 28 November, discovered that Ida had shed her persona as the faintly sinister fairy for something lighter.

The first 'novelty' was a ballet entitled **Nocturne**, composed of choreography by Nijinska and selections from Borodin's music, arranged by Nicolas Tcherepnine. The sets, yet again, were by Benois. The plot was simple and deliberately frivolous: a Spanish night, a young girl (Ida) on her balcony is courted in a grotesque serenade by an old roué with a band of hired musicians in tow. She is 'rescued' by her young lover (Vilzak) and the two run off together at the approach of the night-watchman.

And once again Diaghilev (who had extended his stay in Paris specially to be present) wrote what Serge Lifar admitted was 'another wicked slashing criticism' (Lifar, 1940, pp. 340-1):

The beginning was better than usual. A moonlit scene, Spain, really a great improvement on the rest, firstly because moonshine is always lovely, and secondly because it was dark, and there was less to be seen. The first dance, an **ensemble**, was better than anything else, and for once the costumes weren't so vulgar and the dancing was better. At last we saw something of Lapitzky, a shortish, i.e., fattish Lapitzky, it's true, with his legs going through the floor, but nevertheless dancing well, and very much in the Bronia manner. It really began to look as though the whole thing would turn out better than any of the other ballets, but the moment Unger...appeared, impersonating an old gouty marquis and trying to be fearfully comic,...the whole thing began going downhill. And then, what finished it off completely was the appearance of Ida, with her interminable classic **pas de deux**...As for Tcherepnine's arrangement (of the music), it's simply shocking. Imagine getting a **tenor** to sing the 'cello part of that famous quartet. Why, it's like turning Borodin into restaurant music.

But there was more to the score than just a vamped-up version of the slow movement from Borodin's second string quartet. Paul Bertrand, the **Ménestrel** critic, found it quite inspiring: 'Borodin's **Nocturne** was made up of a collection of pieces taken from the illustrious Russian musician's work...for which a sequence of Spanish scenes has been devised. They adapt themselves marvellously to the music; this underlines yet again the striking affinity of accent and rhythm that exists between the music of two peoples situated at opposite ends of Europe' (1929, p. 248). But, however one reacted to the musical arrangement, nobody disagreed with Emile Vuillermoz's general comment that the ballet was 'only a pretext for serenades and stylized coquetry' (1928, p. 2). It was not intended as anything else.

The second new work of the evening (following a repeat performance of **La Bien-Aimée**) demanded more serious consideration. This was **La Princesse Cygne**, a fairytale ballet based on a poem by Pushkin with music taken from Rimsky-Korsakov's opera **Tsar Saltan**. The story was fantastic and romantic: Prince Guidon, son of Tsar Saltan, is cast away on a desert island with his mother. Seeing a vulture in the act of carrying away a swan, he fires an arrow and kills the predator. The grateful swan puts the prince and his mother to sleep and, by the time they awake with the sun, a city has magically been conjured up. The citizens hail Guidon as their king. Meanwhile, the swan has metamorphosed herself into a beautiful princess and offers her hand to her rescuer.

Finding himself on familiar Russian territory, Diaghilev redoubled the force of his attack. He described the ballet as (Lifar, 1940, p. 341)

Tsar Saltan turned into a bad sort of L'Oiseau de feu. As for the set, that must have come straight from the Casino de Paris, plus a postcard or two by E. Boehm and Solomko...The changes aren't bad, but why the Smolny nunnery should rise from the bottom of the sea passes understanding. The Russian national dances were produced à la the Brothers Molodzov...The only original touch was provided by the Tsarevitch (Vilzak) who dances a wild variation in a crown and mantle, and gives the impression of having got so drunk that he just could not help dancing. Ida did more dancing in this than in any of her other ballets. She appeared dressed like a Pavlova swan, specially got up for some Moulin Rouge performance (her bodice one mass of false diamonds, and her wings all covered with spangles).

With a straight face Charles Tenroc added a further point of detail: 'The appearance of the beautiful Princesse Liebida, queen of the swans, adds the additional sumptuousness of ermine to Madame Rubinstein's wardrobe. King Guidon, having become her husband, drowns in the voluptuousness of the plumage' (1928, pp. 744-5).

But most serious critics appraised the ballet favourably. Louis Schneider declared that 'nothing is more sumptuous and expressive than the staging, the work of...Bronislava Nijinska. The costumes and sets contributed to the fairytale brilliance of the ballet' (1931, p. 561). Henry Prunières was generous with his praise: 'From the purely choreographic point of view the ballet that came off best seemed to me to be Tsar Saltan which was danced to perfection by Ida Rubinstein and all her troupe with costumes and admirable sets by Benois' (1929, p. 244).

The final première of Ida's short season at the Opéra took place on Tuesday, 4 December. This was Henri Sauguet's ballet David. Sauguet's first major essay in the form had been La Chatte, commissioned by Diaghilev and first performed by the Ballets Russes on 30 April 1927. Ida was impressed by the work with its striking music and sparkling orchestration and, while planning her season of ballets, her thoughts turned again to the young composer. She asked him to write a ballet to a scenario by André Doderet (a faithful friend since Phaedre days) and the two men soon found themselves creating a balletic version of the life of David, from the curing of King Saul with the therapeutic strains of his harp to his victory over Goliath with his equally efficacious sling.

Sauguet was overawed by Ida. He found her (Bril, p. 58)

extremely impressive. She remained the character of Schéhérazade whose incarnation she had been. For me, she was also and above all Debussy's Saint Sebastian, rather like an embodiment of my idol's dream. I approached her with a sort of dazzled reverence. Aesthete, in love with beauty, she seemed to be surrounded by an artistic haze, a little as though seated in the clouds. But she also knew how to be caring and generous.

The result of her interest in Sauguet was one of the most original scores of the season and one which the public awaited with great (and growing) anticipation - and not simply because Ida was to tackle yet another transvestite role as the young David. As day after day passed audiences looked in vain in their programmes for Sauguet's **David**. The more pessimistic thought that it would never be ready. And they had good reason: the production was so elaborate, so lavish that endless difficulties had to be overcome before a public performance could be attempted. To make matters worse, the choreographer, Massine, was on temporary release from his New York contract and had to leave before the first night. At that point Nijinska stepped in to put the finishing touches to the ballet and only succeeded in adding to the confusion. Diaghilev learned, with ill-concealed satisfaction, that 'everyone's cursing and disappointed - except, it appears, Bronia (Nijinska), who keeps telling Ida she's a genius' (Lifar, 1940, p. 341).

And when the ballet finally did reach the stage, some were inclined to agree that Ida **was** a genius. Sir Francis Rose was impressed by 'the wonderful music and unique collaboration of the creators' but his impish sense of humour got out of control when Ida 'dragged an enormous papier-mâché head of Goliath across the stage...The hair came off and there was nearly a disaster when the head rolled into the footlights and practically on to the drums in the orchestra' (pp. 135-6). Sir Francis, as always, was exaggerating.

The **Times** critic was less inclined to agree that the music was wonderful but he did admit that 'Massine's choreography...was energetic and effective' (anon., 1928, p. 14). Arnold Haskell took up this point. He thought that 'Massine's **David** had a simplicity and grandeur that gave one a taste of his new development' (1977, p. 153). But Massine himself was apologetic and tried to shift attention away from himself: '**David**...was an opulent affair, with costumes by Benois, but it was not a success. Rubinstein, who was really more of an actress than a dancer, was beautiful and statuesque...I had very little opportunity for original choreography' (pp. 176-7).

Whatever the choreographer thought, that most respected of critics Henry Prunières gained a different impression: 'In the unanimous opinion of all those who saw **(David)**, Ida Rubinstein was a marvel of harmonious and expressive grace in it.' Indeed, he went further and, comparing it with all the other ballets, commended it specifically because of its adventurous choreography. He exclaimed (1929, pp. 244-5):

Why, alas, was this ballet the only one with **Boléro** that was not sacrificed to the tyrannical empire of classical ballet? (And he uttered a word of warning for Ida's benefit:) Let it be said that she is infinitely superior to the artists whose laws she feels she must follow. Let her conform to the rules of her own choreography and abandon once and for all classical dancing for free-style dancing; she will then provide us with visions of radiant beauty and astonishing originality.

But however fiercely the critics might argue among themselves about choreographical interpretations, when the curtain finally came down at the Opéra on 4 December 1928, Ida had the personal satisfaction of knowing that, in the briefest of seasons, she had succeeded not only in mounting more original works than any independent impresario in living memory but also in starring in each and every one of them herself.

CHAPTER 13

The Waltz and the Magic Rose, 1928–1929

Immediately after their last night at the Opéra, Ida and her troupe departed for Brussels. Behind them they left a Paris reverberating with reactions. Stories about the events of the past few weeks were told, retold and made into the stuff of memoirs.

Sir Francis Rose was fascinated – but tried not to sound so – by the audiences who flocked to see Ida's ballets: 'The crowds of fashionably dressed people who wandered through the halls and corridors were of an entirely different kind of elegance to that of the Diaghilev ballet. It was more like the crowd at a gala dinner in a casino on the Riviera or in Biarritz, and it glittered more but sparkled less' (p. 135). (One wonders where this host of socialites hid when the Ballets Russes came to Paris!) Rose was particularly impressed by the sight of Madame Pierre Mayer, wife of the owner of the fashionable men's wear shop Old England, as she arrived for the ballet 'in the first long, plain, black velvet evening dress' that he had ever seen. 'A dog collar of pink pearls the size of pigeon's eggs were her only ornament: she did not even wear the traditional twenty-five carat diamond held by a thread of platinum on her fingers' (p. 135).

But, at least according to Rose, the first-night audience was much more distracted by a vision of quite a different sort (pp. 135-6):

The Garde Républicaine, in shining breast-plates and helmets, lined the famous staircase, and many astonished people recognized the much changed Nijinsky mounting the steps with a vague look on his face and wearing a very heavy overcoat which he refused to remove during the entire performance...

On the way out, Nijinsky, who had never said a word or removed his coat, sat in the middle of the great staircase and refused to move. At last, when the Garde Républicaine had left and the lights of the chandeliers were being extinguished and the cleaners were arriving, he was persuaded to leave, muttering. 'They cannot jump, they cannot jump; none of them can jump.'

Considering that he had just seen his sister Bronislava's choreography for **Boléro**, it is not surprising that his half-crazed mind registered such a distorted impression.

But Nijinsky was in good company because even supposedly sane individuals registered distorted impressions of the Rubinstein ballet. And his old friend Diaghilev was the worst offender. Prince Peter Lieven suggested a psychological reason for his behaviour. Because of his homosexuality Diaghilev had 'many feminine traits in his character' and could be 'extremely jealous of any manifestation of rivalry or competition in his work; it was the cause of many of his quarrels with his friends...If Bakst collaborated with Rubinstein, or perhaps Benois with someone else, Diaghilev would always be moved to recrimination and abuse' (p. 260).

During Ida's 1928 season Diaghilev's fear and jealousy became so overpowering that he was overcome by a nihilistic neurosis. After seeing her ballets, he was plagued by doubt: 'What is the use of it all? No, we need somebody, a Napoleon or the Bolsheviks, to explode a bomb under these old hovels' - by which he meant theatres - 'with their audiences, their sluts who think themselves dancers, their millions spent on buying musicians' (Lifar, 1950, p. 240).

Serge Lifar, to whom Diaghilev poured out his feelings, was profoundly shaken by his attitude. The Bolsheviks of this world might start by blowing up Ida's 'hovels' but 'possibly Diaghilev's ballet would be equally destroyed, and then what would happen?' Lifar was unable to suppress this train of thought (1940, p. 339):

Here, with the utmost cruelty, he attacks these rivals of his, not only Rubinstein, but anyone who dares work with her, Stravinsky, Sauguet, Massine, Nijinska, Vilzak, Schollar and even Unger. Yet all these people once worked with him too; even Rúbinstein herself began with him, and he more than anyone raised her to fame! Thus it was inevitable that I should begin to ask myself whether Diaghilev was not, in his way, striving to wipe out the whole past of his ballet, and his connection with it.

Diaghilev's destructive impulse went further. He gave an interview to a journalist from **Vozrozdenie**, a Paris-based Russian-language journal, and his comments appeared in an article on 12 December. After some pontificating on the dichotomy between classical training in ballet and the classical mode of expression, he hurled thunder-bolts in Ida's direction (Haskell, 1955, pp. 288-9):

Skyscrapers have a classicism of their own; they are palaces of our time. Classicism is a means - but not an end. When it becomes merely a restoration, we must destroy the poison that affects the whole organ. That is how classicism appreared to me in Ida Rubinstein's recent performances. I can say so because twenty years ago I brought into the dance the mysterious, extravagant, biblical Rubinstein. How could she spoil (that unforgettable) impression?

Stravinsky read the article and, while trying to maintain an air of neutrality, wrote indignantly to Gavril Païchadze: 'I don't approve of...his appraisal of the "poor Russian woman", as he calls her...it was foolish and tactless for Diaghilev to lower himself to criticize her, especially since he was appearing immediately after her in the Paris Opéra. I felt embarrassed for Diaghilev's sake' (Stravinsky, Vera, and Craft, p. 287).

Diaghilev's ridiculous outburst made no impression upon the 'poor Russian woman': she carried on regardless. But his own final days were significantly affected by the whole episode. He cast aside Stravinsky as his 'favourite son' and became emotionally involved with the young prodigy Igor Markevitch, in whose talents as a composer he placed more faith than was ultimately justified. More important, he consciously revitalized his flagging interest in his own productions. He took the greatest care over arrangements for his season beginning on 20 December. As Grigoriev remarked, after Ida Rubinstein, 'Diaghilev was taking no chances over our next appearance' (p. 254). If he really thought her efforts so dreadful, one wonders what he was afraid of!

Serge Lifar was worried about the effect upon his health. He noted in his journal: 'Serge Pavlovich is exhausted. His interest in ballet continues to diminish...The discovery of some old Russian book means much more to him than a new ballet' (1950, p. 241). But Diaghilev forced himself to plan an exciting new season, which he only just lived to see. Given his state of mind, how he must have raged when Henry Prunières declared that with her ballets 'Ida Rubinstein was treading in Diaghilev's footsteps'! (1929, p. 242).

While Diaghilev was fulminating about Ida's abuse of classical dance techniques, a quite different Parisian personality added her own comments. Colette put pen to paper immediately after the final performance: 'Since escaping Fokine's rough hand, she has broken the invisible shackle that slowed down Cleopatra's pace and inhibited Schéhérazade's exuberance; she has not stopped wanting to leave the ground, to express herself by verbal means, to cavort about, perhaps to sing' (1958, p. 154). Ida had certainly tried hard to impress, flying like a snowflake as the fairy, leaping higher than a gazelle as David before Saul. And the richness of her productions, the gold lamé, the silver, the jewels, the embroidery, made it clear that Ida loved luxury as other women loved love. Work itself was a kind of drug for her. Judging by the fruits of her labours, she allowed herself no rest whatsoever. But, none the less, Colette hankered after the days when Ida specialized in mimed roles. 'A mime inhabits your stunning body...Mime is your empire,' she told Ida. 'Survey it with the calm passion of impassive voluptuousness' (pp. 156-8).

But the message of another critic was just as clear. Henry Malherbe maintained that Ida had achieved 'the most absolute success, despite the envy of rivals and mediocrities' (1928a, p. 3). He went even further: having started in Diaghilev's company, 'she had just surpassed...her old master.' Malherbe was certainly not the most avant-garde of critics but at least he judged Ida on her own merits, while he dismissed Diaghilev for pursuing novelty at any price, 'grotesquely rigging out his dancers with masks to fit in with the peculiarity of his theatrical conceptions', which Malherbe considered the product of 'a bizarre and tormented imagination'. By contrast, Ida had 'recreated the impression of the original Russian ballet in all its freshness.' And, he concluded, when one looked at the lamentable achievements of other theatre productions, the superiority of Ida's work was all the more apparent (1928b, p. 3).

Malherbe's view was shared by a number of critics. Others echoed Colette's words: Ida was 'really the queen of the (plastic) pose' and she should pursue that vocation in the theatre (Pawlowski, 1928, p. 4). But in the end of the day only Charles Tenroc had a practical suggestion to make as Ida set out on her European tour: her success would be assured if she learned from experience and resisted the temptation to star in every one of her ballets; her achievement as a dancer would be even better (1928, p. 745).

As events turned out, it was not Ida's insistence upon dancing all the star roles that caused problems on the tour but bad organization at the local level. The troupe paraded round the major opera houses of Europe, giving only a few performances in each. There were frequent cancellations and curtailments for technical reasons. More than once dancers found themselves stranded in a strange city. The younger ones took everything in their stride and used the free time to explore the great centres of European culture. For an impressionable Frederick Ashton it was an unforgettable experience, 'rehearsing in one of the lounges in the Scala, seeing Vienna in the snow, Naples in the spring...and rehearsing in the same rooms in Monte Carlo which had seen the creation of so many of Diaghilev's ballets' (Vaughan, p. 30).

A very junior William Chappell called it a 'crazy, half-starved tour' (ibid., p. 30). An irascible Stravinsky used even stronger language. His **Baiser de la fée** opened in Brussels on 7 December and, since the celebrated musical director of the Théâtre de la Monnaie, Corneil de Thoran, conducted, he was able to see his work from the audience for the first time. He was slightly unhappy: he now admitted that there was nothing wrong with the choreography or the dancing but the 'five-to-eight minute pause between the tableaux...sabotaged the work' (Stravinsky, Vera, and Craft, p. 286).

In Monte Carlo the complaint was different. Ida offered only one performance of his work – a Sunday matinée on 6 January 1929: 'It is a mystery to me,' he muttered, 'why Ida Rubinstein offers it only once, since that is hardly worth the expense to which she has gone' (ibid., p. 286). But Ida was impervious to his protests and, after the two performances of **Le Baiser** in Brussels and Monte Carlo, she gave only one more (in Milan) during the rest of her tour. When the time came to broadcast the work in the spring of 1929, Stravinsky was still sulking. On 25 March he wrote to Gavril Païchadze in explicit terms: 'I ask you not to **mandeet** (waste time masturbating) with (Ida Rubinstein), and thus shit up the broadcast' (ibid., p. 286). A curious mixed metaphor that tells one more about Stravinsky's state of mind than Ida's!

Yet, despite inconviences and problems of temperament, Ida achieved some striking successes on tour. For example, the audience at the Vienna opera house was spellbound at the sight of her dancing in **Boléro**: 'With an almost demonic indifference, Ida Rubinstein wheeled round and round without cease, to the stereotype rhythm, on an immense tavern table, while at her feet the men, displayed an unfettered passion, beat themselves till the blood came' (Reich, p. 275).

So satisfied was Ida with her success that she decided to finish off her 1928-1929 season by mounting a few more performances in Paris. This also provided an opportunity for presenting the two new ballets which had not been ready for the winter programme.

Rehearsals began at the Opéra on 29 April 1929 and the run opened on 16 May with performances of **Les Noces de Psyché, David** and **Boléro**. The programme was new to nobody - except Massine, who saw his **David** for the first time. The second ballet choreographed by Massine (to a score by Georges Auric), **Les Enchantements d'Alcine**, received its première in a programme bounded by **Nocturne** and **La Princesse Cygne** on 21 May.

Les Enchantements d'Alcine, Auric's fourth ballet, was based on an adventurous plot drawn by his friend Louis Laloy from Ariosto's **Orlando furioso**. A simple enough story in itself, it was rich in possibilities for an elaborate and luxurious production: two suitors, the poet Roger and the warrior Tancrède, both compete for the hand of the fair Angélique. She seems inclined towards the manly soldier and trips off to her palace hand-in-hand with him. Just then the thorns of a rose-bush catch her dress and her beau prepares to free her by hacking off the offending branch. The disappointed poet stops him in time and gently frees the dress without harming the bush. Left alone, Roger is waylaid by the Rose Fairy, Alcine (Ida), who presents him with a rose, a token of gratitude for his kindness. He is still so wrapped up in his own love that he fails to realize that Alcine has fallen in love with him and, tactlessly, he gives the rose to Angélique. To punish him, the fairy transports him in his sleep to a beautiful enchanted garden where she changes him into a tree. Not satisfied with that, she turns rocks into monsters and flowers into amazons to keep watch over him. But Angélique breaks the fairy's spell with the aid of the magic rose and offers her hand to Roger instead of Tancrède - who takes it all with as much good grace as the disappointed fairy does.

Auric's music sang in harmony with the stage-action and did not pretend to be a symphonic work in its own right. It was eclectic. Hints of Satie, Messager and Chopin could be detected; and, as James Harding later remarked, popular idioms were their happy bedfellows: 'The Flowers sway gracefully to a little melody like those sentimental songs that were to be heard at the tea dances in the Twenties, and Alcine's slow waltz is nothing more or less than a popular café-concert tune' (p. 206).

Paul Bertrand summed up Auric's achievement succinctly: this work was 'perhaps the most complete and richest in effects in all his already abundant output.' Bertrand also enthused about how Benois's splendid sets had enhanced the production and how his beautiful costumes had embellished it. And as for Ida, 'as always one had to applaud the supreme harmony of her poses.' **Les Enchantements** was yet another in the 'series of sumptuous spectacles presented by her with a sense of taste and a magnificence that can only arouse the liveliest admiration' (1929, p. 248).

The second new work presented by Ida in May 1929 was Ravel's **La Valse** and not a freshly commissioned ballet by Nicolas Nabokov, as many expected. Ida had made overtures to him. Diaghilev got wind of her plans and his young cousin, still a novice in the art of theatre-intrigue, chose not to offend his tyrannical patron by consorting with the enemy - an act of loyalty ill-repaid by fate.

The history of **La Valse** is slightly bizarre, mainly because of the part Diaghilev played in it. In 1920 he asked Ravel to compose a ballet for the end of the current season and, with uncharacteristic speed, Ravel completed a short-score, entitled **Wien**, within a month. But when Diaghilev heard his misty choreographic poem based on a drifting waltz theme, he was not impressed. Poulenc was present when Ravel and Marcelle Meyer played him the two-piano version and he recorded his impression of the scene: 'I knew Diaghilev very well at the time, and I had seen his false teeth shift, his monocle move, I had seen that he was very embarrassed, I had seen that he did not like it.' Poulenc knew that he would reject the work and, in fact, his comments were unequivocal: 'Ravel, it is a masterpiece...but it is not a ballet...It is a portrait of a ballet...a painting of a ballet' (p. 179). Ravel said nothing. He simply removed his score and left. When he later learned that Diaghilev had dismissively referred to his work as 'nothing but a waltz', his rage knew no bounds and he almost fought a duel with him over the matter.

Renamed **La Valse**, the score soon proved highly successful as a concert piece. And on 20 October 1926 it was presented by the Royal Flemish Opera Ballet as a choreographical sketch by Sonia Korty. But it was Ida's production of 1929, with its new scenario, that established **La Valse** as part of the modern ballet repertoire. Its staging was dramatic. Nijinska's choreography was simple but telling: swirling clouds fill the stage; through them waltzing couples can be seen dimly. A crescendo of light matches the gradual build-up of the music as a great crowd of dancers, waltzing in groups, becomes visible, finally revealed in a mid-nineteenth-century ballroom with blazing chandeliers. The effect was gripping and rather sinister, like an uncomfortable dream in which some indefinable force can be felt but not seen.

The Paris public had its first opportunity to see **La Valse** on 23 May 1929. Reactions were guarded for the simple reason that nobody knew quite what to make of this unusual but strangely moving work. It could be taken at face value as a subtle poem in music and movement that made out of a snatch of a waltz theme a complete and compelling creation by means of clever rhythmic variations. Some commentators went further and claimed to see in the music 'an expression of personal anguish or premonition, a nightmarish vision, in a word, a **danse macabre**' (Myers, p. 195).

After this première Ida's troupe moved from the Opéra to the Théâtre Sarah-Bernhardt for one - just one! - final evening of ballet on 30 May. Surprisingly, she did not take the opportunity to give a second performance of **La Valse**. Instead, **Le Baiser, Les Enchantements** and **Boléro** were chosen to bring down the curtain on her ballet season. But, for Ida at least, there was still work to be done: she stayed on at the Théâtre Sarah-Bernhardt and, the following week, gave three performances of **La Dame aux camélias** - as if to prove that her theatrical horizons remained unlimited.

However, while she was expending her last ounce of energy on stage, she had to cope with an irritating 'outside' distraction. On 30 May, the afternoon of the opening at the Théâtre Sarah-Bernhardt, she was summoned to court to answer a civil charge brought against her by a cinematographic operator called Sammy Brill. He had done some work for her and presented a bill for 20,000 francs but she, the woman who had reputedly just spent nine million francs on her ballets, was not satisfied with the results and refused to pay him. Despite her riches and her apparently carefree extravagance, Ida never willingly allowed anybody to take advantage of her. She cannot have liked having a writ served on her as Madame Lydia Horwitz (or Gorwitz), a name she always refused to use, even for the sake of convenience. One can imagine the ill-will with which she wrote one of her distinctive Lloyds Bank cheques for a final sum of 22,000 francs when the court-case, predictably, went against her on 15 June (AN, AJ 13. 1293, no. 3).

This apart, as the summer of 1929 came, Ida evidently felt a degree of satisfaction with her year of achievements. Even her more cynical, hard-headed friends shared her feelings. About this time, Bettina Bergery witnessed what she considered a slightly odd scene. She was invited to lunch by Romaine Brooks and arrived to find among the guests Natalie Barney and 'a long-eyed skeleton in an old dress made by Leon Bakst, a scarecrow left over from the Ballets Russes who turned out to be Ida Rubinstein' (Wickes, p. 252). Madame Bergery went on mercilessly: 'She wore a lot of tarnished gold lamé and fishnet, with a terribly thin, pointed face. I remember her wearing a black-and-white coat and white stockings, all very untidy and spilled on' (Secrest, p. 326). One can only imagine that Bettina Bergery's eyes were deceiving her or that Ida really was having an off-day.

But it was not so much the sight of these three old friends that startled her as a remark made by Natalie during the course of lunch: 'We all got what we wanted. I got my salon; Romaine became a painter and Ida became a famous ballerina' (ibid., p. 326) - a statement all the more remarkable because Natalie was the last person in the world to indulge in flattery.

Admittedly Natalie was fixated by Ida as the personification of the androgyne that figures so largely in her own writings. She shared this preoccupation with Romaine Brooks, both using their own chosen art-form to complement each other's expression of it. As early as 1915, the year in which Natalie and Romaine first met, Natalie wrote a poem entitled 'The Weeping Venus', inspired by Romaine's painting of an emaciated nude, inspired in turn by Ida's body. Romaine wanted that 'fragile and androgynous beauty' to represent 'the death of the old gods amid the mutilations of the war' (Wickes, p. 150). Natalie put her own feminist construction on it (Barney, p. 12):

> No crown of thorns, no wounded side,
> Yet as the God-man crucified,
> Her body expiates the sin
> That love and life with her begin!

Since then Natalie had followed Ida's career with interest, paying particular attention to her transvestite roles in the revivals of **Le Martyre**, in **Orphée**, even in **Les Noces de Psyché** and finally in **David** as the Botticellian shepherd-boy. While Ida was charming the soul-sick King Saul on the stage of the Opéra, Natalie was writing a novel on the subject of a suicide who rematerializes in some ectoplasmic form as a sexless androgyne. The work was, in fact, the culmination of a long-term interest in hermaphroditism, represented for her in the figure of Tiresias - so close to T.S. Eliot's male heart. Natalie's novel, unhelpfully entitled **The One Who Is Legion, or A.D's After-Life,** was published privately in 1930, not, one suspects, because publishers were unwilling to accept a work saturated with sexual ambiguities, but because it is almost impossible to understand, unless one is given a 'guided tour' of its symbolic highways and byways.

For Ida, the book's slightly morbid adulation of epicene beauty was fascinating, a curious tribute to the stage-image cultivated by her. She had no reason to fear what construction the general public might put on the work since, until recently, nobody read it - except Natalie Barney's sisters in Sappho and a few male hangers-on.

Coincidentally, Ida's next major stage-role was - yet again - a transvestite one.

CHAPTER 14

Amphion or the Power of Music, 1929-1931

Sometime before her ambitious 1928-1929 season came to an end, Ida Rubinstein began planning ahead. Having built up a substantial repertoire of nine ballets, she intended to use them as the staple diet of future programmes, to which she would add occasional novelties to stimulate the gastric juices of the artistic public. The first addition was a major work entitled **Amphion,** based on a libretto by Paul Valéry.

In the 1890s, as a young poet, scarcely more than an adolescent and still decades away from the Académie Française, Valéry was fascinated by architecture. But far from allowing this to distract him away from poetry, he found himself drawing parallels between the two arts. The correlation between structure and form in architecture and the French language was very close. And when one went further and considered construction in architecture, then, thought Valéry, one came very close to the spirit of composition in the musical sense. 'It is clear that music and architecture are arts that are equally inimitable,' he decided. 'They are arts in which matter and form share a far more intimate relationship than in any other art' (1936 p. 83).

The logical sequence of Valéry's thought led him back to the ancient Greek myth of the invention of music and, through music, the invention of architecture: the sun-god Apollo gives the poet Amphion a lyre and with it he discovers order and form in sound; music, played amid the disordered material of nature, rocks, dense, tangled forests and rivers, charms them into an ordered existence; a temple magically arises, the epitome of classical form and balance; a fountain springs into existence, jetting its waters upwards towards heaven and honouring the deities.

These ideas germinated for a while in Valéry's mind and, in 1894, he shared his thoughts with two friends, Claude Debussy and Pierre Louÿs. They listened with a degree of interest as he sketched out a grand plan for an elaborate stage-work in which instrumental and vocal music, mime and dance would be used to describe the different stages of the gestation and birth of music and architecture through the exertions of Amphion. Valéry hoped that Debussy would agree to provide the vital musical element. But, he noted with regret, 'Debussy gave the idea only the slightest consideration: it appeared so complicated although extremely simple in theory' (ibid., p. 88). Truth be told, Debussy already had enough work to keep him busy for some time. If he had become involved in the **Amphion**-project, his master-work **Pelléas et Mélisande** might never have been completed. Valéry was disappointed by his reaction, although he had no real excuse for complaint since he himself, an unknown twenty-three-year-old, had so far done nothing more than talk about his fantasy.

How fortunate that Valéry did not commit his ideas to paper at this point! The result would almost certainly have been a florid torrent of words, gushing from the wells of contemporary Symbolist imagery. When he finally came to write the work thirty-five years later, even a fragment of juvenalia might have been more of a hinderance than a help.

Valéry did not reveal what rekindled his interest in the subject of Amphion more than three decades later. Perhaps the sight of Ida in Roger-Ducasse's **Orphée** in 1926 provided the vital spark. An introduction to her was easily arranged. They had many friends and acquaintances in common, such as André Gide and, more important, Valéry's Egeria, the brilliant young Duchesse de La Rochefoucauld, who lived a few paces away through the chestnut trees on the other side of the Place des Etats-Unis. The poet discussed his ideas with Ida and, as he freely admitted, she acted as the catalyst that made them crystalize into something tangible: 'Madame Rubinstein was tempted by the very poetic myth and even by all the difficulties that my specific ideas put in the way of its materialization' (ibid., p. 88). One problem she solved immediately: she enlisted the help of Arthur Honegger and commissioned him to write a score to Valéry's libretto.

Honegger was well aware that he was tackling 'a project which Valéry had previously entrusted to Debussy' and he considered this 'a great honour, a heavy responsibility' (1966, p. 109). He was afraid that the subject might prove too much for him. Had he shoulders strong enough 'to carry without weakening the full weight of musical evolution since its birth, from original chaos to forms of the highest sophistication?' (Delannoy, p. 129). But once the libretto (of what Valéry had begun to call his **mélodrame**) took shape, Honegger set to work with a will and, during the early months of 1929, he created an impressive score for reciter (Amphion), baritone solo (Apollo), four women's voices (the Muses), orchestra and chorus. Considering the size and complexity of his task, Honegger completed it with remarkable speed, although Valéry showed signs of impatience when the composer overstepped his deadline of May 1929. But by the end of July the music was ready. On 31 July Valéry wrote to his friend, the art-expert Paul Poujard: 'The other day I heard a first hearing for piano duet and four voices of this unusual work. My impression is not at all bad. My incompetence does not seem to have prevented Honegger from coping...Apollo's monologue, which was neither brief nor easy to set to music, seemed remarkable to me and, a rare thing in this petty age, it seemed **great**' (1952, p. 177).

Valéry ended by telling Poujard that 'Madame Ida' and all her collaborators were to begin work at the Opéra in November. Nothing seemed to stand in the way of **Amphion**'s reaching the stage by spring of 1930. But fate conspired to keep Valéry waiting a little longer to see the brain-child that he had conceived forty years before.

In 1929 signs of a severe recession in the world-economy began to be noticed. Cracks appeared in the agricultural and industrial foundations of the Western world's and America's economic structures. Lost commercial opportunities and irresponsible financial speculation precipitated a crisis, of which the Wall Street Crash of October 1929 was a mere symptom. Like any millionaire, Ida had her worries. But her fortune was well enough managed. She had already survived the effects of the Russian Revolution and she could ride out an economic slump. More important, her friend Walter Guinness survived relatively unscathed: the poor went hungry but apparently did not stop drinking stout. However, until the full implications of the crisis could be assessed, caution was called for and so Ida simply put her theatre-projects into cold storage until she was sure that 'she could do justice to them.

By the spring of 1931 she was confident enough to reassemble her company and plunge into an ambitious season without any apparent financial restraint. It opened at the Opéra on 23 June with a glamorous gala evening that featured revived versions of **Boléro** and **La Princesse Cygne** and the première of **Amphion.** The first two ballets provoked little comment other than a few sounds of approbation. **Boléro,** for example, was hailed as 'a vision at one and the same time simple and grandiose which we owe to the choreography of...Nijinska and the understanding of...Ida Rubinstein' (Schneider, 1931, p. 561).

Almost all the attention was focused on **Amphion.** The spectacular stage-effects, lighting and décor arranged by Benois and Massine's inventive choreography were very impressive. However, the story unfolded by Valéry's text and interpreted by Ida's combination of mime and dance was unfamiliar and, in places, rather puzzling (ibid., pp. 559-60):

Amphion, Jupiter's son by Antiope, leads a rough and savage existence in the forest, where only the springs sing, only the streams murmur. He sees a beast which he can kill for food; but he is persuaded by a mysterious voice that implores him to spare it and, tired by the chase, he falls into a deep sleep. In his dream Apollo reveals that a special mission has been entrusted to him...As soon as Amphion awakes, he sees a marvellous instrument before him on the ground. He picks it up and strikes it roughly, spreading terror among men and upsetting the world of nature. Amphion...realizes that the strings must be touched more gently;

he then produces a caressing sound that enchants all things, animate and inanimate alike. He practices his playing and discovers scales. He has invented music. Rocks are charmed by his melodious strains; they proceed to arrange themselves in impeccable order and form the city of Thebes. A temple in honour of Apollo materializes. By a miracle, the Muses appear and form themselves into the temple's columns. The people marvel. They acclaim the man whose art has just given birth to the science of architecture. They decide to take Amphion into the temple and set up a cult to him. Suddenly, a woman shrouded in mourning veils bars the poet's way; she snatches the lyre away from him and throws it into a rushing stream. She then drags him off to nothingness and thus Amphion is the only one not to benefit from his discovery.

The sight of Amphion disappearing in the arms of this mysterious figure, ambiguously described as either Love or Death, certainly sent a shiver up the spine, but the audience remained uncertain as to why the creator should have to pay this price for artistic sensitivity and be denied the pleasure of enjoying his creation. One critic suggested that more enlightenment would be gained from reading the appropriate entry in **Larousse** (Teramond, p. unnumbered). Some might have found even that a pointless exerise. In the audience a venerable professor from the Collège de France, more of a Hellenist than a music-lover, dozed, lullabied by Valéry's poetry and Honegger's music. As Ida took up the lyre, a foreign woman turned to her neighbour and asked (Horatio, p. 3):

'Is this taking place in Greece?'

The professor woke up with a sudden start: 'Not at all, Madame, it's set in Italy. Can't you see that Amphion is picking up a lyre (**lira**)?'

'Oh yes! You're right!'

Valéry himself was disturbed by how difficult it was to realize his ideas in dramatic form. He had dreamt of combining artistic with spiritual elements. He had tried to give his libretto a quasi-liturgical structure. The problem was that Valéry suffered from a fatal flaw. His devoted friend Edmée de La Rochefoucauld makes it clear that, music-lover though he claimed to be, Valéry could not cope with music played in the 'abstract' context of the concert-hall. He needed the fantasy-world of the theatre to distract and excite him and allow him to experience afresh the unexpected or the essential (pp. 22-3).

Some would have condemned him as a musical amateur in the worst sense of the word. Boris de Schloezer cast a more charitable but still discerning eye on the matter: 'Nothing is more terrible...for a musician than a too perfect text or too poetic a subject.' The problem was 'that the poet and the musician operate on two different planes.' Valéry had produced one of his most 'Apollonian' works, elegant, graceful, a triumph of art. But, Schloezer wondered, 'what is Apollonian art without struggle, without danger?' It could so easily devolve into mere academicism. The result was that the text had caused Honegger to write a very uneven score. The composer of the muscular **Pacific 231** and **Rugby** had found himself writing passages of rather unrobust music. But Schloezer did admit one thing: 'The best episode in the whole score is certainly the fugue which accompanies the construction of Thebes; for that splendid fugue one can pardon the composer for...the first section where the music at certain moments (the monologues of Apollo and Amphion)...cramps the free flow of the text' (1931, pp. 348-9).

This opinion contrasts strangely with the one expressed by Henry Prunières in the **Revue Musicale**: 'One has had the occasion, at times with justification, to reproach Honegger with his indifference to the quality of the texts which he sets to music. This time he has devoted his talent to the service of a great poet's thought. Honegger's tumultuous art becomes classical here without resort to the conventional' (1931, pp. 239, 240).

And what was the critical opinion of Ida's achievement? Gilbert Charles warmed up by commenting on how she had to cope with mime, dancing, declamation and acting, altogether an extremely complex task, but, he continued, 'Madame Rubinstein had already given proof that she dreads only the easy' (p. 5).

Prunières was particularly struck by Amphion's 'long monologue which her musical voice declaimed eloquently to an orchestral accompaniment' (1931, p. 240). Nothing quite so active was needed to please Raymond Balliman: 'Admirably plastic - during Amphion's sleep she has the perfect beauty of an antique marble - eloquent in her gestures,...Ida Rubinstein asserted herself, as always, as an enlightened artist' (p. unnumbered).

Gustave Bret remarked upon how **Amphion**'s theme was 'eminently suitable for the creative imagination of an interpreter such as...Ida Rubinstein, whose gestures, poses, movements have beauty...charged with mystery and harmony' (p. 7).

Georges Guy summed up her achievement both as patron and artist by remarking upon how she had made possible a collaboration between Valéry and Honegger, comparable to Maeterlinck's association with Debussy in the creation of **Pelléas et Mélisande**. That was not all: 'Ida Rubinstein, who is a great artist, and whose life is at the constant service of all that is beautiful, staged **Amphion** sumptuously' (p. unnumbered).

All things considered, **Amphion** was a bold experiment which succeeded as a whole and contained some remarkable moments. As an example of its genre, it taught Ida a great deal and helped to pave the way to the creative heights that were achieved a few years later with Claudel's and Honegger's **Jeanne d'Arc au bûcher.**

The other novel feature of Ida's 1931 season received its première on 25 June. This was a production of Ravel's **La Valse** with completely new choreography by Michel Fokine. Even the sets and costumes were different. Rumour had it that Ravel himself took a hand in their design and began by getting rid of the original gold lamé tunics, which he did not like. There is no doubt that he preferred the new production to Nijinska's original attempt: the dancing and the décors had given little suggestion of place and not much sense of time. It was, in other words, too intangible for a Ravel who would not live to see the abstract ballets of later years.

The revival of **La Valse** provided the critic André Levinson with an opportunity to criticize the state-subsidized theatres in France. He deplored how official Opéra programmes contained only traditional or classical works while a foreign patron, 'with a foreign **corps de ballet,** was left with the task of mounting...Ravel's **La Valse...,** whose triumphal success in the concert hall was undiminished by time and which contained first-rate material for a stage production' (1931, p. 2). Raoul Brunel went further - and with considerably more enthusiasm: 'Ida Rubinstein has lent **(La Valse)** all her lustre as a producer, complemented by her marvellous personal talent. She has been justly rewarded with a great success' (p. 6).

The **Musical Times** critic, W.G. McNaught, was rather more prosaic but just as enthusiastic about **La Valse** (1931, p. 745):

In the whole course of a spectacular season we have seen nothing so lavishly beautiful as the ball-room in which this ballet was danced and the crinolined ladies and military gentlemen...who danced it. There was an artistic parallel between the sumptuous treatment of the waltz on the stage and Ravel's well-known orchestral elaboration, and the result was a unified creation, single and complete, and too strong in its impersonal quality to be affected by what any individual dancer did, or wore, as a unit in the ensemble. For this reason it is the best of the ballets, although the simplest in theme.

As soon as the final curtain came down on her Paris season, Ida found herself being interviewed by Pierre Lagarde, a positively swooning journalist from **Comoedia.** Hailing her as a magician who had just brought off a triumph, he bubbled with excitement at the news that she was leaving for London to present a season of ballets and plays at Covent Garden. (Why he had not heard of her plans before this is a mystery, since she had been preparing the ground with a skilful publicity campaign since early spring.)

If one can judge from Lagarde's account of the interview, he did most of the talking. Ida sat, posed on her divan, and looked mysterious. The only direct quotation that he reproduced was mundane, if startling: 'I am going,' she said with a laugh, 'with one hundred and fifty individuals and baggage weighing seventy-five thousand kilos!' Lagarde waxed lyrical at the sound of her voice: 'But she is going above all with her faith, with the atmosphere of magic that surrounds her - seventy-five thousand kilos of magic! - with her prestige, her lyricism, her will, with her art and her love' (p. 1).

Ida's Covent Garden season ran from 6 to 17 July 1931 and it caused a sensation, if only because London boasted nothing comparable in the way of ballet companies: Marie Rambert at the Mercury Theatre was doing sterling work on a shoe-string; and only two months before, in May 1931, had the Sadler's Wells Ballet launched itself as a permanent British institution. (Truth be told, Ida's company had few serious rivals even in France since Diaghilev's death had left a hiatus that was not filled very satisfactorily for some time.) What immediately impressed London audiences was the ambitious scale of her enterprise. Anybody could tell at a glance that 'she spared no expense. She recognized the finest creative minds of the day and promptly bought them' (Haskell, 1977, p. 152). And, unlike most ballet promoters, she could afford to do so.

The English balletomane's excitement was stimulated still further by the sight of a photograph of Ida in the **Dancing Times**. There she was - with her famous mysterious smile and daringly clad in trousers that disappeared into knee-length leather boots - the woman who, not content with bringing her repertoire of ballets all the way to London, also planned to appear in two of her great acting roles, as Marguerite Gautier and Saint Sebastian. In fact, it was with **Le Martyre** (as a charity gala in aid of the French hospital in London) that she opened her season on 6 July.

The London public had clearly never seen the like of d'Annunzio's drama and were at a loss to know what to make of it. The **Times** critic fell back upon a historical approach: the essence of the 'mystery' as a dramatic form was (or had been) the simplicity of its treatment of a central theme. 'But the theme of **Le Martyre**...is not simple: it begins with martyrdom for a cause...and changes to martyrdom for its own sake...and again...to the even more perverse theme "Each man kills the thing he loves"' (anon., 1931b, p. 12). Ida had disturbed the dread shade of Oscar Wilde - and it continued to haunt the writer. As he discussed the problem of what acting-style, the heroic or the realistic, better suited the play (neither of them, he seemed to think!), he returned to the homosexual theme: 'The emperor...had an easy task from the unheroic nature of his part, and (Maxime) Desjardins made his **crescendo** of interest in Sebastian the Archer a credible thing from real life: he had no occasion to worry whether he was symbolizing anything or not' (ibid., p. 12). And Desjardins, surprisingly, did not sue him for libel!

Ida was paid a qualified compliment: 'The dancer's use of her arms, her poise and her stillness brought dignity, which was sometimes lost by the more histrionic acting of the rest of a numerous cast' (ibid., p. 12). The production, thought the **Times** critic, was 'beautiful but opulent' - whatever he meant by that. And as for the music, that too was 'beautiful, though fragmentary, but Debussy could not write heroics - he made no attempt to do so here - and so...it is not part and parcel of this magnificent piece' (ibid., p. 12).

For his part, W.G. McNaught of the **Musical Times** was more interested in the music than in the text and would have welcomed the chance to 'listen to the music in a concert room' (1931, p. 746). But choice did not enter into the matter: this was the last occasion upon which Ida ever performed **Le Martyre** in public. And more than a decade had to pass before another actress tackled the work.

On 7 July the programme began with **La Princesse Cygne** - 'a pleasing example of the manner familiarized before the war by Fokine' (anon., 1931c, p. 12). It continued with Sauguet's **David,** which the **Times** critic thought 'sober in colour and at times surprisingly sentimental' (ibid., p. 12). The evening ended with **Boléro,** during which enlightenment suddenly came to the **Times** critic, who already knew it as a concert piece: 'the less expression is put into the performance, especially in the matter of tempo, the more effective it becomes. It gains enormously from performance as a ballet, since the spectacle provides an antidote to its mechanical monotony' (ibid., p. 12). McNaught thought the opposite: 'That crescendo of music spells a crescendo of human passion and all that the ballet gave us was human movement...Nothing more drastic happened than a mock fight...It seemed too uneventful a scenario, in these days of popular bloodshed, for such melodramatic music...**Boléro** was deficient in gore' (1931, p. 745). McNaught was clearly addicted to gangster movies.

As for Ida's performance, after a gap of twenty years, London had forgotten about her distinctive style and comments on it were rather gauche: 'While the movement of her arms are graceful and her poses well conceived, she seemed to be a mime rather than a dancer' (anon., 1931c, p. 12). But that preoccupied her public a lot less than the excessive length of the intervals. Feelings ran high among a section of the audience. 'A natural impatience' (ibid., p. 12), thought the man from **The Times,** although he later changed his tune and talked about an 'unmannerly demonstration' on the part of some of the audience (anon., 1931d, p. 12). Ida took the hint and curtailed the ordeal of waiting on subsequent evenings.

On 8 July the programme consisted of **Nocturne** and a repeat of **La Princesse Cygne,** preceded by a perfomance of **La Valse,** which monopolized all critical attention. Ravel's work attracted glowing critical reviews, partly because he had designed the beautiful sets and costumes - or so the programme said! Alas, Ida earned herself a hint of criticism, but not for her performance. The intrepid **Times** critic thought that 'the only thing that detracted from the perfection of the spectacle on stage, which must rank with the finest ballet we have seen, was Madame Rubinstein's dress. It is unfortunate that the chief character, to whom we owe these delights, should choose to wear dresses which have no relation to the carefully planned designs of the scenic artists' (ibid., p. 12). They had, none the less, designed them, even if Ida's costumes had been executed by Worth and Lanvin!

On 9 July Ida broke into the exacting sequence of ballet programmes and gave a performance of **La Dame aux camélias.** In England Dumas's work, though familiar in its operatic form, was practically unknown as a play - and still less in the original French. It impressed the audience. For one thing, few were in a position to make comparisons with Sarah Bernhardt's 'standard' intepretation and this was reflected in their verdict: 'The performance was...a display of the kind of acting, no less genuine than accomplished, which we do not often see today...Marguerite and Armand (Maurice Donneaud) wept, declaimed, and fainted as vigorously as Dumas could have wished.' Ida's acting - in the grand manner - attracted particular attention (anon, 1931e, p. 12):

Never for a moment...did Madame Rubinstein show by any exaggeration of gesture or excessive fervour of speech that she expected us to be too sophisticated for the play...she, so evidently,...kept her control. Even when, in the interests of the sentimental or overtly dramatic, her beautifully modulated voice had to break its even flow, that break was...equally a carefully and rigidly controlled artifice. Dumas's persistent assaults on the emotions were thus perfectly and persistently foiled. She even died with so artificial a touch of nature that this outrageous scene had no power to bring any shamefaced sob to the throat or even to induce any deliberate and protective cynicism. This, of course, was infinitely better than any parody, however sympathetic, and one came away delighted that the two dangers of sophistication and sentimentality had been so scrupulously avoided.

A generous enough compliment, even if Ida, as a courtesan, seemed to possess remarkably suburban virtues!

The London première of **Amphion**, on 10 July, attracted a deal of attention but that was scarcely surprising considering the renown of the librettist and the popularity of the composer. Even Ravel, conducting his own magnetic **Boléro** on the same evening, failed to steal its thunder. W.G. McNaught explained (1931, pp. 745-6):

> **Amphion** brought us face to face with tremendous issues...At a touch of the lyre, Amphion caused the walls of Thebes to rise, and incidentally gave birth to music and architecture. A heavy programme, this...and it was left to...Honegger to bring us into contact with the remote and mystic affairs of mythology...his music subtly conveyed a sense of the vast and inhuman. It was the most interesting score among the novelties.

Two of these so-called novelties only appeared in the final days of Ida's season, **Les Noces de Psyché et de l'Amour** and **La Bien-Aimée**. They provoked no interesting comment. And **David**, admired as 'a Botticellian projection of the story of David, Saul and Goliath', ended the final evening of the season (ibid., p. 746).

As a young man, Arnold Haskell sat through all of Ida's performances and, although he admitted a personal bias of interest in Ludmilla Schollar and let this colour his appreciation of Ida, he and his contemporaries agreed that the great trouble and expense to which Ida had gone had resulted in one of the most spectacular and sumptuous programmes of plays and ballets seen in London in the inter-war period.

Praise or guarded comments, what strangers said about her meant little to Ida. She pressed on with her work with undiminished zeal. A few days after her return to Paris she received a short note from Rouché promising to reserve five days in April 1932 for her next season at the Opéra (BN Opéra, Ida Rubinstein, dossier II, fol. 21).

CHAPTER 15

Seasonal Bigamy, 1932–1934

At the beginning of 1932 a close friendship began to develop between Ida Rubinstein and the pianist Marguerite Long. Though almost ten years her senior and a virtuoso performer in her own right, she had admired Ida from afar ever since her first appearance in Paris. For over two decades her devotion survived on the slightest of acquaintances until it blossomed into a much warmer, more tangible relationship. Marguerite Long, who could flatter better than anybody when necessary, had nothing to gain professionally from championing Ida and yet she had nothing but the most fulsome praise for her. She was unashamedly direct in her admiration. On one occasion she turned to Ida and said: 'All that you have done for poetry and music is so beautiful and so great that it always seems to me beyond belief.' Others would have wilted with embarrassment or swelled with pride at such an emotional statement. Ida's reply was simple and unaffected: 'They are my jewels!' (Long, 1971, p. 41).

Years after her death, when Ida was beyond the reach of flatterers, Marguerite openly expressed her feelings for her: 'If I recall her memory with emotion - for I knew her, admired and loved her dearly - it is not only because she was the creator of a particular aesthetic but also on account of the magnificent blossoming of works of art brought about by her generous patronage...Her kindness to her composers, her poets and her musicians was legendary' (pp. 38, 44).

The person who did most to weld their friendship together was Maurice Ravel. Ida saw a great deal of him in a professional capacity and also cherished him as a friend. While in London for Ida's 1931 season Ravel was preoccupied with the composition of his Piano Concerto in G Major, which, he confessed, he was looking forward to performing in public. But as the year drew to its close, his deteriorating health forced him to abandon the idea. Instead, he assigned the task to Marguerite Long, to whom he dedicated the work, and he confined himself to conducting it at the première in the Salle Pleyel on 14 January 1932. The concerto was presented as the centre-piece of a Ravel 'festival' and, quite apart from the fact that her own commission, **Boléro,** also featured on the programme, Ida came along to pay homage to a great composer. She was dazzled by the new concerto and by Marguerite Long's interpretation. Thereafter, Marguerite 'never peformed that work without receiving from her the most beautiful flowers' (p. 44).

After her initial surprise, Marguerite soon became used to Ida's mildly eccentric attitude towards personal relationships. She realized that her sudden, secret journeys to distant parts and her periodic withdrawal into herself constituted the natural counterpoise to an overexposed public and professional life. Marguerite was quick to learn that 'her long absences never lessened the loyalty of her feelings. She would leave one without news, and then, from the other side of the world, a telegram of epistolary dimensions, charged with remorse, and overflowing with joy at a meeting soon to be, would suddenly arrive' (p. 44).

Against the background of this new friendship the strange, sad history of Ida's last commission to Ravel unfolded. Before mounting a new season, she planned to change her repertoire radically by commissioning at least five new major works, this time almost entirely 'original' from the musical point of view. Because her plans were so ambitious, it soon became clear that the season planned for April 1932 would not be feasible. And, indeed, it was not until the spring of 1934 that a programme of new works impressive enough to match her previous efforts was ready. The unusually long delay was partly caused by Ravel.

After finishing work on the Piano Concerto and completing a harrowing four-month concert tour of Europe with Margueite Long, he settled down in the late spring of 1932 to plan a ballet for Ida - a **pantomime arabe**, he called it - based on the story of Ali Baba and the Forty Thieves in the **Arabian Nights** (translated into French some decades before by the husband of Ida's friend Lucie Delarue-Mardrus). The work, entitled **Morgiane**, stimulated Ravel to great flights of musical fantasy. Yet, he managed to sketch out no more than a few themes, although the form of the work was clear in his mind's eye.

No entirely satisfactory explanation for the brain disease from which Ravel suffered in the last five years of his life has ever been put forward but it seems clear that some form of cerebral deterioration may have begun even before October 1932 when a Paris taxi, in which he was travelling, crashed and knocked him unconscious. He only just managed to complete his three songs for the film of **Don Quixote** but after that he composed nothing more. Anxious friends hoped that this was only a temporary state of affairs and waited for the moment when his hands could again co-ordinate themselves with the dictates of the brain. More than anybody else, Ida tried very gently to encourage him and confidently awaited the appearance of a masterpiece, although, as time slipped by, not even a flicker of creative life showed itself in him.

A second project upon which Ida set her heart also failed to materialize - at least not in time for the 1934 season. This was a ballet full of medieval pageantry and courtly love, entitled **Oriane le sans-égale**. Ida decided to give the commission to her old friend Florent

Schmitt. However, when the idea came to her in August 1932, Schmitt was far away in his country retreat at Artiguemy in the Hautes-Pyrenées. Ida was undaunted. Schmitt was impressed by her determination, as he later recalled in reverential tones (p. 4):

One beautiful summer afternoon, I was in Artiguemy,...facing an incomparable southern peak, untouched by snow, as I stretched out under the apple trees, thinking no evil thoughts, when a sound like an earthquake cause me to jump. A motorcar, rashly tackling the goat-path, had just smashed itself open against the great oak tree and deposited two women on the ground.

The oak tree had only a few, easily healed scratches. As for Madame Ida Rubinstein, everybody knows that she is above such contingencies: tracing the line of the oak tree, as erect, as high and still smiling, she scarcely realized that she had just escaped the most picturesque of deaths. By her side, no less unscathed was Madame Fauchier-Magnan, (a friend of Ida's).

They came - eight hundred and seventy-three kilometres - to offer me **Oriane le sans-égale**, this ballet...which became in time a **tragédie dansée** in two acts...

The medieval period with all its contradictions, from the charm of the Court of Love to the despair of the Dance of Death. In between, the amorous capers of a dwarf, the excitement of a Mongul fair, a poet's madrigals, the triumph of the Prince of Love, the incoherence of the Feast of Fools. The Middle Ages a little barbarous, as is only fitting, but without torture and without hangings,...this subject, at one and the same time modern and archaic, direct in colour, immediately captivated me, especially considering the talent of the principal interpreter.

Alas! Schmitt's faith and enthusiasm were ill-rewarded. He worked solidly upon his score until the early months of 1934. But as the production date drew near, it became clear that, since other commissions were taking up all available rehearsal time, **Oriane** would not be ready by the opening night, although press notices included it on the programme until the very last minute. Then the inevitable postponement was announced. Madame Rubinstein would include it in a season planned for the following autumn when, she hoped, Ravel's **Morgiane** might also be ready. But, in the event, no autumn season was possible and she never mounted **Oriane**, even though she spent a substantial sum commissioning the score.

Schmitt was annoyed at being left with an unperformed work on his hands. Worse still, he was afraid that it would be unperformable, since it had been written very much to Ida's specifications. As Reynaldo Hahn remarked, the problem was that Ida had wanted to personify a strange and prestigious heroine, to exercise her talents as a mime and to do so in the context of a lavish stage production (1938, p. 5).

However, under the modified title of **Oriane ou le prince d'amour**, it was adopted as part of the official repertoire of the Paris Opéra and given its première on 7 January 1938 with décors by Pedro Pruna and choreography by Serge Lifar. But many difficulties had to be overcome, largely because the Opéra did not have the limitless means of an Ida Rubinstein to spend on an individual production; nor did any of its stars possess her qualities as a mime.

Ida's lack of luck with **Morgiane** and **Oriane** (and, so it seems, with plans to base a ballet on Debussy's **Ibéria**) was far outweighed by her success in mounting three new large-scale works, all products of illustrious pens: **Perséphone** by Igor Stravinsky and André Gide, **Diane de Poitiers** with Jacques Ibert's music to a libretto by Elisabeth de Gramont, and **Sémiramis**, a second collaboration between Arthur Honegger and Paul Valéry.

Ideas for a ballet based upon the myth of Persephone began to form in Ida's mind in mid-January 1933. Dining with his friend Maria van Rysselberghe on 19 January, André Gide revealed that he had seen Ida a few days before and that in the course of their conversation he found himself discussing ballet with her. As he confessed, 'I do not know what brought me to tell her that I had a little ballet which had lain dormant for thirty years, **Proserpine**; she asked to see it, and lo and behold! she raved with enthusiasm!' She immediately decided that Stravinsky was the man to write the music and that José-Maria Sert should designed the sets. In other words, it would be a spectacular work executed on a grand scale because, Gide added significantly, 'she would like...to give it as her swan-song' (1974, p. 283).

But that piece of news scarcely impressed the poet. As always, he only considered his own feelings: 'For my part, it's all the same; I believe less and less in the theatre; I don't attach any importance to it, but the challenge will amuse me. It will provide me with a month's work on putting the thing in shape; a little text, the rest pretexts for movement and for dances' (p. 283). Not, one would have thought, the most helpful of attitudes to adopt when embarking upon a major project!

Ida went straight ahead and approached Stravinsky. He jumped at the chance to work with her again, although for some reason he seemed to think that Paul Valéry would be his librettist. (And time proved that he would have been much better off with Valéry.) But when he learned the truth, he received reassuring words from Gavril Païchadze: 'I had a long conversation with Ida Rubinstein, who told me that...André Gide...had written a remarkable piece for her, the subject of which will please you. I understood that it is a classical text, with chorus' (Stravinsky, Vera, and Craft, p. 314). What both men did not seem to realize was that the text was not only thirty years old but also that Gide would put little effort into bringing it up to date. But, for the moment, Stravinsky was not concerned about textual details: he was only interested in settling the fees for the commission - the same as for **Le Baiser de le fée** - and for conducting the new work.

Meanwhile, Gide was working himself up to fever pitch with excitement. On 20 January he wrote to Stravinsky, then on tour in Germany: 'The thought of attaching my name to your name in a work that has been close to my heart for a very long time fills me with extreme pride and joy. A word from you would call me to Berlin or elsewhere to talk about it - and the sooner the better. I will dine Monday the 23rd at Ida's with Sert, who is very enthusiastic and would like to do the settings' (Stravinsky, Igor, and Craft, 1960, p. 146). And on 30 January poet and composer did meet - in Wiesbaden and not in Berlin (then on the hinge of history as Hitler took over the reins of power.)

The meeting went well, if one can judge from the entry in Gide's **Journal:** 'Trip to Wiesbaden, where I meet Stravinsky...Perfect agreement' (1951, p. 1159). And two weeks later Gide sent Stravinsky a copy of his verse for the first tableau - care of Ida in Milan. By 5 March the text of the second tableau was in his hands and he had to write flattering words to the anxious poet: he was 'seduced by the beauty of his magnificent words celebrating the ancient mystery of **Perséphone.**' But he wanted a little time to gauge the libretto's potential as a stage work before writing music worthy of his 'beautiful verses' (Stravinsky, Vera, and Craft, p. 316).

In reality Stravinsky was more than happy not to have to think about the work until his return to Paris to conduct a programme of his works at the Salle Pleyel on Sunday, 19 March. Ida and Gide turned out to support their collaborator. Gide brought Count Harry Kessler along with him, although he seems to have been more interested in Ida than Stravinsky. He noted in his diary: 'We...met there Ida Rubinstein and Guy de Pourtalès. I had not see her since 1914. She has become an old woman, strangely shrivelled' (p. 450). True, Ida at forty-seven no longer looked like a woman of twenty-eight and certainly advancing years did not suit her emaciated looks. But after nineteen years what changes must she have seen in Kessler?

Even at this point Stravinsky was still mainly concerned about settling his contract with Ida and details continued to worked out over the following month. But Ida was clearly more interested in the creation of a new work of art than in contractural clauses and assiduously cultivated Stravinsky, whom she knew was worried and distracted by severe, apparently chronic colitis. She invited him to dinner: **'Cher maître et ami,** please give me the great pleasure of coming to my house next Friday April 17 with Madame Debussy and Nadia Boulanger...We will dine according to your diet' (Stravinsky, Vera, and Craft, p. 299). One can only hope that he had abandoned his diet of the previous year when mashed potato was the only item on the evening menu. That may not have worried Ida but Emma Debussy and Nadia Boulanger needed more to sustain them.

By the beginning of May 1933 Stravinsky had begun composing **Perséphone,** a major task that took him months to complete. But the work did not confine him completely to his desk. At the end of May Ida took him and Gide along with her to Saint-Louis-des-Invalides to listen to a boys choir, which they 'dreamed of borrowing for the third tableau of **Perséphone'** (Gide, 1951, p. 1171). In the event, a choir capable of tackling the music had to be imported from Amsterdam.

Otherwise, Ida tried to make herself useful by helping Stravinsky to find a suitable flat in Paris where he could work in peace. He was very grateful, although he was less pleased when she kept making discreet inquiries about the progress of his work. He thought it strange that she should telephone him one day and ask Païchadze about the project the next day. Païchadze made a rather sharp retort to his complaint: 'Why are you so astonished that Ida Rubinstein talks to **me** about your work? What else can she talk about? She wants to know not only from you but from other people, too, which only shows the trepidation and respect she feels for you' (Stravinsky, Vera, and Craft, p. 316). But this was only a minor irritation compared with the problems that Gide soon began to cause the composer.

Gide's **Perséphone** was a relatively straightforward treatment in verse of the Homeric hymn to Demeter, the Greek myth of the changing seasons: Persephone, the daughter of Mother Earth, Demeter, is ravished by Pluto, god of the Underworld, and carried off to be queen in his sombre kingdom. Winter descends on the earth and spring only returns when Persephone is brought back to the living world to join her terrestial husband Triptolemus. But into the myth Gide tried to inject social concepts inspired by his current enthusiasm for communism. Persephone is greeted in the Underworld by a crowd of shades who look hopefully to her as a ray of sunlight in their dark world. The narrator Eumolpus exclaims (Stravinsky, Igor, and Gide, pp. 35-6):

> Perséphone, un peuple t'attend.
>
> Tout un pauvre peuple dolent

                    Qui ne connaît pas l'espérance.
And Persephone responds to their joyless plight by redeeming them
through self-sacrifice - the concept is strangely close to immolation in
the Christian tradition. She brings the light of spring to them for six
months in the year by returning to live in the Underworld with her
infernal husband Pluto.

   Just before rewriting the poem Gide paid a visit to a coalmine and
instantly conceptualized the situation: the miners represented the
prisoners in the Underworld, the down-trodden labouring masses. Like
Persephone's shades, they too awaited the coming of a humanitarian
social system in which all would enjoy an equal share of the light.

   Whatever Ida and Stravinsky thought of Gide's romantic concept of
communism, nobody could take it too seriously in the context of his
poem: it was heavily overladen with symbolism and imagery that had gone
out of fashion almost forty years before. Persephone, for example, is
tempted to stay in Hades permanently by being offered a jewelled cup
with water from the River Lethe; she first realizes the misery of the
shades by gazing into a narcissus; she is reminded of her earthly duties
by eating a pomegranate - appealing in its own way but too effete to be
the language of political polemics!

   Stravinsky took the law into his own hands. He consulted Gide on the
syllabification of his poem and proceeded to impose upon it rhythmic
patterns that stressed the importance of the music rather than the
words. Stravinsky himself thought his approach so revolutionary that it
warranted an explanatory article in **Excelsior** at the time of the
première (1934, p. 4):

   In music, which is time and regulated pitch, as distinct from the
   confusion of sound found in nature, there is always the syllable.
   Between it and general sense - the style permeating the work
   -there is the word, which channels straying thought and succeeds
   in making discursive sense. Now the word, more often than aiding
   the musician, constitutes a cumbersome intermediary for him. For
   Perséphone I only wanted syllables, beautiful, strong syllables,
   and then a plot. In this wish, I congratulate myself in having
   encountered Gide, whose text, highly poetic but unstartling, came
   to provide me with an excellent syllabic structure.

   For music is not thought. One says **crescendo** and **diminuendo**:
   music that is really music does not rise or fall according to the
   temperature of the action...Music exists solely in order to create
   order: to pass from an anarchic and individualistic to a
   controlled state, perfectly conscious and provided with guarantees
   of vitality and durability.

Stravinsky was not altogether sympathetic towards Gide. He later grumbled: Gide had been 'warned in advance that I would stretch and stress and otherwise "treat" French as I had Russian' and yet 'the musical accentuation of the text surprised and displeased him' (Stravinsky, Igor, and Craft, 1960, p. 150). Stravinsky was probably nearer the truth when he suggested another reason for the poet's reaction: 'The...explanation is simply that he could not follow my musical speech. When I first played the music to him at Ida Rubinstein's, he would only say **"c'est curieux, c'est très curieux"**, and disappeared as soon afterwards as possible' (ibid., p. 150).

Gide went further. He refused to attend rehearsals and was not to be seen at any of the performances, although he did appear at a private unstaged preview presented at the home of Stravinsky's old friend and staunch champion, the Princesse Edmond de Polignac. But that was a far from happy occasion and it left a clearer impression on the composer than the première itself: 'I can still see the Princess's salon, myself groaning at the piano, Suvchinsky singing a loud and abrasive Eumolpus, Claudel glaring at me from the other side of the keyboard, Gide bridling more noticeably with each phrase' (Stravinsky, Igor, and Craft, 1968, p. 36).

Stravinsky grew less and less charitable about Gide's libretto. He dismissed it as **'vers de caramel'** and later suggested that for any revival of the work his 'first recommendation...would be to commission Auden to fit the music with new words' (ibid., p. 37).

On 24 January 1934 Stravinsky completed the full score for **Perséphone**, a major landmark in his output (and his only commission for performance in France in the ten years after Diaghilev's death), a **mélodrame** for orchestra, baritone solo (sung by the narrator Eumolpus), full chorus and boys choir (functioning jointly as the traditional Greek chorus) and reciter (the role of Persephone herself). But long before this date Ida had engaged Jacques Copeau to produce it. By mid-October 1933 he had chosen to work with the young designer André Barsacq, with whom he had just collaborated on a production of **Le Mystère de Sainte Ursula** in the cloisters of Santa Croce during the May Festival in Florence.

On 20 October Gide went to a working dinner at Ida's house with Copeau, Barsacq and Stravinsky and soon found his ideas for a 'realistic' production being briskly waved aside. He left a bitter description of the event (1952, pp. 20-1):

'You see,' my friend Copeau said, 'there is no question of presenting the action of the drama itself to the public. We must proceed through illusions.'

'Yes,' Stravinsky then exclaimed, 'it's like the Mass...The

action itself must be implied...'

'So I thought to myself,' Copeau continued, 'that everything could take place in a single place, thanks to the narrator who would just give a recital, a reflection, of the facts themselves. Everything in a single place: a temple, or better, a cathedral...'

I felt lost for Ida and Stravinsky tried to outdo each other in their approval.

'But, dear friend,' I tried to object, 'I did clearly indicate for the first act : a sea-shore...'

'Yes, the narrator will make that clear.'

'It's marvellous,' Ida said.

'And the second act, which must take place in Hades. How in your cathedral...?'

'Old friend, **we have the crypt,**' Copeau continued with such assurance that, that very evening, giving up the game, I set out for Syracuse to see again the ancient setting that I just happened to want.

At every stage in, the process of **Perséphone**'s creation Gide's preconceived ideas were more of a hindrance than a help. No self-respecting director would have stood for his interference, even if devoid of ideas of his own. The truth was that Copeau's plan to set the whole work in the framework of a Greek temple, with different backdrops to indicate the change of scene from the sea-shore to Hades and then to a hillside back on earth for the rebirth of spring, was ingenious. But nothing would soften Gide's attitude. Long after the event he continued to dismiss Copeau's ideas as boring, even though he saw nothing of the final production.

If Copeau's high reputation in the theatre guaranteed him no immunity from Gide's self-opinionated carpings, he was equally not immune from Stravinsky's spite, although on much more material grounds. The composer wanted him to engage his son Theodore as his designer. Copeau naturally refused: he had already put Barsacq to work on the project and, in doing so, had passed over an established artist in the person of José-Maria Sert.

By comparison with these difficulties, the choreographer's problems were slight. Ida had taken the bold step of employing Kurt Jooss - 'the one flower from the German dungheap', as her agent described him (Lester, fol. 1). The brilliant young English dancer Keith Lester had been engaged as one of the principals (his height made him doubly valuable to Ida) and with a mixture of awe and amusement he watched the choreographer at work: 'When an artist of Kurt's integrity searches for the true movement to fit the exact moment, then one must wait on his

Muse...Kurt's Muse was occasionally dilatory...Sometimes rehearsals stretched into the abyss of Time...; one was wracked with the ennui of being needed but not wanted. The expansion of minutes to enormous intervals of silent waiting for the flash of incandescent wings, for...Frau Muse herself, was benumbing' (fol. 6). But the results were worth waiting for. When Lester gave a display of some of his choreography to that lovable tyrant of the practice-room, Olga Preobrajenskaya, whom Ida had appointed as ballet-mistress, she instantly recognised its quality: 'Ah, Jooss looks for beauty and simplicity; he seeks a truth for himself' (fol. 11).

As for Ida, Keith Lester was not entirely uncritical of what he called her 'intrusion into the unlikely world of Movement' but he did develop a strong bond of sympathy for her. For one thing, with such a composite work as **Perséphone**, he felt that 'Ida was the only factor that truly fulfilled its function in such an assembly of the Arts and that the professional dancers leaped at the periphery of its meaning' (fol. 13).

Lester had been given one of the three leading male parts, Pluto's Servant, and all went well during rehearsals. Then Ida arranged that, in the final tableau, he should also dance the role of Triptolemus, her earthly husband. He was excited by the idea - until he came to rehearse the part: he had to kneel with his big toe bent under in true Greek style, while the newly arisen Persephone recited a long speech: 'Gide had gone to town,' recalled Lester, 'and by the time Ida got to what I thought was **"O ma terre reste pure"** I was in agony. It turned out that she said **"O mon terrestre époux"** but by then neither I nor my big toe cared very much whether it was bigamy or not' (fol. 13).

Only at the final working-rehearsal did his role as Pluto's Servant become complicated because he had no opportunity until then to work with his 'prop', the cup of temptation designed to seduce Persephone into staying in Hades. It had just been delivered from Cartier. Their biggest and best and made of silver, it 'weighed a ton'. When Ida saw it, she uttered a shriek: 'I'm meant to drink from it, not wash in it...Change it.' But the order was not carried out and Lester had to make the best of a bad job. He soon 'learned how to resist its centrifugal pull in turns and managed to get rid of it rather earlier than had been intended' (fol. 16).

Despite all these difficulties **Perséphone** impressed the audience as a balanced and well-rounded work when it reached the Opéra stage on 30 April 1934. Critical comment was predictably mixed. It was, after all, one of Stravinsky's boldest scores to date. What failed to impress some were qualities in others' eyes. Paul Le Flem voiced his opinion: 'The music...has nobility and grandeur...one rediscovers in it the mastery, the skilfulness of a musician who, renouncing the splendours of yesteryear, today prefers the neatness of a deliberately stripped-down style' (p. 9). Henry Prunières agreed: 'The work is magnificently balanced...The choruses are superb...counting among Stravinsky's greatest achievements. The music is austere, powerful, at times possessing an emotion of the rarest nobiltiy' (1934, p. 381).

Ida's performance earned some high praise. The critic from **Le Cri du Jour** went into raptures: 'Ida Rubinstein, sculptural in her poses, enchanted us with the silhouette of her impeccable lines and with her musical voice' (anon., 1934, p. 11). Elisabeth de Gramont waxed even more lyrical: 'Ida Rubinstein scans André Gide's poem equally with her voice and her poses. She seems like a great jet of white water under a faint rainbow.' Next to her in the audience a fascinated spectator, overwhelmed by such physical gifts combined with such spiritual ardour, murmurs: 'She's a supernatural being' (1937, p. 146).

This impression is all the more remarkable when one realizes what agonies of nerves Ida was suffering on stage. Keith Lester was amazed when he approached her during the second tableau: 'I found Ida in convulsions of stage fright, cowering on a palatial lie-low, the tongue, an inheritance from the pre-Olympian gods, working overtime to moisten and refresh the fevered lips, if not the fevered brow' (fol. 16). But all that the public saw was Ida 'incarnating Persephone in the most moving fashion, a living statue with poses at one and the same time natural and hieratic, as befitting a sacred mystery' (Prunières, 1934, p. 381).

Ida's role as a patron caused some comment. That was nothing new. But, for once, one of her critics made his point clear by spelling out his own terms of reference. Henry Bézanet felt that 'nobody would have a word to say against a patron as lavish as...Ida Rubinstein, if our composers, in spite of her solicitude, were producing masterpieces. We should learn to lose our patience and...simply ask Monsieur Rouché to mount, for the pleasure of our eyes and ears, such unpretentious and delightful ballets as **Gisèlle** or **Coppélia**' (p. 8). The voice of real authority spoke when Henry Prunières commented that he was well aware that the Paris theatre-going public was old fashioned to the point of being positively philistine, but that was no excuse for Bézanet's conclusion: 'The whole spectacle gives one a grand impression and one must congratulate Monsieur Rouché for having procured for the Opéra's public such a beautiful expression of art' (1934, pp. 380, 382).

Ida was proud of her part in the creation of this extraordinary and controversial work, although she only gave two more stage performances of it, on 4 and 9 May. It did, however, adapt quite well as a concert-piece. In this form it enjoyed considerable public success - and also some private success. On 18 May the Princesse de Polignac gave it a second hearing in her salon. Afterwards the young writer Julian Green confided to his diary how impressed he was by its 'rhythms of Cyclopean power' (p. 215).

Whatever her plans were, whatever Gide expected, Ida did not use **Perséphone** as the setting for her swan-song as a dancer. But it missed that distinction only by a matter of days.

CHAPTER 16

Royal Mistress and Amazon Queen, 1934-1935

The curtain came down on **Perséphone** and the audience flowed out into the corridors and moved towards the bar (Rivollet, p. 7):

> Crowned with their top hats, the nice, timid season-ticket holders are cautious. It appears that the **fauves** are there, menacing: you know them well...these dictators of taste, these vehement oracles who force their likes and dislikes on one, these mysterious augurs followed by their thurifers: negresses dyed blonde, the smallest of duchesses naked under swathes of cellophane, a **lady** in a jet dinner jacket with gold facings, who strain their ears, and, of course, the potentates of fashion, Chanel and Schiaperelli...
>
> Is the Prince Jean-Louis de Lucinge trying to defend the cause of **Perséphone** by himself?...
>
> 'Another whisky!'

During the first interval at the Opéra on 30 April 1934 opinion - predictably - was divided. By the second interval - again predictably - there was a much greater concensus of opinion: **Diane de Poitiers**, a masque-like ballet with music by Jacques Ibert to a libretto by Elisabeth de Gramont, had just been given its première.

Ida initiated the project in May 1933 when she approached her friend and fervent admirer Elisabeth de Gramont, a voluntary exile from high society in Natalie Barney's 'alternative' world. She was looking for a plot for a new ballet. She wanted something other than a classical subject, perhaps for a change something from the Renaissance period.

Elisabeth de Gramont responded by sketching out a delightful scenario consisting of three decorative tableaux, based on the life of Diane de Poitiers, the influential mistress of Henry II of France. Diane is first shown surrounded by her court, in which Venetian ambassadors, Russian dancers, boyars, Spanish lords, captive Incas and a merchant from Orvieto vie with each other to pay homage to their beautiful hostess. They offer her a bow and she dances a **divertissement** in honour of her mythological namesake, the equally beautiful (but chaste) goddess Diana the Huntress. The second scene depicts the king returning from the chase to surprise her in her garden, bathing her body in the morning dew, an allusion to Acteon's intrusion into the goddess's private world but a happier intrusion because it leads to a rapturous **pas de deux** between the lovers. The final tableau takes place on a summer night in a great port where crowds of sailors and workers, women and great ladies, press round to join the king in honouring his beloved Diane.

This literary confection inspired Jacques Ibert to write a sparkling score, based largely on themes from sixteenth-century songs and dances. In the first tableau it is not difficult to recognise the strains of Passereau's madrigal **Il est bel et bon.** (An **oboe d'amore** and a basset horn slipped into the orchestra to provided additional 'period' flavour.) In the second scene Jannequin's **Chant des oiseaux** provided a thematic ground-work. And in the last episode dances by Claude Gervaise were reworked to create the right atmosphere. The overall result was masterly, colourful and, as always with Ibert, effervescent. The whole score fell neatly into the three main movements of the symphony: **allegro, andante** and **finale**; and later on Ibert had no difficulty in recasting the music as two popular symphonic suites.

Ida recruited Alexandre Benois to create suitably grand sets and costumes to enchance the late Renaissance ambiance of the music and the scenario. The choreography was arranged by Fokine - his first task on his return to Paris after a lengthy absence in Australia and the United States.

According to Keith Lester, Fokine's arrival in Paris was largely instrumental in preventing open warfare from breaking out in Ida's troupe. The Russian émigré dancers - the **gaspoda,** as they were familiarly known - were insanely jealous of non-Russian interlopers in the ballet world. Any mark of favour shown to an outsider provoked reprisals. 'All Russians have a built-in persecution complex that, like a thermostat, warns them that life is getting too much for them,' Lester concluded. The **gaspoda** had the 'slave mentality of Czardom in their souls' that only responded to the master-figure, such as Fokine or Ida. 'Their abasement, always laced with resentment, was a demand for protection.' This love-hate relationship with the necessary master often resulted in petty bitchiness. In the wings one evening Lester overheard the **gaspoda** discussing Ida. They were in fine form: 'Madame's dancing has improved since her sixty-ninth birthday.' Lester's comment was just as uncharitable: 'They were too kind: it had not' (fol. 3).

Fokine's arrival not only contained civil war in the company; it also resulted in some original choreography. For **Diane** he successfully created dances in a sixteenth-century style, unlike anything else in his whole output. He visited libraries and researched as thoroughly as possible the dance patterns of the early modern era. And one day, quite by chance, he came across interesting documents that helped him to 'recreate' an Inca serpent dance for the first scene - though how Incas came to be at the court of a French king in the first place is a question that defines the historical imagination!

Diane's première provoked a flood of compliments. Pierre La Mazière declared that it was 'brilliant, lively, graceful and entertaining'

(p. 20). Bézanet thought the choreography pleasant and the score ingenious (p. 8). In the **Revue Musicale** Alexandrine Troussevitch described the dances as 'rich and precise...the spectator's dream of bliss' (p. 395).

André George focused on Ida as Diane: 'Madame Rubinstein possesses the royal bearing, the elongated elegance that Jean Goujon bestowed, so precisely, on his **Diane d'Anet,** or Cellini on his **Nymphes**' (p. 8). Henry Prunières commented on the sumptuous overall effect of the ballet and commended Fokine's 'admirable mastery'. He concluded by confessing how much he like the pavane and galliard, the central **pas de deux** danced by Ida and Vilzak (1934, p. 382). (This partnership was rather apt because the discrepancy of ten years in the dancers' ages reflected the exact age-gap between the historic Diane de Poitiers and Henry II, whose relationship bordered on the OEdipal.)

Ida's opening night ended with a familiar work, **Boléro.** If all else went wrong, it could be counted on to send the audience home in a good mood. On stage Keith Lester, as one of the men sent wild by Ida's dancing, was less happy (fols 18, 21):

> On...her enormous, circular table, the size of a skating-rink...Ida did her utmost to be Andalusian, passionate, flexible, savage and voluptuous. We all crept round and round, crouched over the rim of the table till at last the music ended and the descending curtain released us from what must have looked like a procession of lumbago sufferers at some gypsy Lourdes, conjuring the divinity of Flamenco Chorea...We could hardly forgive Ravel for **Boléro.**

But if Lester really expected an ounce of sympathy from a Paris audience, enchanted by the ballet's exotic sights and sounds, he would wait in vain.

On 4 May this final item on the programme was replaced - for the sake of variety - by Ravel's **La Valse** with choreography by Fokine. It too enjoyed a predictable success, although some people were less moved by Fokine's version because, though 'expert enough, it lacked Nijinska's strangeness' (ibid., fol. 17).

The last ballet added to the repertoire for 1934 was **Sémiramis.** It first saw the light of day at a **répétition générale** on 6 May. The première followed five days later on 11 May. Compared with the other new works, it had a long gestation. Scarcely had the curtain come down on **Amphion** in the summer of 1931 before Ida asked Paul Valéry to provide her with a libretto for a new **mélodrame.** Honegger could be relied on to produce a suitable score. But well over a year passed before the composer received the text. Valéry had already dealt with the chosen theme in an early poem but, recasting it for the stage, he felt that he must create an altogether more substantial work.

The story of Sémiramis, the amazon Queen of Babylon, made a splendid subject for a spectacular ballet. In the first scene Sémiramis (Ida) appears as the warrior, conqueror of empires, entering her capital in triumph. After walking over the backs of abject and submissive captive-kings, she makes them pull her chariot, while a cohort of amazons surrounds her like a palatine guard. The idols of the conquered are beaten down, broken up and burned. Then follows a love scene between the tyrannical queen and a handsome captive. Having enjoyed the ecstasy of the erotic moment, the prisoner receives a present from his royal lover: a dagger, with which he must kill himself as he is cast from her tower. In the last scene Sémiramis, after a long monologue in which she accepts the fate written in her horoscope, allows herself to be immolated as a loving sacrifice to the sun-god.

Honegger received the libretto late in 1932 and composed the music to a deadline of May 1933. Ida clearly had plans to mount **Sémiramis** that season but postponed it at the last moment - too late to benefit Honegger, who regretted having to rush the work: he was attracted by the text and would have liked more time to develop his ideas with Valéry. He later recalled the collaboration in wistful tones: 'He submitted a fine project to me which, alas, we did not have the leisure to complete. This would have begun with a text in prose; then the prose would have been relaxed towards a more rhythmic poetry, which, in turn, would have given way to music at the precise moment when the power of words came to a halt' (1966, p. 109). And Valéry's well-intentioned attempts to solve their problems were not always very helpful. Honegger revealed that Valéry thought of **Sémiramis** as an almost religious work and so (1934, p. 4)

had wanted all the music in the first scene to be written for organ; this instrument, with its coldly majestic character, seemed the most suitable for the purpose.

This idea was impracticable. It was in effect nearly impossible to find in any theatre an instrument with the necessary power and volume. We then decided to replace the organ with an ensemble of wind instruments, in an attempt to recreate an archaic colour, tender and barbaric at the same time.

Boldly I went to the Opéra to see Monsieur Sax, director of the brass section, who, with completely good grace, showed me an extraordinary collection of all sorts of instruments constructed by his father...and by himself. I heard there a double-bass trombone descending to unusual depths, bass-trumpets, a strange trombone with several bells, as well as the whole family of saxhorns.

Alas! with the composer's characteristic faint-heartedness, I did not dare introduce into the orchestra all these instruments whose addition could, however, have been so effective. I was afraid of making the work impossible to perform in every theatre except the Opéra. So I contented myself with the saxophone, the double-bass trombone, the double-bass clarinet, to which I added two sets of ondes Martenot.

Honegger may have achieved a happy enough compromise over that problem but Valéry continued to make impracticable suggestions. Honegger wondered out loud how he should treat Sémiramis's long speech in the third scene: 'When I wanted to halt the music for the words, to give the text its full value, Valéry half jokingly, half seriously said, "Run a little tremulo under it for me!" And the monologue lasted for seventeen minutes!' (1966, p. 109). None the less, Honegger did relish 'the joy of work accomplished at Valéry's side. He was not only a great poet but a charming man as well. At every moment he found the opportunity or pretext to develop an idea with an extraordinary power of expression' (ibid., p. 109).

Honegger need not have had so many doubts about **Sémiramis**: his score was - and remains - a masterly and accomplished piece of work that aptly conveyed the atmosphere of the Assyrian world. The dark eroticism of the second scene, in which the ondes Martenot underline the sinister voluptuousness of the cruel queen, was particularly effective.

Honegger's uneasiness over the music affected his feelings about Fokine's choreography. Keith Lester, who had been given the role of Sémiramis's ill-fated lover, found that 'his music was at first difficult to move around in. As in swimming one has to get used to the new element' (fol. 18). Honegger was clearly aware of this and overreacted by interfering whenever he thought that some piece of choreography created more problems than it solved (fol. 19):

'If that part remains in,...people will laugh.'

Fokine drew himself up to his full classic height and beetled his brows. 'I have mounted a hundred ballets; no one has ever laughed.'

'Oh dear,' thought Lester, 'how awful! Two of them were comedy ballets.'

But before the work reached the stage Lester had many other eye-opening experiences. One of the most astonishing occurred while at Ida's house for a private rehearsal. He was given a little room to change in: 'Around the walls...were shelves on which were drawn up a legion of shiny cardboard boxes of oval shape. After a few days I could resist the temptation no longer...I had a look into one of them...It contained a pair of shoes, a hat and a pair of gloves all to match. I peered in expectant amazement at several others: their contents were the same. I was astounded and slightly repulsed' (fol. 10).

Yet Lester developed a strangely close relationship with Ida. He knew how to make her relax and laugh. And Fokine, appreciating how perfectly he could complement her stage movements, enlisted his help to overcome basic problems. One day, 'weary with teaching Ida how to stand without the traditional hand-on-hip of the **diseuse,** he said to (Lester): "She likes you. Try to stop her doing that terrible position"' (fol. 10).

But, occasionally, Fokine had to come to Lester's rescue. During a private rehearsal he informed him that he had a hole in his tights. Madame might find it embarrassing. Lester 'hurried to close the offending gap and hoped that it had not caused any psychological upheaval' (fol. 10).

What Lester meant by a 'psychological upheaval' is not clear - unless one wants to read something into another 'incident': he found that his costume for the first scene was very scanty, 'a diminutive, mini-skirt, that went only three quarters of the way round, leaving the right side of the body completely bare...A charming design but accident prone... Mounted on a fairly reliable G-string, the effect was achieved, but it would not have withstood a tug...Fortunately the first act was comparatively static and Ida had on so much armour that she could not get very excited' (fol. 19).

The second tableau might have proved more compromising, since they both ended up in bed, but it was 'so large a playground that the intimate gestures of love were more like long-distance signals.' Moreover, the captive-lover 'spent most of his time on the floor, whilst Ida, mistress of Valéry's lines, struggled with Fokine's' (fol. 20). Indeed, Lester was sure that Ida was beginning to find the physical effort of dancing a considerable strain. She was much more at ease when reciting her lines and he admired her 'ringing voice: for, let there be no doubt about it, Ida had a splendid and resonant tone that did justice to the wonderful verse. The sound was full stereophonic, tinted with Victoria plums' (fol. 9).

The critics' reaction to the première on 11 May ranged from the muted to the enthusiastic. Gilbert Chase of the **Musical Times** cast an objective eye over the whole production and then focused on the music: 'There were vigorous rhythms, the strident brass, the acidulous harmonies. Technically, this was good ballet music' (p. 557). But then it was so difficult to judge the public's reaction to a new work such as

Sémiramis. Honegger's biographer, Marcel Delannoy, was highly sceptical about 'the "sophisticated" Parisian first-night audience, who, when in the dark, sneered on hearing Paul Valéry's text, and then applauded when the lights went up' (p. 133).

There was nothing hypocritical about the praise lavished on the **mélodrame** by Suzanne Demarquez. She thought that 'Honegger's music, from its first bars, exactly reflected...Valéry's thought, as did Jacovlef's sets.' And after a detailed discussion of the finer musical points, she turned to Ida who, she thought, had 'found, in Sémiramis, a role which suits her plasticity perfectly. Her appearance on the war-chariot, the triumphant movement of her ascending towards her throne, the gesture of death that ended in tender supplication, are visions which will long be remembered' (p. 46).

Memories, indeed, were all that were left. When the curtain came down on the last night of Ida's ballet season on 21 May 1934, Parisian audiences never saw her dance again. However, despite confiding to Gide that after **Perséphone** she would give up dancing, she does seem to have contemplated mounting at least one more season. For one thing, her correspondence with Jacques Rouché between June and August 1934 make it clear that she intended to employ the Opéra's musicians and choirs in the following season. Indeed, there was a sharp exchange between her and Rouché over paying the musicians during the summer recess. She lost the duel and cheques to the tune of 50,000 francs were duly handed over (BN Opéra, Ida Rubinstein, dossier I, fols 40-6).

But it would be wrong to overstress the differences between Ida and the Opéra's management. They did crop up from time to time but Ida's and Rouché's relationship was generally very good. Rouché put up with a lot of thoughtless public criticism for letting her use the Opéra, a state-subsidized theatre, for her productions. He made no bones about his admiration for her as an artist and **animatrice.** And indeed, it was largely due to his efforts over a number of years that she was made a **chevalier** of the Légion d'Honneur on 21 July 1934. He and Gabriel Astruc first began to campaign for the decoration in January 1926. They submitted lengthy lists of her charitable works and of the theatre productions mounted by her - but to no avail.

One reason for official reluctance to make the award, meagre enough in the circumstances, may have been her position as a stateless person. Her naturalization as a French citizen was given official approval only in February 1935, after Rouché personally interceded on her behalf with the Prefect of Police (ibid., dossier II, 25 Feb. 1935). But by this juncture her contribution to French cultural life, not to mention her and her company's nomination as the 'representatives of French artistry' at the 1934 Salzburg Festival, was enough to gloss over this technical problem and lubricate the wheels of the French honours-machine.

Rouché was the first to send her the good news. His letter was delivered to her yacht, the **Roussalka**, anchored at Cherbourg: 'I am happy to announce that the event that I wanted for you is official...my most sincere congratulations' (ibid., dossier I, fol. 20). Henry de Jouvenel and Paul Léon, who had lent support to her nomination, were given the task of delivering what Marguerite Long described as 'the modest ribbon to which the government limited its tribute...to Ida Rubinstein...and to her marvellous artistic gifts' (1971, p. 40).

Ida's yacht remained at Cherbourg no longer than it took the news to arrive because it was needed for her summer expedition. That year Walter Guinness (more lavishly honoured by his country with his elevation to the peerage as Lord Moyne on 1 January 1932) allowed his own yacht, the **Rosaura**, to be commandeered by the Prince of Wales for the fateful cruise that made public property out of his association with Wallis Simpson.

Ida returned to Paris later that summer to find a letter from Rouché waiting for her: as she requested, he had reserved the Opéra between 12 and 27 April 1935 for her next season; on-stage rehearsals would start on 15 March (BN Opéra, Ida Rubinstein, dossier I, fol. 22). The season was subsequently postponed until the end of May. Ida made advance payments to Rouché (ibid., fols 57-8) but nothing came of her plans. She did, however, dip into her ballet repertoire for performances outside Paris.

On 28 November 1934 Sir Henry Wood presented an all-Stravinsky concert in the Queen's Hall in London. He himself conducted the first part and after the interval the composer directed a concert performance of **Perséphone.** Although the choirs and orchestra were recruited locally, Ida made a point of reciting Persephone's part herself. René Maison also made the journey from Paris to sing the part of Eumolpus.

The concert was broadcast by the B.B.C. and it made some impression on the British listening public. The critic from the **Musical Times** thought that 'the music was agreeably free from shocks to the ear. Some of the chorus writing for female voice was delicately pretty' (McNaught, 1935, p. 65). For his part, Stravinsky confessed himself 'completely satisfied' with this performance - by contrast with the Paris performances where, he complained, his 'participation was limited to conducting the music'. And, for once, he was generous about his collaborators: 'Ida Rubinstein lent her valuable services, and so did René Maison, the excellent tenor who, with his musical flair, had so admirably rendered the songs of Eumolpus at the Paris performances'

(1975, p. 173).

Ida's final appearance as a dancer took place on 27 January 1935 in the Palais des Beaux Arts in Brussels. Her old friend the poet and diplomat Paul Claudel, French ambassador to Belgium, organized a gala concert in his capacity as honorary president of an association of Belgian mothers who were raising funds to help Russian mothers resident in Belgium. Why they chose Claudel as their president is a mystery, but it turned out to be a wise move. He suggested inviting Ida and her company because, with her impressive record of charitable works, he could almost guarantee her acceptance. She did accept and performed her last three ballets, **Perséphone, Sémiramis** and **Diane de Poitiers**, to an extremely enthusiastic audience. The applause lasted for a very long time after the final curtain came down - a happy conclusion to any dancer's career.

Many have speculated on the reasons for Ida's decision to give up dancing. Had her style become out of date? The **Times** obituary writer commented: 'Around her there clung till the end the atmosphere of a period which died with the First World War and was buried in the great slump' (anon., 1960, p. 15). There is perhaps a grain of truth in this statement: the lavishness of her productions was unusual in the inter-war period. But this tended to provoke her rivals' envy, not their condemnation. Otherwise work commissioned by her came from thoroughly modern, if not always radically avant-garde artists, writers and composers. Her penchant for classical or historical themes could be criticized. But she was certainly not alone in this and, besides, it was clear that she did not see them as opiates for refugees from the harsh realities of life, as d'Annunzio had suggested in a fit of post-war euphoria. Although some of her stage-works did have a predominantly decorative quality, most dealt with fundamental human problems that were as relevant to her own age as to the world of the Ancients. One thing is certain: her classical tastes did not inhibit the public from flocking to see her work. She seldom performed before anything but completely packed houses, a fact that some of her critics conveniently overlooked.

Money problems may have influenced her decision. The cost of mounting ballets was inhibiting for somebody like herself who combined a passion for extravagance in the theatre with the shrewdest business-sense in the stockbroker's office. She spent a fortune of her own (and others') money on her enterprises but, contrary to some opinion, she did not ruin herself in the process.

The simple truth was that, having reached her fiftieth year, she was too old to cope with the strain of a full ballet programme. She was psychologically incapable of standing aside and using her money, influence and good taste to create ballets in which she did not take a leading part. As soon as the burden of this vocation became too much to sustain, she simply abandoned the genre. She had always found dancing something of a physical strain and all her collaborators knew that she suffered agonies of stage-fright before - and even during - her ballet performances. Nobody understood why she persisted in pursuing a career that took such a toll in physical and nervous energy. Her whole career had been motivated by an overwhelming egoism that had resulted in some spectacular successes, as well as a few near failures. But then, exactly the same could be said of Diaghilev's career. If either of these unique individuals had refused to take artistic risks, the twentieth century would be the poorer for a legacy of remarkable cultural achievements.

One thing is certain: Ida gave up dancing when she felt that she could no longer adequately serve her Muse and not when critics or admirers felt she should.

CHAPTER 17
The Wise Virgins and the Maid, 1935-1938

Ida Rubinstein seriously contemplated mounting a season in 1935 with a significant choreographical element in the programme. Until March or even April she was still toying with the idea. External circumstances put paid to it but they did not significantly affect her decision to end her career as a dancer. They only brought her swan-song forward by a matter of months.

At the beginning of 1935 Ida was still nurturing the hope that Ravel would write a score for her **Arabian Nights** ballet **Morgiane**. Nothing came of a plan to include it in a season of ballets in October 1934. In February 1935 he still had not put pen to paper. In fact, he was incapable of doing so. The disease that progressively possessed his brain left his thoughts clear but his body was unable to articulate them. By the end of 1935 he could scarcely even sign his name. But his friends continued to hope that the disease would abate. Among those who tried to encourage him during his ordeal Ida was one of the most unobtrusive and the most practical. She arranged for Ravel's friend, the sculptor Léon Leyritz, to take him on an extended holiday to Spain and North Africa. Perhaps the rest would hasten his recovery. Perhaps the sights and sounds of Moorish Spain and Morocco would awaken his dormant creative forces.

On 15 February 1935 the two friends set off through Spain, going by way of Madrid and Algeciras to Tangiers and then to Marrakech, where they stayed for two weeks. Every evening, Ida telephoned to ask how the expedition was going and to arrange excursions for them. While at Marrakech she had them invited to a spectacular evening at the desert palace of one of El Glaoui's sons. Ravel was 'enchanted by the oriental splendour of the pageant arranged in his honour, with a hundred dancing girls, a native orchestra and Arab warriors leading magnificent black deerhounds' (Myers, p. 88).

At Fez the director of Fine Arts gave him a conducted tour of his spectacular residence and gardens. He wondered if their opulence would inspire Ravel to write a truly Arab work. The composer's answer was quick: 'If I wrote anything Arab, it would be far more Arab than all this!' (ibid., p. 88). **Morgiane** was clearly still very much in his thoughts.

The two friends' journey back through Spain, from Seville to the pass at Roncevaux, was equally colourful and stimulating. Their eyes absorbed the sights of ancient and traditional Spain, architecture and bullfights, all to the accompaniment of native music, food and wine.

Meanwhile, Ida had left for Bali on a much less conventional journey that involved a flight over the Easter Islands in a two-seater aeroplane. But before long she was winging her way back towards Europe again. At two o'clock in the morning Ravel and Leyritz were wakened by a ringing telephone. It was Ida just back from Bali: 'I can't tell you how beautiful the sunrise on the Acropolis at Athens was this morning!' (Jourdan-Morhange, p. 231).

But although the pleasure afforded Ravel was worth all Ida's efforts, his ideas on **Morgiane** remained unarticulated. There was only one last glimmer of hope. On the day of Paul Dukas's funeral in May 1935 he confided to his old friend, the composer Charles Koechlin: 'I have written down a theme. I can still write music' (ibid., p. 240). Alas, fate had played a cruel trick on him. That was all that he ever wrote of **Morgiane**. Not another note came from his pen during the last two tragic years of his life.

Ida's ultimate concern was for Ravel as a person. Even in February 1935, when organizing his holiday, she could scarcely have expected him to produce a score in time for a season in May 1935. Besides, by then she was preoccupied with other projects.

On 27 March 1935, at the Théâtre de la Monnaie in Brussels, she appeared in the role of Clytemnestra in Paul Claudel's translation of Aeschylus's Orestian drama **Les Choéphores.** Darius Milhaud had written an elaborate score for the tragedy as early as 1915 but, despite attempts by both poet and composer, nothing came of plans to have the work performed at that point. (Even then Ida was to be their Clytemnestra.) Only the music was given a hearing at one of the Concerts Delgrange on 15 June 1919. That in itself was a great success: the public realized that 'Milhaud had constructed an entirely revolutionary score in which percussion instruments accompanied human voices uttering cries of grief and groans of anguish together with natural sounds like those of wind' (anon., 1974, p. 20). But a decade and a half passed before a complete performance of the play with the music was arranged.

It did at last reach the stage because Claudel, as ambassador in Brussels, was anxious to make an ostentatious gesture of solidarity between France and Belgium in the face of the growing menace represented by Nazi Germany on their borders. During the first half of 1935 he presided over a series of cultural events in what he described as a Paris-Brussels season. But he naturally took a personal interest in the production of **Les Choéphores** and, although it was officially in John Dolman's hands, he was invited to supervise it. Claudel certainly made his presence felt. As Milhaud recalled, 'for the costumes and décors, he called on his faithful collaborator Audrey Parr, who...did her best to translate in her sketches the exact ideas he endeavoured to express to her in words...The spoken choruses were delivered by 'Les Renaudins' under Madeleine Renaud-Thévenet whose interpretation closely...followed Claudel's own idea of what he had been trying to convey' (p. 183).

He also tried hard to make Ida conform to his plans for staging and production but he found that a more difficult task - as his correspondence with Milhaud clearly shows. However, the end result was highly satisfactory. Claudel described the three performances that took place in Brussels (on 27 and 28 March and on 17 May 1935) as 'unforgettable'. And he made a point of adding: 'Ida Rubinstein who took the part of Clytemnestra was admirable in it' (1965, p. 421) - so admirable that he made every effort to extend the life-span of the production.

Successful performances were given in Rennes in 1936 and immediately Claudel thought of bigger and better things. But there was a hitch in his plans. On 20 September 1936 he wrote to Milhaud: 'I know nothing at all about Ida who seems to have disappeared into thin air. This is a pity: for I should very much like to engage her to revive **Les Choéphores**. It is exactly right for the 1937 Exhibition. With the necessary adjustments the effect would be remarkable' (1961, pp. 234-5). But Claudel's plans were thwarted. A completely new, 'authentic' production of **Les Choéphores,** in a translation by Paul Mazon with music by Natalie Barney's erstwhile friend, Eva Palmer Sikelianos, elbowed its way into the official programme for the Exhibition and monopolized the stage of the Salle Pleyel in June 1937. However, performances of Claudel's version were given the following year in various French towns.

But all this was in the future and, while Ida was working with Claudel and Milhaud on the 1935 production, they were already deeply involved in another project, one that was on the point of going through a crisis. The work in question (which finally emerged with the title of **La Sagesse**) owed its conception to a combination of circumstances that occurred early in 1934. As Milhaud later recalled (pp. 212-13),

At one of Madame Long's receptions, we met...Ida Rubinstein, and talked to her about the Ohel players from Palestine, who differed from all other Jewish theatrical companies, usually strongly under Russian influence, and were playing at the Théâtre de l'Ambigu at the time. The primitive, rustic style of the production, its savagery almost, and the authentic flavour of the acting so delighted us that we had gone several times...Ida Rubinstein asked to be allowed to accompany us. At the end of the evening, she asked me if I should be interested in writing her a work based on a Biblical theme. I suggested a collaboration with Claudel, and she enthusiastically agreed.

But Claudel would first have to be persuaded, so Milhaud went to see him in person at his château at Brangues. Milhaud's intuition was quite correct: 'Claudel...at first refused point-blank to agree to a Biblical subject. What? Which one? He would not do it. Next morning at breakfast, Henri Claudel told (Milhaud) that his father had asked not to be disturbed, as he was working. About eleven o'clock, he came in with the completed scenario of **La Sagesse,** based on the Parable of the Wedding Feast' (p. 213).

By August 1934 Claudel had drafted out the script of what was, in effect, a lyric drama. He provisionally called it **Le Festin de la sagesse.** (It is a mystery why he finally gave it the title of **La Sagesse** with all its associations with an imprisoned Verlaine in a frenzy of self-flagellation after his affair with Rimbaud.) But, for once, Claudel was unsure of himself. He positively invited suggestions for modifications. Milhaud made a few. Claudel adopted them and then wrote to him on 14 August: 'My project is entirely at your disposal and you may do with it what you wish. Let's hope that it will please Ida. If for her part she has some proposal to make, I am ready to listen' (1961, p. 219).

Milhaud took Claudel up on the point and suggested that they should wait for Ida's comments before finalizing the text. 'The whims of patrons must be considered,' Milhaud remarked with the voice of experience, 'and one must take into account the possibility of her preferring another scenario' (ibid., p. 220). Claudel accepted his advice and waited for confirmation before going ahead with the work. He wrote to tell him so on 30 August and added: 'Above all don't have the **least scruple** about letting me know if **la patronne** prefers something else. I fear that my project may be a little severe and may not lend itself sufficiently to feminine display and so-called sumptuous productions' (ibid., p. 220).

In the end of the day Claudel's fears were justified. Ida responded amiably; plans went ahead but nothing was settled very quickly. She may well have felt that the Parable of the Wise and Foolish Virgins – surely one of the least colourful in the whole Gospel – lacked stage-potential. She may have hesitated over Claudel's ideas on her own role in the drama. As he explained to Milhaud on 2 October, 'I.R. **(sic)** would only have a mimed and choreographed part' (ibid., p. 221). But how was he to know that at that precise moment she was contemplating abandoning her career as a dancer?

Be that as it may, by December 1934 he had recast the last three parts of **La Sagesse** and was convinced that the public would be stunned by it.

Meanwhile, preparations for the various Brussels productions of 1935 distracted Claudel, while Milhaud threw himself into the task of writing the music. By the beginning of May the first two parts of the score were complete enough for him to play them to Claudel and Ida at her house in Paris.

On 20 June Claudel wrote to Milhaud asking him to join him and his family and Ida at Aix-les-Bains for discussions but, he added, 'It would be very useful if we could have a little council of war beforehand' (ibid., p. 226). The two collaborators did discuss production details but Claudel remained unhappy. On 22 July he complained to Milhaud that Ida had not given him any money and had said nothing more about the project. Would she keep her promise? He had gone to an enormous amount of trouble and all that he had received was a note from her secretary saying that they were in complete agreement. 'If I thought that Ida were not as good as her word,' he declared, 'I should break off everything immediately' (ibid., pp. 228-9).

But Claudel did continue his work and, by the beginning of August 1935, he completed a major revision of the text. He contacted Ida on her travels and, in reply, received - as he put it - 'one of those effervescent telegrams of which only she has the secret.' Now she was on the point of leaving for Jaffa 'in order to take a rest(!)' - or was it Java? Claudel was not sure (ibid., p. 230). But one thing he did know: she would not return until the end of September. Meanwhile, the Opéra had been definitely booked for the end of March 1936.

La Sagesse's production was, in fact, postponed again and again. As late as September 1938 a contract was signed for its première at the Opéra on 29 November. Ida had Claudel's text printed by the **Nouvelle Revue Française** but went no further than that. The first performance of the work took the form of a broadcast on French radio in 1946. No stage version was mounted until the Venice Festival of 1949 - long after Ida had lost interest in it.

There are no grounds for assuming, as Claudel did, that she was lukewarm about the project from the beginning, although she clearly had reservations about it. The main problem was that she planned to mount **La Sagesse** in a double bill with another work that turned out to be more substantial than expected and infinitely more colourful and robust. The result was that, like a cuckoo in the nest, it edged **La Sagesse** out. Ironically, Claudel was also the author of its text and Milhaud was partly instrumental in bringing it into existence. Indeed, without him, **Jeanne d'Arc au bûcher**, Ida's most important commission after **Le Martyre de Saint Sébastien**, may never have come about.

Around 1933 the arts students at the Sorbonne were gripped by a passion for performing thirteenth-century mystery plays, the sort of things that mendicant friars went from town to town performing before popular audiences. A friend of Ida's since **Martyre**-days, Gustave Cohen, was largely responsible for this wave of enthusiasm. When Ida attended one of their productions in the beautiful Salle des Thèses of the Sorbonne in April 1934, she too was carried away by the general excitement.

Although completely absorbed in her Opéra season at the time, she did find a moment to discuss the idea of commissioning a modern 'mystery' with Honegger and Jacques Chailley, who, as an expert in early music and professor of musicology at the Sorbonne, had acted as musical director for the students' productions. Could the life of Joan of Arc be adapted as a suitable theme for a dramatic oratorio? They were taken by the idea and so Ida looked around for a writer with flair and imagination enough to produce an attractive libretto. Several names were considered, one of whom, a woman of letters (nobody seems eager to name her), specified that Honegger should be dropped in favour of a protégé of her own. Ida demurred and the awkward librettist found that she was the one who was dropped.

Perhaps Claudel was the man for the job. Ida hestitated. It was only a month or so since he had shown every sign of reluctance about tackling **La Sagesse**. But then he had changed his mind afterwards. So Ida enlisted Milhaud's help. Could he approach Claudel for her and ask him to write a scenario on the subject of Joan of Arc for Honegger? Milhaud caught the poet in Paris while **en route** for Brussels and passed on the request. The response was quick and abrupt: 'What...another Joan of Arc? No, I won't.' But, added Milhaud with a touch of deliberate naïvety, 'the rhythm of the train must have touched off his imagination, for on arrival in Brussels, his plan for **Jeanne d'Arc au bûcher** was already drawn up, and Madame Rubinstein received the precious manuscript a few days later' (Milhaud, p. 213).

Claudel's own account of how the springs of inspiration welled up is more picturesque. There is no doubt that to begin with he was not happy about the suggestion (1954, pp. 302-3):

> I have never liked the idea of taking a great person as the subject for a piece, because the author feels restricted by a situation too well-known to give him sufficient freedom of movement.
>
> I have recounted many times how I changed my mind, how a sign from Joan of Arc forced itself upon me during my train journey from Paris to Brussels. I saw clasped hands making the sign of the cross and, immediately after, the complete libretto of **Jeanne au**

bûcher was, so to speak, thrust upon me. On the whole I write pretty slowly, whereas the libretto of **Jeanne au bûcher** was written in a few days.

Divine promptings apart, a more mundane consideration may have influenced Claudel: the new work, with its enormous dramatic potential, could act as a foil to the much less exotic **La Sagesse,** if coupled together on the same programme. This would solve a problem that had been troubling him.

Considering how composers and writers had overworked the Joan of Arc theme about the time of her belated canonization in 1920, Claudel succeeded in producing a text that was sufficiently fresh in approach to stimulate even the most jaded of palates: Joan stands at the stake awaiting death throughout the drama that unfolds. One of her voices, Saint Dominic, calls to her. A dialogue between her and a monk, one of her accusers, follows. He explains her crimes and brands her as a 'heretic, sorceress, relapsed, cruel, the enemy of God', while Dominic reassures her that man's justice is not divine justice. Joan recalls the horror of her trial. She hears the sound of pens on parchment, scratching out words that she cannot read. Her judges appear like a pack of wild beasts, a ferocious tiger, a sly fox, a perfidious serpent and, aptly, a pig in Bishop Cauchon's mitre.

Dominic explains to Joan why her king has abandoned her. The Dukes of Bedford and Burgundy play courtly games with each other and she is the victim of the contest between Charles VII and Henry VI.

As bells sound, announcing that Charles, the King of Bourges, has become king of all France, the people hailing him with traditional songs from the provinces, Joan is secured to the stake. Visions of her childhood well up before her eyes, thoughts of spring in Domrémy, a symbol of hope after the cold and snow of winter. Joan reaches out for Saint Michael's sword: it is the symbol not of Hate but of Love; and the greatest act of love is to give one's life for one's loved-ones. Sinister, yelping voices penetrate her consciousness and suddenly, as the flames begin to crackle, Joan feels fear, like Christ on the cross. Then, as the flames mount, they make a mantle that envelops her body and she dies.

Honegger responded sympathetically to Claudel's libretto. He produced a score for full orchestra and chorus, with solo voices (taking the parts of the saints) and with a recited part for Joan except for a little snatch of song, which she sings in a thin, pathetic voice, all the more effective for not being professionally trained. Some of the orchestral sonorities were ingenious: ondes Martenot, insinuating and unctuous, underlining the tones of Joan's enemies, and pianos 'prepared' in mid-performance to sound like harpsichords at the court of Charles VII.

According to Honegger, Claudel was quite specific about the musical language in which his text should be expressed and provided him with line-by-line instructions. This would have infuriated a less confident composer. Honegger was charmed by his musical imagination, although he found it difficult to comply with some of his suggestions, such as, 'the music imitates the sound of beating a carpet' (Honegger, 1966, p. 111). But on the whole he appreciated Claudel's collaboration. Indeed, he confessed (ibid., pp. 110-12):

> One of the greatest joys of my life had been to have Paul Claudel as librettist...Unlike many literary figures, he showed great interest in whatever touched music...In the theatre, he knew how greatly music could contribute and...add value to the text...He forced me to penetrate the atmosphere, feel the density, the melodic contour, which he wanted, and which he entrusted to me to express in my own language...It was sufficient to hear Claudel read and re-read his own text. This he did with such plastic force...that the whole musical pattern emerged in relief, clear and precise, for whoever possessed a modicum of musical imagination.

Honegger worked on the lengthy score (eighty minutes worth of music) at Rigi Klösterli and at Perros-Guirec during the summer of 1935. A vocal version was completed on 30 August and the full score was ready by 24 December.

Meanwhile, Claudel was labouring under the misapprehension that plans for the production were advancing. On 30 September 1935 he wrote rather grandly to Milhaud: 'For **Jeanne d'Arc** I shall leave the work (on the sets) to Jacovlef or the painter that I choose. I am not concerned about it' (1954, p. 231). Alexandre Benois was finally engaged to provide designs but not until two years had elapsed. Because of production difficulties, lack of support from the Opéra's staff and finally the overburdened programme for the Exhibition in 1937, **Jeanne d'Arc au bûcher** did not see the public light of day until 1938 at a concert performance in Basle. French audiences had to wait until 1939. By that time Claudel had become very concerned, not to say alarmed at the slow progress of Ida's production plans for the new work and also for **La Sagesse**.

Her intentions were not at all clear. And the situation was further complicated by the fact that in 1934, the same year as the inception of **Jeanne d'Arc** and **La Sagesse**, she commissioned a third major work, **Le Chevalier errant**, which, unlike the other two, was to be a ballet with reciters and a choir. Ida almost certainly planned to mount it during some final ballet season that ultimately failed to materialize. Whatever her intentions, the resulting work was a substantial creation, a minor masterpiece in its own right.

Delighted by the success of **Diane de Poitiers**, Ida asked Jacques Ibert to write her a work based on Cervantes's **Don Quixote**. Once again she engaged Elisabeth de Gramont as librettist. However, although she sketched out an admirable scenario, consisting of four scenes from the life of the Don, the composer was less happy when he saw the verses that she expected him to set. Instead, he suggested that Alexandre Arnoux, a specialist in Spanish literature, should write the text. Arnoux obliged with every sign of enthusiasm and produced verses that aptly complemented Elisabeth de Gramont's scenario. They were exactly what Ibert wanted.

Le Chevalier errant was conceived of as a grand ballet in the eighteenth-century Italian manner and the Don himself was 'visualized, not as he is usually represented, the sad caricature of a hero tossed in the blanket of his own illusions, with his goatee-beard, cropped hair and haunted expression, but as he sees himself in the adventures which he lives through with great intensity, the true knight who, by giving himself, triumphs over his enemies' (Michel, p. 108).

Ibert completed his substantial score before the end of 1935 and delivered it to Ida. But by that time her plans were even more vague than before. She delayed so long that that Second World War intervened before anything definite was settled. It was not until 26 April 1950 that what turned out to be one of Ibert's best works reached the stage when the new director of the Opéra, Georges Hirsch, gave it a magnificent production. Serge Lifar created the choreography and also danced the role of Don Quixote. The part of Dulcinea was taken by a different dancer in each of the four scenes in order to highlight different aspects of her image. It was a clever device, though certainly not part of the original plan. In fact, Ibert had been very anxious to see Ida interpret the role and even resisted Jacques Rouché's and Charles Munch's suggestions for a production during the Occupation when she could not have taken part. But with the return of peace Ida adamantly refused to resume her stage career and alternative plans had to be made.

However, in 1935, when Ibert was writing **Le Chevalier errant**, Ida had no thought of giving up the theatre. She had every intention of keeping on the role of Clytemnestra in **Les Choéphores**. She was also concerned to prevent some of her commissions from failing into oblivion. On 23 February 1936 she played her part in presenting two of her brain-children to the public in their orchestral guise at one of the

Concerts Pasdeloup. After Ibert had conducted one of his symphonic suites from **Diane de Poitiers**, Ida joined the orchestra to recite her part in a performance of **Sémiramis**, conducted by Honegger. Both works created a good impression upon the audience, although Denyse Bertrand complained about what she considered Honegger's overaddiction to the use of ondes Martenot. Their strident abrasive tones, so she thought, did not blend well with orchestral textures. 'Be that as it may,' she added with a touch of generosity, 'one recognizes in **Sémiramis** Arthur Honegger's vibrant personality, his taste for vast works, his breadth of thought, expressed with power and clarity.' As for Ida, she had put all her 'style and seductiveness at the disposal of Sémiramis the Proud' (1936, p. 69).

And the following year Ida began to contemplate reviving another major work, even though three commissions still awaited their premières. She seemed intent on staging **Antoine et Cléopâtre** again. On 9 September 1937 Gide noted in his journal: 'Occupied all these last days on the translation of **Antoine et Cléopâtre**. The task which I undertook, at Ida Rubinstein's request, with the purpose of reducing the number of sets (and, therefore, the number of scenes), I really must master, as well as sewing together the scenes and filling in the gaps' (1951, p. 1272).

Why should Ida have wanted a scaled-down version of the play? Economic pressures? More likely she had learned a lesson from the public impatience with the excessive length of the 1920 production. Besides, by the late 1930s, endlessly lavish realism in the theatre was no longer very fashionable. But, whatever Ida's ultimate aim was, it is enough to say that the project went no further than Gide's agonizing at his writing desk.

But there could have been another reason for Ida's second thoughts about an opulent production of Shakespeare's tale of passion and death. As the years went by and her affair with Walter Moyne faded into a beautiful friendship, she became increasingly wrapped up in religion. Born a Jew and brought up with an inevitable veneer of Russian Orthodoxy, she turned more and more towards Catholicism during her years in France and finally joined the Church in September 1936 - an experience which, according to Claudel, made her 'drunk with joy' (1969, p. 157). A religious or, at least, a spiritual thread had run through many of her stage-productions since the creation of **Salomé** in 1908 (whatever the Holy Synod thought about the matter!) But from 1934 all the new works commissioned by her were religious in tone, even **Le Chevalier errant** where the emphasis is upon Don Quixote's own vision of himself as the true Christian knight.

The gathering of ominous political storm-clouds in the late 1930s only served to intensify Ida's almost mystical spiritual life. Acts of charity and personal renunciation motivated her existence. War itself would be the final turning-point in her life but, for the moment, it was a personal sense of loss that most affected her.

During the latter half of 1937 Maurice Ravel's disease worsened and he consulted Dr Thierry de Martel, a famous neuro-surgeon, a pioneer in his field. Extensive tests convinced him that there would be no point in operating on his brain. Neither Ravel nor some of his friends accepted this verdict as final and Ida set off by aeroplane to discuss the case with leading neurologists and neuro-surgeons in Germany, Switzerland and the United Kingdom. She saw anybody who could provide a ray of hope. Finally Dr Clovis Vincent agreed to operate to find out if the trouble was being caused by a brain tumour, although he basically agreed with Martel's opinion.

The operation was performed on 19 December but without any very conclusive results. Ravel rallied slightly but soon sank into a post-operative coma. On 28 December he died without regaining consciousness. During the whole period Ida and Marguerite Long were seldom far from his ‘bedside, hoping desperately for his recovery. Knowing that the operation had, in effect, cut short his life, their only consolation was that a creative artist's nightmare of seeing his expressive faculties atrophy before his eyes was over.

And within a very short time another great friend of Ida's was dead. On 1 March 1938 Gabriele d'Annunzio suddenly suffered a cerebral haemorrhage and died within a matter of hours. His death was not of the same tragic order as Ravel's. D'Annunzio had lived a full life and it had run its natural course: he died within twelve days of his seventy-fifth birthday and was by then something of a spent force. None the less, Ida was deeply affected by the death of the man whom she had loved with a sisterly affection for more than a quarter of a century and whom she had championed to the end. When, on 17 March 1933, André Gide had been tactless enough to express the opinion over her luncheon table that d'Annunzio was above all an actor, Ida rushed to his defence: 'People believe that everything is show with him. On the contrary he is very sincere.' Gide checked himself from commenting: 'True and that's what is so terrible about it' (Gide, 1974, p. 290).

Ida was much more sympathetic to those who showed unqualified admiration for the poet. One detects this in her correspondence with Gabriel Faure, a writer famed for his travel-books. In May 1933 he sent her a copy of his **En Veneto**, a description of Venetian scenes. She was touched by its poetic style and confessed: 'With your incomparable gift of evocation, you have made me nostalgic to see these places again.' And she expressed her impatience to read the book on d'Annunzio on which he was then working (BN, 16420, fols 83-4). The result, **Au pays de Gabriele d'Annunzio,** a twenty page guide to the countryside around Pescara, his birthplace, was slighter than expected. But when Ida found a copy waiting for her on her return from London at the end of November 1934, she was effusive in her praise: 'How enchantingly you evoke all the flowers and beauty spots. In a word what a magnificent presentation' (ibid., fols 97-8).

In 1935 d'Annunzio repaid her devotion by including a beautiful passage in his **Libro segreto,** in which he described the exquisite vision she had been in the far-off days of **Cléopâtre** and **Schéhérazade.**

The real tragedy of d'Annunzio's death was the way in which, after keeping him in virtual confinement for the last ten years, his 'jailer' Mussolini gave him a grand funeral. The poet may have been the prophet of Italian fascism, but its Messiah, Mussolini, all too clearly had become the personification of its defects and he was the man who stood by his graveside and uttered a mock-heroic panegyric while his true friends nursed their grief in private. Ida paid her last respects in her own distinctive way by giving two private performances of **Le Martyre de Saint Sébastien** in his memory during the summer of 1938.

D'Annunzio's death occurred while Ida was preparing for the long-awaited première of **Jeanne d'Arc au bûcher** (in a German translation by Hans Reinhardt) at Basle on 12 May 1938. She had to learn and rehearse her part, but the process also involved a retreat at the Dominican convent of Saulchoir at Tournai, where she prepared herself spiritually for an event which she regarded as a protestation of faith. Some of her friends were surprised to see her leave Paris in a chauffeur-driven car with her maid and her hairdresser in tow, but few doubted the sincerity of her feelings.

Meanwhile, in Basle Paul Sacher (in his own right a great patron of music, arguably the greatest in the twentieth century) is rehearsing the Kammerorchester and Kammerchor. Honegger, who has arranged the première with him, looks on. All goes smoothly until an orchestral player pretends not to understand his part. Should he play an F natural or an F sharp? 'Play what you like,' says Honegger with an apparent lack of concern. Laughter all round. Sacher is relieved to let the point pass. 'But, of course,' he reassures himself, 'Honegger knows that it should be an F sharp.'

The première of **Jeanne d'Arc** as a concert-oratorio was hailed as Honegger's greatest triumph since **Le Roi David** in 1921. With evident satisfaction Claudel noted in his journal: 'Immense success. 1000 in the audience. Endless ovations' (1969, p. 232). The critics offered only praise. They admitted to being staggered by the work's colour and dramatic impact (Appia, pp. 159-60):

> Paul Sacher was the moving spirit of this performance. His lucid and vital love of music gives him give the most natural sureness of touch. His faith causes him to overcome all difficulties, and his art allows him to translate the deep meaning of the works that he mounts...
>
> Ida Rubinstein portrayed Joan. Her intelligence and her personality fit her for so many exceptional roles that it is scarcely necessary to praise her.

Fair praise but greater was to come when she gave French audiences an opportunity to assess the masterpiece.

CHAPTER 18

Lucifer and the Gods of War, 1938–1940

The success of the Basle première of **Jeanne d'Arc au bûcher** encouraged Ida Rubinstein to forge ahead with plans for a new season at the Opéra in Paris. Productions of **Jeanne d'Arc** and **La Sagesse,** arranged for the period between 15 and 24 February 1938, were rescheduled for June. But even then the preparations were not completed in time. Ida was undeterred: she looked further ahead and engaged the Opéra for 29 November and 1 and 6 December 1938 for productions of **Jeanne d'Arc** and **La Valse** – which would not tax anybody's balletic skill. At the same time she booked the theatre for performances of **'Jeanne d'Arc, La Sagesse, Le Chevalier errant** etc.' (BN Opéra, Ida Rubinstein, dossier I, fols 72-3). She did not specify what was meant by 'etc.' but it is clear that, despite the backlog of commissions waiting to be mounted, she was planning to commission more works to add to her repertoire. And one of them was to be yet another stage work by Paul Claudel.

What made Ida turn again and again to Claudel for inspiration was probably not so much his reputation as France's most eminent poet as his intense spirituality. As her own interest in mysticism and religion took on almost obsessional proportions, his example meant a great deal to her. She once revealed something about his effect upon her when she said to Marguerite Long: 'If you knew my feelings...on seeing this great Christian, this great poet, Claudel – candle in hand, (in the Ash Wednesday) procession in Notre Dame!' (Long, 1971, p. 47). And the subject of her new collaboration with him was – predictably – religious, the story of Tobias and Sarah, taken from the Book of Tobit.

In 1936 Claudel had published an exegesis on this obscure Biblical book in **La Vie Intellectuelle.** Whatever its spiritual merits (and few theologians have ever taken it very seriously), the Book of Tobit had great dramatic potential. After all, there was something theatrical about Tobias's beloved Sarah who, before meeting him, 'Had been given in marriage seven times and...Asmodeus, that worst of demons, had killed her bridegrooms one after the other even before they had slept with her as man and wife' (Tobit 3.8). As for Tobias's encounter with the angel and his triumphant struggle with the fish in the River Tigris, that had all the ambiguity of a painting by Botticelli, all the more meaningful for a post-Freudian audience. When Ida approached Claudel in the late spring of 1938, the dramatic plan which they sketched out together emphasized the ambiguous element by casting her in the transvestite role of Tobias himself. The three planned acts were designed to stress the purely dramatic aspects of the story, but at the end of each act there was to be 'a long mimed development...for Ida' (Claudel, 1961, p. 240).

And who should be commissioned to write the music for **L'Histoire de Tobie et de Sara**? Ida had no hesitation in approaching Stravinsky. She had maintained a relatively close friendship with him since the production of **Perséphone**. She had played a part in patching up the long-standing quarrel between him and his erstwhile friend, Ravel's pupil Maurice Delage. In 1923 Delage had been foolhardy enough to criticize Stravinsky's development of a neo-classical style and the resulting rupture between them was not mended until 1938 when Ida, at Manuel Rosenthal's suggestion, invited them both to dinner at her house. And when she asked Stravinsky to compose music to Claudel's libretto, a piece that would be 'of large proportions, with chorus and declamation (an oratorio with staging)' (Stravinsky, Vera, and Craft, p. 318), he was quite sympathetic - surprisingly so since he disliked Claudel. It was Honegger who put his finger on Claudel's fatal flaw: 'Perhaps musicians might find his opinions a bit disconcerting: for example, an inexplicably tender feeling for Berlioz was balanced by a solid animosity towards Wagner' (1966, p. 110). In fact, only recently, on 26 March 1938, Claudel had published an article entitled 'The Wagnerian Poison' in **Le Figaro Littéraire**. It had infuriated Stravinsky, who thought it too stupid for words.

None the less, on 31 May discussions on their collaboration began and by 21 June Stravinsky's agent had worked out the business arrangements with Ida. However, one vital detail remained to be settled. Stravinsky was not in the least interested in the story of Tobias and, instead, insisted that the myth of Prometheus was a more suitable subject. Claudel was adamant and, on the same day as Ida was settling contractural details, he wrote to Stravinsky rejecting his **Promethée**. The inspiration for **Tobie** was flooding fast and nothing could stem it.

Claudel was naïve to imagine that Stravinsky would stand for his inflexibility and he soon found himself without a composer. But not for long. At the beginning of August 1938 Darius Milhaud wrote to him. He had seen Stravinsky's son a few days earlier and learned from him that 'his father would not do **Tobie**.' Milhaud had a proposal to make: 'If you are continuing with this work, I should really like to do the music' (Claudel, 1961, p. 239).

Claudel liked the idea and on 15 August wrote to him: 'I have already written to Ida that St(ravinsky) has backed out and that...you would seem to me the one most qualified to write the music.' Ida was clearly annoyed by this turn of events because Claudel received no reply from - as he put it - 'that elusive personality'. But he was undeterred and determined to take a hard line with her over **Tobie**: 'In any event, I want to grant her only an option limited to a certain time...I don't want to sell her the work purely and simply, as I did with previous scenarios. I have learned from experience' (ibid., p. 240). Experience might also have taught him that Ida had just as strong a will as he had.

It was almost certainly Claudel's attitude that dampened Ida's interest in the project. On 5 September one finds him explaining to Milhaud the contractural conditions that he wanted for the newly completed libretto: 'I have no intention...of selling the piece to Ida, but simply of giving her an option, say for two years, reserving for myself the right to intervene over its distribution etc.' (ibid., p. 241). What use would a two-year option have been to Ida? Claudel had surprisingly little idea of the practical difficulties involved in mounting full-scale theatrical productions. He was only concerned about his precious libretto and went on to describe the work in rapturous terms: 'The piece comprises three great spoken scenes and in addition what I call **lyric** parts where the music can come in, but in a **very subdued** manner, a little like in the litury or Erik Satie's **Socrate**. I should like to see inspiration mounting from a murmur to the vowel, the consonant, the word, the note, the chant and from there subside again' (ibid., p. 241).

But, despite their enthusiasm, both poet and composer were cautious enough to do no more than talk about the project until Ida returned from holiday in mid-October. And then she made it abundantly clear that she was not entirely happy with **Tobie**. On 16 November Claudel wrote Milhaud a sober note, saying that Ida approached the work without any sense of perspective: 'So for the sake of prudence I should not ask you to commit yourself to a difficult task. I have already landed you with enough white elephants.' And he added skittishly: 'After all I am only seventy years old and beginners must show patience!' (ibid., pp. 243-4).

The great scheme did, in fact, come to nothing. Milhaud did not attempt to write a score. And less than a month later, on 16 December, one finds Claudel writing to the founder of the Théâtre de l'Atelier, Charles Dullin, to arrange a reading of the text alone: 'This reading is of interest to a cettain number of friends. Don't forget that it should include a lot of music, mime and even cinema! - the thing having been written at the behest of that madwoman Ida Rubinstein' (1966, pp. 197-8).

Foolhardy she may have been but she certainly had her feet more firmly on the ground than the otherworldly poet. Besides, she had more than enough to do with all the preparations for her 1938-1939 season. She was also preoccupied with the creation of yet another new work, **Lucifer ou le mystère de Caïn,** her last completed commission.

This time her collaborators, René Dumesnil, who created a libretto out of Lord Byron's poem **Cain**, and Claude Delvincourt, who wrote the score, were more amenable to her suggestions. But there were other problems. Despite his achievement as winner of the Prix de Rome in 1913 and despite his eminent position as director of the Conservatoire at Versailles, Delvincourt was not at all sure that he could cope with a full-scale stage oratorio in three acts with a prologue. He was flattered by her confidence in him but maintained that 'she was deceiving herself and that he was not the right musician for her; up till then there was nothing in his work that justified such a choice and marked him out for an enterprise of such scope. Ida Rubinstein held firm, and because of her insistence and the advice of his friends, Claude Delvincourt let himself be convinced, though with difficulty and against his will' (Viollier, p. 12).

Delvincourt had good reason to hesitate: Dumesnil's libretto began with a prologue relating the expulsion from the Garden of Eden; it then elaborated the story of Cain up to his murder of Abel, wove in a substantial part for Lucifer himself and ended up with a choral section in which, against the background of Cain's remorse, the Redemption was foretold. But Ida's enthusiasm won the day. Here was a work that was as specifically Christian in its orientation as **Le Martyre de Saint Sébastien** and **Jeanne d'Arc** and, as such, more meaningful than **L'Histoire de Tobie**. She gave Delvincourt all possible encouragement and during **Lucifer**'s composition she even accompanied Dumesnil on a visit to the musician's family home in the priory of Hacquenouville near Dieppe. Dumesnil recalled a touching incident that took place during this visit (1960b, p. 8):

> I don't know how we came to talk about the organ of Saint-Jacques where Delvincourt was the titular organist: the fancy to go and hear it took him. Night was falling; Delvincourt had the keys to 'his church'; he took us there, and in secret, for her alone, we were treated to one of the most beautiful and moving recitals, completed by an improvisation on the **finale** of the new work intended for her.

Lucifer was finally completed in 1941 (the same year in which he achieved the distinction of being made director of the Paris Conservatoire.) It was accepted by Jacques Rouché for production at the Opéra but, because of wartime conditions, the two authors urged him to wait until more adequate financial resources became available. As a result **Lucifer** did not reach the Opéra's stage until 1949. It was, nevertheless, the theatre's first major creation since the Liberation and, as such, attracted a deal of attention. Serge Lifar's sterling work as producer and choreographer clinched its success. Ida herself had nothing to do with the production, although she had the satisfaction of knowing that **Lucifer** had finally gained the recognition that it deserved. The work that Delvincourt had been so reluctant to tackle in 1938 had turned out to be the crowning glory of his career.

Meanwhile, when work on **Lucifer** was still in its early stages, Ida was being pressed to produce the commissions already completed. But a disagreement between Serge Lifar and Honegger was standing in the way of **Jeanne d'Arc**'s French première. Claudel was perturbed by this but took it as a sign that Ida would press ahead and mount **La Sagesse** at the Opéra at the end of November 1938. But not so. She had the libretti of both works published, but on 20 October announced that their production would have to wait until the following April. On 24 October an angry trio, Milhaud, Honegger and Claudel, confronted Ida, who 'after a stormy explanation promised to mount the two pieces first in concert form, then on stage next May.' Claudel was still sceptical and scribbled in his journal: 'I don't believe a word of it' (1969, p. 248).

Jeanne d'Arc au bûcher, at least, did receive its French première in May 1939 but not at the Opéra. Monseigneur Courcoux, Bishop of Orléans, suggested that Ida might mount the work in Orléans on 6 May as part of the celebrations for the saint's feast day, which fell two days later. She accepted and, having rehearsed the work in Paris, she performed it as an oratorio before an illustrious audience spangled with representatives from the army, the church and the state. The papal nuncio Valerio Valeri presided over the proceedings.

Claudel noted in his journal that the work achieved 'the greatest success' (ibid., p. 268). And the critics agreed with him. Romain Rolland wrote in the **Ménestrel**: 'A première is a rare thing at Orléans, all the more so that of an incontestable masterpiece like **Jeanne d'Arc au bûcher**. One rediscovers in it the richness of inspiration of **Judith** and **Le Roi David**...The performance under the baton of (Louis) Fourestier was impeccable...Ida Rubinstein added the charm of a moving recitation to it' (p. 149).

René Dumesnil - in his official capacity as critic of the **Mercure de France** - enthused about Ida: She 'has just added an incomparable jewel to the crown of beautiful works which her good taste has created. She was an admirable Joan - and so was doubly associated with the authors when a transported public...gave the work a triumphal welcome at the Théâtre (Municipal) in Orléans' (1939, p. 198).

Claudel, however, was still not satisfied. Less than two weeks later, on 18 May, he noted in his journal: 'In effect Ida is not keeping her promise to mount the two works at the Opéra. Yet another illusion!'

(1969, p. 269). But Ida was not idle. On 15 June she gave a repeat performance of **Jeanne d'Arc**, if not at the Opéra, at least in the newly-built theatre in the Palais de Chaillot and achieved what Claudel himself agreed was 'an immense success' (ibid., p. 273), even though this time the work was given without the sets designed by Benois and without the choreographed section arranged by Boris Romanov for the performance at Orléans.

Denyse Bertrand confirmed Claudel's impression. She spoke for most when she said (1939, p. 171):

> The dramatic oratorio...is an authentic masterpiece. This word is much abused but here one must use it in its highest and fullest sense. The other evening, in the vast nave of the Palais de Chaillot, there was a breath of grandeur, nobility and pure emotion that wafted the audience towards the spheres. (And she lavished praise on all the artists, particularly Ida.) One must...pay her the homage that her marvellous initiative merits. Patronage on such a masterly scale, what can be more priceless? But...Ida Rubinstein is above all a very great artist. As much in her sculptural beauty as in the quality of her voice, she is an extremely moving Maid. The accents, the silences, everything is exactly right - and with such art and such natural ease!

Truth be told, some of the enthusiasm for **Jeanne d'Arc** stemmed from the fact that it appealed to national sentiment at a time when once again France was being menaced by an enemy with scant respect for her traditions and culture. The French government realized the patriotic significance of Ida's work and, on the strength of it, awarded her the grand cross of an **officier** of the Légion d'Honneur on 24 May 1939.

But no amount of national fervour could inhibit the fury of Hitler's Germany and on 3 September the two countries found themselves officially at war. For Ida this was a tragedy of monumental proportions. It was bad enough for her adopted country to be threatened with imminent invasion, but she was also in personal danger because of her Jewish origins, which no amount of Catholicism could conceal from the eyes of the Gestapo, especially when an attractively large fortune was involved. And if one can deduce anything from the impression she made on Paul Valéry during a chance encounter, she was still in a slightly stunned state two weeks after the outbreak of hostilities. In a letter to Gide, Valéry recounted how he had gone to Potin, the grocer, to buy pickled tunny-fish when there 'entered a long black form which presented me with an extremely pale face and a very forced smile between locks of white-blonde hair. It was Ida, who had come, in person, in a magnificent motorcar, to buy canned foodstuffs. We chatted a little about everything and nothing. And that's all!' (Gide and Valéry, p. 518).

But if she withdrew into herself as far as society was concerned, this was far from true of her vocational life. Soon after her reception into the Catholic Church, she had become one of the Dominican Order's tertiary sisters and dedicated herself, as a laywoman, to a life of charity in the world. The outbreak of war gave her activities a sharper focus. Her spiritual headquarters, the Dominican convent of Saulchoir at Tournai, transferred itself to Etioles - of Pompadour fame - near Corbeil and Ida set up a hospital in one of its wings.

And when she could tear herself away from her nursing duties, she continued her personal war-effort in another way. She mounted several performances of **Jeanne d'Arc** in France and abroad, mainly as morale-boosting exercises but also to gain money for charity. On 22 February 1940 the work was broadcast on Radio-Paris from a live performance at the Salle Pleyel and it attracted a great deal of attention - partly because an interview between Ida and Germaine Dacaris had been published in **L'OEuvre** two days before.

This newspaper article is interesting because it outlined, with unusual frankness, Ida's aims for the future and her thoughts about the past. Her immediate concern was to raise money to help aged musicians. After all, they had spent their lives, often without a thought for the morrow, delighting audiences. Now that their sons were fighting for France, it was not right that they should be left without financial support. Ida's second aim was to help the Secours Universitaire of the Académie de Paris. From her earliest days in France she had poured money into student charities and was enormously popular with the university community. She confessed to Germaine Dacaris (Dacaris, pp. 1, 5):

> Students have always honoured me with an affection full of an extraordinary delicacy..., Ah! if you knew the charming letters which I have often received after my performances. When I gave my grand seasons at the Opéra, it was booked up in advance. In the cheaper seats, there was scarcely anybody except young people. They were not the sort of people who wanted to be seen in a box. No. They were children who deprived themselves of dinner for it.

A touching tribute to faithful supporters and also a neat dismissal of the critics of a lifetime!

And what were her plans for the future? She intended to revive **Le Martyre de Saint Sébastien,** that 'marriage of the French genius of Debussy and the Latin genius of d'Annunzio'. (Italy had yet to declare war on France.) Like **Jeanne d'Arc,** it was a perfect synthesis of words and music (ibid., p. 5). Apart from that she was planning to give a performance of **Jeanne d'Arc** in front of the cathedral in Lucerne in summertime. Meanwhile, she would take the work on tour in Belgium as a tribute to the Belgian people's noble stand against Germany. 'We are in a period,' she concluded, 'when we must seek out ways of bringing people closer together' (ibid., p. 5).

And, in fact, Ida left for Belgium immediately after the broadcast of 22 February. Helped by the Chorale Sainte-Cécile of Antwerp, she repeated her performance in Liège and Antwerp. On 29 February Claudel, sitting next to that renowned music-lover Queen Elisabeth of the Belgians, was present at the Palais des Beaux-Arts in Brussels to witness the tumultuous reception accorded to the work. Claudel's terse note in his journal tells one everything: 'Immense success, acclamations, cries of **Vive la France**, etc.' (1969, p. 305).

In the following years **Jeanne d'Arc au bûcher** continued to be performed, often by groups of amateur musicians, in the French Free Zone and other parts of unoccupied Europe as a gesture of defiance against tyranny and oppression. But Ida was unable to have anything to do with these productions. She even had to abandon her plans for the performance at Lucerne. As Hitler unleashed his **Blitzkrieg** against the Netherlands and Belgium, at the beginning of May 1940, and poured troops across the French frontier, she made a last-minute dash to the south of France.

CHAPTER 19

Death in Vence, 1940-1960

Ida Rubinstein had been very loath to abandon Paris. She was even more reluctant to leave the country. But she was well aware that the fragile truce, made between Marshal Pétain and the Nazi invaders on 24 June 1940, could be shattered at a moment's notice, so she and her devoted young secretary Madeleine Koll undertook the dangerous journey across the Mediterranean to Algeria. There, at least she could remain on French territory. But that proved to be only a temporary expedient and, after months spent in persuading Ida to leave, Walter Moyne was finally able to arrange for the two women to go to Casablanca where an aeroplane was ready to take them to Portugal. The journey from Lisbon to England was as hazardous as any imaginable at that moment but finally they arrived unscathed in London in the late spring of 1941.

Ida was now completely cut off from any source of income but Moyne was only too willing to support her - and very handsomely. He installed her in a suite in the Ritz Hotel in Piccadilly and that became her only permanent base during her years in England. The more cautious rich preferred the concrete safety of the Dorchester. But the Ritz's air of bygone splendour had a homely familiarity (at least for Ida) and that justified the risks involved. Yet, truth be told, neither German bombs nor personal discomfort caused her much concern. Her life-style had altered radically since the mid-1930s and in England she put the finishing touches to the change. She made no attempt to mix in high society. She avoided all forms of publicity. And despite a lifetime's devotion to the theatre, she refused to attend stage productions of any kind.

She still saw as much of Walter Moyne as his political duties permitted. Even at the age of sixty he was still an extraordinarily handsome, charming and gregarious man with a gift for light-hearted and imaginative conversation. There was certainly no suggestion of any residual sexual element in their relationship. Moyne never lacked mistresses; his friendship with Ida was now of a completely different order. Those who saw them together were struck by their contrasting yet strangely complementary characters. Ida gave the appearance of a woman who had never known jealousy of any sort. She was quite impassive in the face of distress and personal or material loss - except in one instance.

One day, soon after her arrival in London, Moyne took her to visit a young Poliakoff kinswoman of hers, the actress Véra Lindsay, who lived nearby in Charles Street. At the time she was the main B.B.C. correspondent covering the activities of the Free French Forces and, as such, she kept a fairly powerful wireless in her flat, a considerable attraction for Ida, who was always eager to hear news from France. However, she arrived to find that the house had been bombed the previous night and everything was in chaos. Véra Lindsay had been unable to warn her not to come, so they sat on the stairs and chatted. Miss Lindsay was struck by Ida's perfect skin and facial structure (although she seemed older than her fifty-five years) and by her calm, serene and impenetrable look. The only thing that made her shown any sign of anxiety was the thought of what might have become of her library of books and manuscripts left behind in Paris at the mercy of the German authorities. For three decades she had assiduously built up a unique collection of twentieth-century literature, Russian, English, Italian and, above all, French novels and poetry, always in first editions and many of them very rare. In addition she owned the manuscripts of the innumerable works commissioned by her since 1908. They represented a small corner of Western civilization but one which Nazi ideology branded as decadent. Her worst fears were justified.

Once settled in England Ida devoted herself entirely to charitable work. The Free French Forces stationed in and around London became the focus of her attention. She resumed her nursing activities. At first she concentrated upon caring for French patients in the British Legion sanitorium in Preston Hall in Kent. She then set up her own medical unit at Camberley. Although Lord Moyne supplied all the necessary finance, Ida was completely in charge and she amazed everybody with her efficiency and administrative skill - although this is scarcely surprising when one thinks of the superhuman feats of co-ordination and organization that she was used to achieving in the French theatre.

Mrs Sylvia Crawford, who worked closely with her during this period, preserved touching memories of her philanthropic activities (p. 15):

> Only those close to her knew the great extent of her benevolence but many of the Free French Forces, recovering from injury or sickness in different hospitals in the South of England, will surely carry for ever the recollection of her tall elegant figure, not walking but floating along the wards...(They) know how unsparingly she worked for them with a rare sympathy, modesty and sensitivity.

Marguerite Long also recalled how she busied herself with the wounded, in particular those of 'the "Alsace" contingent, to which she was as a godmother' (1971, p. 46).

And in time she acquired another object of her godmotherly attention. Sylvia Crawford eventually persuaded her to come with her and her husband to a performance of Terence Rattigan's 'Air-Force' play **Flare**

Path at the Apollo Theatre in London. 'She was spellbound and within a few days she had adopted an air squadron - a gesture typical of her generosity' (Crawford, p. 15).

Ida's selfless activities were carried out against a background of personal sorrow and concern. Until the threat of a German invasion of Britain subsided, she could have no guarantee of security. She also had to endure with mounting horror the snippets of news about the persecution of ethnic Jews in Europe. But the tragic death of Walter Moyne came as the most terrible blow of all.

In 1941 Moyne had been appointed Leader of the House of Lords and Secretary of State for the Colonies and, in this latter capacity, he had to deal with the intractable problem of regulating Jewish immigration into the mandated territory of Palestine. In the 1930s the indigenous Arab population had consistently protested, often violently, about what they saw as an insidious take-over of their country. They had only just liberated it from Turkish domination and were determined to retain their sovereign integrity and national identity. By the mid-1930s the British authorities were having to cope with a full-scale revolt. This state of affairs continued until 1939 when a compromise was reached: Jewish immigration in the future would be regulated more carefully on the basis of an annual quota. However, with the coming of war, a flood of European Jewish refugees made for the coasts of Palestine. The situation was explosive and the British government made frantic efforts to control the tide of illegal immigrants.

It was during his period at the Colonial Office that Moyne witnessed the appalling tragedy of the sinking of the **Struma,** a leaky converted coal-ship, grossly overcrowded with 769 Roumanian Jews, **en route** for Palestine. On 12 December 1941 it set sail from Constanza but, at the request of the British government, the Turkish authorities stopped the ship at Istanbul. Whatever else this action did, it did not solve the refugees' problem. Eventually, after weeks of delay, the Turks lost patience and, on 23 February 1942, they towed the ship out into the Black Sea as if to send it back to pro-German Roumania. One torpedo sufficed to sink the vessel and drown all but one of its human cargo. The world was shocked. Zionists were outraged and Abraham Stern, the terrorist leader, marked down Lord Moyne for revenge, even though he was personally sympathetic towards the Jewish cause.

Later the same year Moyne was sent to Cairo as Deputy Minister of State and remained there in virtual control of political affairs until 1944. Then, on 6 November, as he was being driven to work, he and his driver were gunned down in the street by Stern's terrorists. Neither of them survived the attack. The public reaction was, predictably, one of shock and horror. Moyne's body was flown back to Britain for an official funeral service, followed by a private cremation attended only by members of his family.

Ida's feelings about the assassination and about her exclusion from the public and private obsequies were one of grief compounded by more grief. However changed her own life, she still knew him as the only man whom she had ever loved, a man who, avoiding all forms of extremism himself, finally met a tragic end at the hands of extremists.

But by this time the war in Europe was drawing to a close. Peace came in May 1945 and, as soon as her services were no longer needed, Ida wound up her affairs in England and returned to Paris only to find herself technically homeless. During the Occupation the Nazis had ransacked her house in the Place des Etats-Unis. They stole or destroyed its entire contents and razed the building itself. Ida eventually had the site cleared and a fairly elegant block of flats was built on it. Paris had been her only real home. Now she no longer identified with the city. The last remnants of her public life had gone with the war. She now felt no sympathy with the materialism and superficiality of metropolitan life. She disliked the futile attempts at expiation for the sin of collaboration. Very soon she left the capital to stay in Biarritz. Finally, in 1950, she bought a villa called 'Les Olivades' on the hillside outside the picturesque town of Vence in the Maritime Alps behind the French Riviera. And there she stayed until her death. She seldom returned to visit Paris.

André de Fouquières quipped: Ida has exchanged her sets of silk underwear for a hair-shirt (p. 270). He was not far from the truth. She fulfilled all her obligations as a tertiary sister, reciting the little office of the order, saying the rosary and reading the lessons for the day, without any of the fuss and ostentation of a fellow tertiary, her old friend Cécile Sorel, the Comtesse de Ségur, who insisted on wearing 'a highly fanciful nun's habit, with silk chiffon veils. She used to wear it to all sorts of society parties until the Pope, in a letter, criticized her behaviour as being out of keeping with her station' (Erté, p. 72).

For her part, Ida used her vocation as a channel for works of charity, although often of a rather impersonal kind - or so it seemed to the outside observer. She was concerned about poverty and want almost as abstract phenomena, while remaining a little detached about particular cases of material distress. After the Liberation one of her kinswomen, Loulou Warschawsky, came to her with news of members of the Rubinstein and Horwitz families still living in Russia. She suggested sending them medical supplies, food and clothing through the Red Cross. But Ida surprised, even shocked her by showing little interest in the idea. Quite simply, Ida saw suffering as a general human problem and not one to be tackled at the whim of subjective impulses.

In fact, she was then in the process of disposing of a large part of her still substantial fortune. (Many believed that she had already spent most of it on her stage productions. This was not the case. Even a quick glance at her accounts tells one that most of her expenses were paid for out of current income and not out of capital reserves.) She had more than enough money to live on until the end of her days, when the residue went to her order. But before her death she was anxious to disburden herself of many material possessions, sometimes of the most personal sort. For example, she gave Marguerite Long the 'princely gift of certain letters that d'Annunzio had written her at the time of the conception of **Saint Sébastien**' (Long, 1960, p. 168).

A lot of Ida's past now meant very little to her, although, as a patron, she had left an enormous legacy to posterity. She was relatively unmoved by revivals of works created for her and even the belated premières of some of her commissions, such as the radio version of La **Sagesse** in 1946 and the stage production of Claudel's **L'Histoire de Tobie et de Sara** at Roubaix in 1947, **Lucifer** in 1949 and **Le Chevalier errant** in 1950. Even the revivals of **Le Martyre** in France and Italy in 1949, 1951 and 1952 and finally in 1957 at the Opéra, under the direction of Serge Lifar, afforded her limited satisfaction. For one thing her two main successors as Sebastian, Véra Korène and Ludmilla Tchérina, were - to put it mildly - far too well-blessed with female endowments to be very convincing in the role of the adolescent saint. Marguerite Long confessed that, after attending a rehearsal for **Le Martyre** in 1957, she was distressed to note that everybody seemed to have forgotten how Ida had created the work in the first place. Only a brief account of her efforts appeared in a special number of the **Revue Musicale** issued to mark the revival. Ida was probably not as upset as her friend.

In the last years of her life Ida was content to be alone and unnoticed. Above all she refused to be pitied like other ageing actresses who present tragic shadows of their former beauty and talent. She had no intention of suffering the same fate as Proust's Berma. She preferred solitude. As Marguerite Long remarked, quoting Villiers de l'Isle-Adam: 'There will always be solitude for those who are worthy of it.' Ida, she added, was worthy of it (1971, p. 47). And with an inner serenity, she contemplated the prospect of life after death. She still ate very little and slept scarcely at all. Often she would sit on her terrace all night long, gazing at the stars and investing them with a mystical significance.

Even when she came to Paris, little was seen of her. René Dumesnil, who, with Marguerite Long, Alexandre Benois and Maurice Delage and his wife Nelly, counted himself among her few remaining friends, left an engaging description of her visits (1960b, p. 8):

> For weeks or months we were left without news of her. And then, on the occasion of some anniversary or celebration, one would receive a basket of fruit or an enormous box of chocolates at the same time as a telegram, a hundred words long, expressing her best wishes, after phrases such as: 'I am a monster! Will you ever excuse my silence?' Or perhaps there would be the telephone call that one had ceased to hope for, and it was not a voice from beyond the tomb...but one full of gaiety, uttering protestations of friendship and promising imminent reunion: 'When I arrive in Paris, I shall let you know.'
>
> Days and weeks would again pass, and then she would emerge...: 'What day will you come to lunch? I'll send Albert to pick you up.'
>
> And we should find ourselves, five or six of us more or less, in the suite which she occupied at the George-V on each of her visits.

Her friends clearly looked forward to the meeting with some apprehension but Ida would be effervescent: 'We must laugh, mustn't we?' Everybody relaxed and, as Dumesnil noted, 'among her friends she was like a child, completely spontaneous' (ibid., p. 8).

During these reunions she seldom gave any outward sign of unhappiness, although Marguerite Long - who was as close to her as anybody - had cause to wonder about this (1971, p. 47):

> I cannot help thinking that, in her retirement, there was some bitterness towards and also nostalgia for her own country. She loved to recall Russia, and when I returned from Moscow, she came to Paris to hear my impressions and to talk to me of her youth; when I said, 'We shall go together', for the first time I saw that secret and impenetrable being with tears in her eyes.

Apart from that, the only thing that interfered with Ida's serenity was her feelings for Romaine Brooks. After the war Romaine spent most of her time in Nice, not so very far from Vence. Ida would send her fond invitations and even arrange for friends to drive her there but Romaine made no attempt to see her. 'She is no longer like an orchid,' was her only, unfeeling comment (Secrest, p. 327). Romaine herself had never looked like an orchid and in old age she looked even less prepossessing. Nor did her sociability and temper improve with the passing of time. And especially after the only real love of her life, Natalie Barney, had fallen hopelessly in love with a younger woman (at the advanced age of seventy-seven), Romaine became even more inconsiderate towards her friends. Ida was one of the unfortunate victims of her bitterness.

The unrepentant pagan Romaine was unsympathetic towards Ida's pre-occupation with religion. And perhaps it is just as well that she passed over the opportunity (which otherwise she would have taken) to criticize it because it was the one thing that sustained Ida to the end.

Since her early days as an orphan in St Petersburg, Ida had always consciously had to create psychological anchors for herself. She had no mature experience of parental love and, after leaving Russia, she enjoyed only two relationships that amounted to anything in emotional terms: her turbulent and partly one-sided affair with Romaine Brooks and (despite the fact that she was basically lesbian) her long, tender relationship with Walter Guinness. But even that lacked any domestic dimension. Guinness's commitments as a married man and as a statesman, not to mention the demands of Ida's own profession, kept them apart for the best part of each year. Even when Guinness could come to Paris, they did not 'officially' live together , since he maintained an establish-ment of his own in the rue de Poitiers. And when his wife died in 1939, there was no question of his and Ida's marrying. Long since then she had conditioned herself psychologically to do without the support of such a formalized relationship since her art, her stage-work, her commissions, her pursuit of beauty and truth (as she would have put it in her Montesquiou-days) provided her with a focus and purpose in life. Indeed, as far as she was concerned, that was life itself. Acquaintances thought that her existence was either two-dimensional or contained a secret element that was kept well-hidden from the public eye. Neither of these things was true. In her work Ida was as obsessive as an ideologue and the exoticism and fantasy of the theatre-world very easily spilled over into her private life. It coloured her leisure moments. Her travels to far-off places, her big-game hunts, her wild-animal pets, her yachts, her aeroplanes, her motorcars, they all provided her with more pleasure, excitement and distraction than most individuals would experience in a lifetime.

Ida's religious faith was the second strongest motive-force in her life. It was there from the very beginning and, far from being a strand of her existence separate from her theatre-work, it threaded its way through it and in later years held the whole fabric of her public life together. When Ida no longer felt capable of sustaining her role as a Diaghilev, a Sarah Bernhardt and a Tamara Karsavina rolled into one, her spiritual life quite simply filled in the gap left by its loss and provided her with the strength to end her days in an atmosphere of serenity and hope.

Ida's death came unexpectedly and quite suddenly after a heart attack on 20 September 1960. Only her faithful secretary and a doctor were present and few of even her closest friends learned the news before her funeral, which according to her strict instructions, took place in almost total secrecy in the local cemetery at Vence two days later.

However unintentional, Ida's last request for privacy turned out to be one of the most dramatic gestures of her life. Almost a month passed before the news of her death became generally known and, as a result, a rash of guilt-ridden obituaries appeared in the international press. They surveyed her life as though it had been one long piece of theatre and vied with one another to praise her.

Jean Cocteau shed a real tear: 'With Ida Rubinstein, once again a little of my youth slips away...There she is on her way on the River of the Dead, she who came from the Russian ghetto wrapped in Cleopatra's carpet' (1960, p. 11).

René Dumesnil reflected lyrically upon the different facets of her character (1960b, p. 8):

A sphinx, an enigmatic being, an unyielding character, forced to be subtle by her will of iron, a character bursting with puzzling inconsistencies, suborned by itself, by the unexpected, by the suddenness of her reflexes, she seemed to come from another world where she would have been sovereign despot. Ida Rubinstein's life was a series of difficult, dangerous victories over her contemporaries but the most perilous of them were won at her own expense.

But when he dropped this contrived poetic tone and summed up Ida's achievement, Dumesnil spoke words telling in their simplicity: 'We shall not forget that she succeeded in exercising a significant influence upon the evolution of contemporary art...Her name will continue to be associated with some of the twentieth century's most important lyrical works' (1960a, p. 15).

Ida Rubinstein could have asked for no better memorial.

SOURCE NOTES and BIBLIOGRAPHY

Very little manuscript material belonging to Ida Rubinstein survived the Second World War and even less survived her death in 1960. However, some documents relating to her life are still preserved in private hands. In addition, a large cache of her letters has come to light in the Comte Robert de Montesquiou's papers, now deposited in the Bibliothèque Nationale, Paris. The Bibliothèque de l'Opéra in Paris, now under the direction of the Bibliothèque Nationale, has extensive documentation relating to Ida Rubinstein's theatre projects. Material relating to the Opéra's productions is also to be found in the Archives Nationales, Paris. This includes a rich store of Leon Bakst's letters. Legal documents in Somerset House, London, proved invaluable. Mr Keith Lester very kindly lent me a copy of the manuscript of an article of his, entitled 'Rubinstein revisited'. This is now published in a shortened form (in **Dance Research**, vol. 1, no. 2, 1983). I have chosen to quote from the fuller original manuscript.

Material from the institutions mentioned above are referred to by the following abbreviations:

AN   Archives Nationales, Paris.
BN   Bibliothèque Nationale, Paris. (All references are to material catalogued in the category of 'nouvelles acquisitions françaises' and, therefore, the prefix of n.a.fr. is omitted.)
BN Opéra   Bibliothèque de l'Opéra, Bibliothèque Nationale, Paris.

The bibliography is mainly limited to works quoted or referred to in the text. All source notes are incorporated (in brackets) into the text. These always refer to works listed in the bibliography. Where reference is made to an author in the text, only a page number reference is supplied. Otherwise, reference is also made to the author's name. When more than one work by an individual author is cited, reference is also made to the date of publication, the works in question being listed chronologically in the bibliography:

Anon. (1913), 'Nouvelles diverses', Le **Ménestrel**, vol. 79, no. 40, 4 Oct. 1913.
    (1922a), **'Artémis troubléee et Frivolant', Le Journal**, 4 May 1922.
    (1922b), 'Mme Rubinstein a loué pour sept jours le Théâtre de l'Opéra', **Petit Bleu**, 15 June 1922.
    (1922c), 'Grand Prix Ball', **The Times**, 27 June 1922.
    (1928), 'A Paris Ballet Season', **The Times**, 7 Dec. 1928.
    (1931a), 'French Ballets and Plays', **The Times**, 2 July 1931.
    (1931b), **'Le Martyre de Saint Sébastien', The Times**, 7 July 1931.
    (1931c), 'Mme Rubinstein's Ballets', **The Times**, 8 July 1931.
    (1931d), 'Ravel's **La Valse'**, **The Times**, 9 July 1931.
    (1931e), **'La Dame au camélias'**, The Times, 10 July 1931.
    (1934), 'Les Ballets d'Ida Rubinstein', **Cri du Jour**, 5 May 1934.
    (1960), 'Miss Ida Rubinstein', **The Times**, 18 Oct. 1960.
Antongini, Tom, **D'Annunzio**. London, Heinemann, 1938.
Appia, Edmond, **'Jeanne d'Arc au bûcher'**, Le **Ménestrel**, vol. 100, no. 22, 3 June 1938.
Armory, M., **'L'Idiot**. La Soirée', **Comoedia**, 2 Apr. 1925.
Ashton, Frederick, 'Miss Rubinstein', **The Times**, 21 Oct. 1960.

Astruc, Gabriel (1929), **Le Pavillon des fantômes**. Paris, Grasset, 1929.
(1958), **Papers**. Genève, Rauch, 1958.
Balliman, Raymond, 'Spectacles de Mme Ida Rubinstein', **Le Soir**, 27 June 1931.
Bardac, Henri, 'Marcel Proust devin', **Hommage à Marcel Proust, 1871–1922**. Paris, Nouvelle Revue Française, Jan. 1923.
Barney, Natalie Clifford, **Poems et poèmes, autres alliances**. Paris, Emile-Paul; New York, G.H. Doran, 1920.
Barrès, Maurice, **Mes cahiers, 1908–1911**. Paris, L'Honnête Homme, 1968.
Batilliot, Charles, 'Louange à Ida Rubinstein', in Tribout, Georges, **Dessins sur les gestes de Mlle Ida Rubinstein**. Paris, La Belle Edition, 1913.
Benois, Alexandre (1941), **Reminiscences of the Russian Ballet**. London, Putman, 1941.
(1964), **Memoirs**, vol. 2. London, Chatto and Windus, 1964.
Bert, Charles, **'Artémis troublée'**, **Petit Bleu**, 2 May 1922.
Bertrand, Denyse (1936), 'Concerts Pasdeloup', **Le Ménestrel**, vol. 98, no. 9, 28 Feb. 1936.
(1939), **'Jeanne au bûcher'**, Le Ménestrel, vol. 101, no. 25, 23 June 1939.
Bertrand, Paul (1922), **'Artémis troublée'**, Le Ménestrel, vol. 84, no. 18, 5 May 1922.
(1929), 'Les Ballets de Mme Ida Rubinstein', **Le Ménestrel**, vol. 91, no. 22, 31 May 1929.
Bézanet, Henry, 'Les Ballets de Mme Ida Rubinstein', **Petit Parisien**, 2 May 1934.
Bidou, Henry (1911), **'Le Martyre de Saint Sébastien'**, **Journal des Débats**, 29 May 1911.
(1912), **L'Année dramatique, 1911–1912**. Paris, Hachette, 1912.
Blanche, Jacques-Emile, **Portraits of a Lifetime**. London, Dent, 1937.
Boissy, Gabriel, **'L'Idiot'**, **Comoedia**, 2 Apr. 1925.
Bourman, Anatole, **The Tragedy of Nijinsky**. London, Robert Hale, 1937.
Bret, Gustave, 'Representations de Mme Ida Rubinstein: **Amphion'**, **L'Intransigeant**, 25 June 1931.
Bril, France-Yvonne, **Henri Sauguet**. Paris, Seghers, 1967.
Brisson, Adolphe, **'Le Martyre de Saint Sébastien'**, Le Temps, 29 May 1911.
Brown, Frederick, **An Impersonation of Angels. A Biography of Jean Cocteau**. London, Longmans, 1969.
Brunel, Raoul, 'Les Ballets de Mme Rubinstein', **L'OEuvre**, 28 June 1931.
Bruyez, René, 'D'une scène à l'autre', **Le Théâtre**, no. 25, Jan. 1924.
Buckle, Richard (1971), **Nijinsky**. London, Weidenfeld and Nicolson, 1971.
(1979), **Diaghilev**. London, Weidenfeld and Nicolson, 1979.
Busoni, Ferruccio, **Letters to his Wife**. New York, Da Capo Press, 1975.
Calvocoressi, M.D., **Musicians Gallery**. London, Faber and Faber, 1933.
Casselaer, Catherine van, **Lot's Wife: Lesbian Paris, 1890–1914**. Liverpool, Janus, 1986.
Catulle-Mendès, Jane (1922), 'Ballet en un acte de M. Léon Bakst', **La Patrie**, 2 May 1922.
(1926), **'Orphée'**, La Patrie, 14· June 1926.
Chagall, Marc, **My Life**. London, Peter Owen, 1967.
Chalupt, René. **Ravel au miroir de ses lettres**. Paris, Laffont, 1956.
Channon, Sir Henry, **Chips. The Diaries of Sir H.C.** London, Weidenfeld and Nicolson, 1967.
Chantavoine, Jean, 'Orphée', **Le Ménestrel**, vol. 88, no. 25, 18 June

1926.

Charles, Gilbert, 'Amphion ou les débuts au théâtre de M. Paul Valéry', Le Figaro, 22 June 1931.

Chase, Gilbert, 'Music in Paris', Musical Times, vol. 75, June 1934.

Claudel, Paul (1954), Mémoires improvisés de P.C. Paris, Gallimard, 1954.

(1961), Cahiers P.C., vol. 3. Correspondance P.C.-Darius Milhaud. Paris, Gallimard, 1961.

(1965), Accompagnements, in OEuvres en prose. Paris, Gallimard, 1965.

(1968), Journal, vol. 1. Paris, Gallimard, 1968.

(1969), Journal, vol. 2. Paris, Gallimard, 1969.

Clermont-Tonnerre, Elisabeth de, Robert de Montesquiou et Marcel Proust. Paris, Flammarion, 1925. (See also under Gramont.)

Cocteau, Jean (1913),'Notes on the Ballets', in Alexandre, Arsène, The Decorative Art of Léon Bakst. London, Fine Art Society, 1913.

(1960), 'Dans le tapis de Cléopâtre', Le Figaro, 17 Oct. 1960.

Cohen, Gustave, Ceux que j'ai connus. Montréal, L'Arbre, 1946.

Colette, Sidonie Gabrielle (1958), Paysages et portraits. Paris, Flammarion, 1958.

(1961), Lettres de la vagabonde. Paris, Flammarion, 1961.

(1971), Le Pur et l'impur. Paris, Hachette, 1971.

Corpechot, Lucien (1922), 'Sous la cupole de l'Opéra', Le Gaulois, 14 June 1922.

(1923), 'La Dame aux camélias. Programme', 27 Nov. 1923.

Cossart, Michael de (1978), The Food of Love: Princesse Edmond de Polignac (1865-1943) and Her Salon. London, Hamish Hamilton, 1978.

(1983), 'Ida Rubinstein and Diaghilev: a one-sided rivalry', Dance Research, vol. 1, no. 2, 1983.

Crawford, Sylvia, 'Miss Rubinstein', The Times, 21 Oct. 1960.

Cuttoli, Raphael, 'Le Martyre de Saint Sébastien: création et réprises', Revue Musicale, numéro special, no. 234, 1957.

Dacaris, Germaine, '"En ce moment on ne peut vivre séparé des autres," nous dit Mme Ida Rubinstein', L'OEuvre, 20 Feb. 1940.

Debussy, Claude, 'Avant Le Martyre de Saint Sébastien', Comoedia, 18 May 1911.

Delannoy, Marcel, Honegger. Paris, Pierre Horay, 1953.

Delarue-Mardrus, Lucie, Mes mémoires. Paris, Gallimard, 1938.

Delluc, Louis, Chez de Max. Paris, L'Edition, 1918.

Demarquez, Suzanne, 'Sémiramis, d'Arthur Honegger, aux Ballets de Mme Ida Rubinstein', Revue Musicale, vol. 16, no. 147, June 1934.

Dézarnaux, Robert, 'Artémis troublée', Liberté, 3 May 1922.

Doderet, André, Vingt ans d'amitié avec Gabriele d'Annunzio. Paris, private, 1956.

Dostoyevsky, Feodr, The Idiot. Harmondsworth, Penguin, 1978 (1955).

Dumesnil, René (1939), 'Jeanne au bûcher', Mercure de France, vol. 293, 1 July 1939.

(1960a), 'Ida Rubinstein', Le Monde, 16 Oct. 1960.

(1960b), 'Souvenirs sur Ida Rubinstein', Le Monde, 26 Oct. 1960.

Durand, Jacques, Quelques souvenirs d'un éditeur de musique, vol. 2, 1910-1924. Paris, Durand, 1925.

Erté, Things I Remember. London, Peter Owen, 1975.

Ferroud, Pierre-Octave, Autour de Florent Schmitt. Paris, Durand, 1927.

Feyran, M., 'L'Idiot', Le Ménestrel, vol. 87, no. 15, 10 Apr. 1925.

Flers, Robert de, 'Le Martyre de Saint Sébastien', Le Figaro, 19 June 1922.

Fokine, Michel, **Memoirs of a Ballet Master**. London, Constable, 1961.
Fouquières, André de, **Mon Paris et ses parisiens. Les Quartiers de l'Etoile**, vol. 1. Paris, Pierre Horay, 1953.
Gatti, Guglielmo, **Vita di Gabriele d'Annunzio**. Firenze, Sansoni, 1956.
George, André, 'Le Premier Spectacle de Mme Rubinstein', **Nouvelles Littéraires**, 5 May 1934.
Georges-Michel, Michel (1913), 'La Pisanelle ou la mort parfumée', **Comoedia Illustré**, 20 June 1913.
(1944), **Dames étranges**. Paris, Parizeau, 1944.
Germain, André (1924), **De Proust à Dada**. Paris, Sagittaire, 1924.
(1951), **La Bourgeoisie qui brûle**. Paris, Sun, 1951.
Ghéon, Henri, 'M. d'Annunzio et l'art', **Nouvelle Revue Française**, vol. 3, no. 31, 1 July 1911.
Gheusi, P.-B., 'Les Ballets de Mme Ida Rubinstein à l'Opéra', **Le Figaro**, 24 Nov. 1928.
Gide, André (1951), **Journal, 1889-1939**. Paris, Gallimard, 1951.
(1952), **Ainsi soit-il ou les jeux sont fait**. Paris, Gallimard, 1952.
(1974), **Cahiers A.G.**, vol. 5. Les **Cahiers de la petite dame, 1929-1937**. Paris, Gallimard, 1974.
Gide, André, and Valéry, Paul, **Correspondance, 1890-1942**. Paris, Gallimard, 1955.
Girard, Maxime, 'A propos de **L'Impératrice aux rochers**', **Le Figaro**, 26 Feb. 1927.
Gramont, Elisabeth de (1932), **Years of Plenty**. London, Jonathan Cape, 1932.
(1937), **Mémoires**, vol. 4. **La Treizième Heure**. Paris, Grasset, 1937. (See also under Clermont-Tonnerre.)
Green, Julian, **Journal, 1928-1934**, vol. 1. Paris, Plon, 1938.
Grigoriev, S.L., **The Diaghilev Ballet, 1909-1929**. Harmondsworth, Penguin, 1960.
Guy, Georges, 'Amphion', **Griffe Littéraire**, 9 July 1931.
Hahn, Reynaldo (1911), 'Le Martyre de Saint Sébastien', **Le Journal**, 23 May 1911.
(1938), 'Oriane et le prince d'amour', **Le Figaro**, 20 Jan. 1938.
(1946), **Thèmes variés**. Paris, Janin, 1946.
Harding, James, **The Ox on the Roof**. London, Macdonald, 1972.
Haskell, Arnold (1955), **Diaghileff. His Artistic and Private Life**. London, Gollancz, 1955.
(1972), **Balletomane at Large**. London, Heinemann, 1972.
(1977), **Balletomania then and now**. London, Weidenfeld and Nicolson, 1977.
Heugel, Jacques, 'Phaedre', **Le Ménestrel**, vol. 85, no. 24, 15 June 1923.
Honegger, Arthur (1934), 'Arthur Honegger nous parle d'**Amphion (sic)**', **L'Excelsior**, 29 Apr. 1934.
(1966), **I am a Composer**. London, Faber and Faber, 1966.
Horatio, 'Humeur et érudition', **Comoedia**, 28 June 1931.
Howell, Georgina, 'A Bomb filled with Silks and Coloured Lights', **Observer Magazine**, 4 Mar. 1979.
Jourdan-Morhange, Hélène, **Ravel et nous**. Genève, Milieu du Monde, 1945.
Jullian, Philippe (1967), **Robert de Montesquiou. A Fin-de-Siècle Prince**. London, Secker and Warburg, 1967.
(1972), **D'Annunzio**. London, Pall Mall, 1972.
Karsavina, Tamara, **Theatre Street. Reminiscences of T.K.** London, Heinemann, 1930.
Kessler, Count Harry, **The Diaries of a Cosmopolitan, 1918-1937**. London,

Weidenfeld and Nicolson, 1971.

Kirstein, Lincoln, **Fokine**. London, British-Continental Press, 1934.

Kochno, Boris, **Diaghilev and the Ballets Russes**. London, Allen Lane The Penguin Press, 1970.

Kraemer-Taylor, Pierre, 'La Pisanelle ou la mort parfumée', Comoedia Illustré, 5 June 1913.

Lagarde, Pierre, 'L'Art magique d'Ida Rubinstein', **Comoedia**, 26 June 1931.

Laloy, Louis, 'Un nouvel **Orphée**', **Ere Nouvelle**, 14 June 1926.

La Mazière, Pierre, 'Les Ballets d'Ida Rubinstein à l'Opéra', **Cadet Rousselle**, 11 May 1934.

La Rochefoucauld, Edmée de, **Images de Paul Valéry**. Strasbourg, Le Roux, 1949.

Le Flem, Paul, 'Le Premier Spectacle des Ballets Ida Rubinstein', **L'Intransigeant**, 2 May 1934.

Legrand-Chabrier, M., Légende et verité', **L'Intransigeant**, 2 Apr. 1925.

Le Senne, Camille, 'La Musique et le théâtre aux salons du Grand-Palais', **Le Ménestrel**, vol. 80, no. 18, 2 May 1914.

Lester, Keith, 'Rubinstein revisited' (manuscript version, c.1970).

Levinson, André (1922), **'Artémis troublée...Frivolant'**, Comoedia, 3 May 1922.

(1923), **Bakst. The Story of the Artist's Life**. London, Bayard Press, 1923.

(1931), 'La Danse au théâtre en 1931', Le Temps, 20 July 1931.

Lieven, Prince Peter, **The Birth of Ballets-Russes**. London, Allen and Unwin, 1936.

Lifar, Serge (1940), **Serge Diaghilev, His Life, His work, His Legend**. New York, Putnam, 1940.

(1950), **Histoire du Ballet Russe depuis les origines jusqu'à nos jours**. Paris, Nagel, 1950.

Long, Marguerite (1960), **Au piano avec Claude Debussy**. Paris, Julliard, 1960.

(1971), **Au piano avec Maurice Ravel**. Paris, Julliard, 1971.

McNaught, W.G. (1931), 'Ida Rubinstein Ballet', **Musical Times**, vol. 72, Aug. 1931.

(1935), **'Perséphone'**, **Musical Times**, vol. 76, Jan. 1935.

Malherbe, Henry (1928a), 'Chronique musicale', **Le Temps**, 28 Nov. 1928.

(1928b), 'Chronique musicale', **Le Temps**, 5 Dec. 1928.

Massine, Léonide, **My Life in Ballet**. London, Macmillan, 1968.

Michel, Gérard, **Jacques Ibert**. Paris, Seghers, 1967.

Milhaud, Darius, **Notes without Music**. London, Denis Dobson, 1952.

Montesquiou, Robert de (1909), 'La Dame bleue', **Le Figaro Littéraire**, 19 June 1909.

(1912), **Têtes d'expression**. Paris, Emile-Paul, 1912.

(1913), **La Divine Comtesse, étude d'après Madame de Castiglione**. Paris, Goupil, 1913.

(1923), **Les Pas effacés**, vol. 3. Paris, Emile-Paul, 1923.

Moustiers, Yvone, 'Ballets à l'Opéra', **France Militaire**, 30 Apr. 1934.

Myers, Rollo, **Ravel. Life and Works**. London, Duckworth, 1960.

Nijinsky, Romola, **Nijinsky**. London, Sphere, 1970.

Nin, Joaquin, 'Comment est né le **Boléro** de Ravel', **Revue Musicale, numéro spécial**, Dec. 1938.

Nozière, Fernand, **Ida Rubinstein**. Paris, Sansot, 1926.

Orledge, Robert (1974), 'Debussy's orchestral collaborations, 1911-13. 1: **Le Martyre de Saint Sébastien'**, **Musical Times**, no. 1582, vol. 115,

Dec. 1974.

(1982), **Debussy and the Theatre.** Cambridge University Press, 1982.

Ouvray, Pierre d', 'Le Secret **du Sphinx**', **Le Ménestrel,** vol. 86, no. 9, 29 Feb. 1924.

Pawlowski, G. de (1912), 'Hélène de Sparte', **Comoedia,** 6 May 1912.

(1928), 'Les Ballets de Mme Ida Rubinstein', **Le Journal,** 24 Nov. 1928.

Petit, Raymond, '**Phaedre** par Arthur Honegger', **Revue Musicale,** vol. 9, no. 9, 1928.

Poueigh, Jean, 'Le **Martyre de Saint Sébastien**', **Ere Nouvelle,** 21 June 1922.

Poulenc, Francis, **Moi et mes amis.** Paris, La Palatine, 1963.

Proust, Marcel (1930), **Correspondance générale,** vol. 1. Paris, Plon, 1930.

(1956), **Lettres à Reynaldo Hahn.** Paris, Gallimard, 1956.

Prudhomme, Jean, 'Les Premières: Théâtre de l'Opéra', **Le Matin,** 24 Nov. 1928.

Prunières, Henry (1927), '**L'Impératrice aux rochers**', **Revue Musicale,** vol. 8, no. 5, Mar. 1927.

(1929), 'Les Ballets d'Ida Rubinstein à l'Opéra', **Revue Musicale,** vol. 10, no. 3, Jan. 1929.

(1931), '**Amphion** d'Arthur Honegger et de Paul Valéry', **Revue Musicale,** vol. 12, no. 119, Oct. 1931.

(1934), '**Perséphone**', **Revue Musicale,** vol. 15, no. 146, May 1934.

Rageot, Gaston (1926), 'Ida Rubinstein, Saint-Georges de Bouhélier, Honegger', **Le Gaulois,** 2 Jan. 1926.

(1927), 'A propos d'un grand spectacle: **L'Impératrice aux rochers**', **Revue Politique et Littéraire (Revue Bleue),** vol. 65, no. 5, 5 Mar. 1927.

Reich, Willi, 'In Memoriam Maurice Ravel', **Revue Musicale, numéro spécial,** Dec. 1938.

Rivollet, André, 'Le Retour de l'Ida prodigue', **1934,** 9 May 1934.

Rolland, Romain, 'Le Mouvement musical en province: Orléans', **Le Ménestrel,** vol. 101, no. 21, 26 May 1939.

Rose, Sir Francis, **Saying Life.** London, Cassell, 1961.

Rostand, Maurice, **Confessions d'un demi-siècle.** Paris, Jeune Parque, 1948.

Rouché, Jacques, 'Souvenirs', **Revue des Deux Mondes,** 1 Nov. 1951.

Rubinstein, Ida, 'Ma première rencontre avec d'Annunzio', **Conferencia,** vol. 21, no. 19, 20 Sept. 1927.

Sabaneev, Leonid, 'Dawn or Dusk? Stravinsky's New Ballets: **Apollo** and **The Fairy's Kiss**', **Musical Times,** no. 1035, vol. 70, May 1929.

Saegel, P. (1920), '**Antoine et Cléopâtre**', **Le Ménestrel,** vol. 82, no. 25, 18 June 1920.

(1927), '**L'Impératrice aux rochers**', Le Ménestrel, vol. 89, no. 8, 25 Feb. 1927.

Schloezer, Boris de (1929), 'Chronique musicale', **Nouvelle Revue Française,** vol. 31, 1929.

(1931), '**Amphion**', **Nouvelle Revue Française,** vol. 37, 1931.

Schmitt, Florent, 'Florent Schmitt nous parle d'**Oriane-le-sans-égale**', **L'Excelsior,** 29 Apr. 1934.

Schneider, Louis (1920), '**Antoine et Cléopâtre**', **Le Gaulois,** 15 June 1920.

(1926), '**Orphée**', **Le Gaulois,** 13 June 1926.

(1931), '**Amphion**', **Revue de France,** vol. 11, no. 15, Aug. 1931.

Scize, Pierre, 'M. André Caplet refuse de conduire l'orchestre',

Bonsoir, 19 June 1922.

Secrest, Meryle, **Between Me and Life,** a Biography of Romaine Brooks. London, Macdonald and Jane's, 1976.

Sombreuil, H. de, 'A propos de La Dame aux camélias', La Rampe, 9 Dec. 1923.

Sorel, Cécile, **An Autobiography.** London, Staples Press, 1953.

Spencer, Charles, **Erté.** London, Studio Vista, 1970.

Strauss, Richard, and Rolland, Romain, **Correspondence together with Fragments from the Diary of R.R.** London, Calder and Boyars, 1968.

Stravinsky, Igor (1934), 'M. Igor Stravinsky nous parle de Perséphone', **L'Excelsior,** 1 May 1934.

(1975), **An Autobiography.** London, Calder and Boyars, 1975 (first published 1935).

Stravinsky, Igor, and Craft, Robert (1960), **Memories and Commentaries.** London, Faber and Faber, 1960.

(1968), **Dialogues and a Diary.** London, Faber and Faber, 1968.

Stravinsky, Igor, and Gide, André, **Perséphone.** London, Boosey and Hawkes, 1949.

Stravinsky, Vera, and Craft, Robert, **Stravinsky in Pictures and Documents.** London, Hutchinson, 1979.

Tenroc, Charles (1919a), 'Imroulcaïs, le roi errant', Courrier Musical, 15 Mar. 1919.

(1919b), '**La Tragédie de Salomé**', Courrier Musical, 15 Apr. 1919.

(1922), '**Le Martyre de Saint Sébastien**', Comoedia, 19 June 1922.

(1928), 'Les Ballets de Mme Ida Rubinstein', **Courrier Musical et Théâtral,** 25 Dec. 1928.

Teramond, Guy de, 'Ballets de Mme Ida Rubinstein', **Nouvelles Littéraires,** 1 Aug. 1931.

Thomas, Louis, 'Le Peintre Bakst parle de Mme Ida Rubinstein', **Revue Critique des Idées et des Livres,** vol. 36, no. 221, Feb. 1924.

Tosi, Guy (1948a), ed., **Claude Debussy et Gabriele d'Annunzio. Correspondance inédite.** Paris, Denoël, 1948.

(1948b), 'Debussy et Ida Rubinstein', **Opéra,** vol. 5, no. 146, 3 Mar. 1948.

Troussevitch, Alexandrine, 'La Chorégraphie dans les ballets de la Ida Rubinstein', **Revue Musicale,** vol. 15, no. 146, May 1934.

Valéry, Paul (1936), 'Histoire d'**Amphion**', in **Variété,** vol. 3. Paris, Gallimard, 1936.

(1952), **Lettres à quelques-uns.** Paris, Gallimard, 1952.

Vaughan, David, **Frederick Ashton and His Ballets.** London, Adam and Charles Black, 1977.

Vestris, 'Billet de minuit', **Comoedia,** 14 June 1912.

Viollier, Renée, 'La Création de **Lucifer** à l'Opéra de Paris', Tribune de Genève, 31 Dec. 1948.

Vuillermoz, Emile (1920), 'Autour du **Martyre de Saint Sébastien**', Revue Musicale, vol. 1, no. 2, Dec. 1920.

(1922a), '**Artémis troublée**', L'Excelsior, 3 May 1922.

(1922b), '**Le Martyre de Saint Sébastien**', Revue Musicale, vol. 3, no. 6, Aug. 1922.

(1928), 'Les Ballets de Mme Ida Rubinstein', **L'Excelsior,** 3 Dec. 1928.

Wickes, George, **The Amazon of Letters. The Life and Loves of Natalie Barney.** London, W.H. Allen, 1977.

INDEX

(Principal Names Cited)